ABRAHAM LINCOLN AND CIVIL WAR AMERICA

Abraham Lincoln at the time of the Gettysburg Address (Illinois State Historical Library)

ABRAHAM LINCOLN

and

CIVIL WAR AMERICA

A Biography

WILLIAM E. GIENAPP

OXFORD
UNIVERSITY PRESS

2002

OXFORD
UNIVERSITY PRESS

Oxford   New York

Athens   Auckland   Bangkok   Bogotá   Buenos Aires
Cape Town   Chennai   Dar es Salaam   Delhi   Florence   Hong Kong   Istanbul
Karachi   Kolkata   Kuala Lumpur   Madrid   Melbourne   Mexico City   Mumbai
Nairobi   Paris   São Paulo   Shanghai   Singapore   Taipei   Tokyo   Toronto   Warsaw

and associated companies in
Berlin   Ibadan

Published by Oxford University Press, Inc.
198 Madison Avenue, New York, New York 10016

Oxford is a registered trademark of Oxford University Press

Library of Congress Cataloging-in-Publication Data
Gienapp, William E.
Abraham Lincoln and Civil War America : A biography /
by William E. Gienapp
p. cm.
Includes bibliographical references and index.
ISBN 0–19-515099–6 – ISBN 0–19-515100–3 (pbk.)
1. Lincoln, Abraham, 1809–1865. 2. Presidents—United States—
Biography. 3. United States—Politics and government—1861–1865.
4. Lincoln, Abraham, 1809–1865—Military leadership. I. Title.
E457.G46 2001
973.7′092—dc21 [B]   2001050056

973.7
GIE

Book design by Mark McGarry, Texas Type & Book Works, Inc.
Set in Monotype Dante
1 3 5 7 9 8 6 4 2
Printed in the United States of America
on acid-free paper

For my sons,
William and Jonathan

I shall do nothing in malice.
What I deal with is too vast for malicious dealing.

CONTENTS

PREFACE

"LINCOLN NEVER poured out his soul to any mortal creature at any-
time and on no subject," his longtime law partner, William Herndon,
once declared. "He was the most secretive—reticent—shut-mouthed
man that ever existed." Judge David Davis, who had known Lincoln
for many years from his practice on the judicial circuit and who served
as a close adviser in Illinois politics, agreed. Using almost the same
words, Davis confirmed that, "he was the most reticent—Secretive
man I Ever Saw—or Expect to See." With considerable understate-
ment, Lincoln himself conceded in 1861, "I am rather inclined to
silence."

Abraham Lincoln is a difficult subject for a biographer. Born into
an undistinguished frontier family, he grew up in obscurity and left
almost no written record until he entered politics as a young man.
He said little about his family or youth, even to friends. Leonard
Swett, who had practiced law with Lincoln on the judicial circuit and
who was a longtime political associate, recalled that he "never heard
him speak of any relative, except as connected with his boy history."
Indeed, Swett sheepishly acknowledged that he did not even know
Lincoln had had a step-brother. Our knowledge of his formative years
comes almost entirely from the series of interviews and recollections
that Herndon collected in the years after Lincoln's death. Most of these
recollections were written down years after the events described, and
while invaluable they are difficult to use as historical sources. Few of
these early acquaintances were as candid as George Spears, who, when
asked about Lincoln's career as a shopkeeper in New Salem, admitted,
"At that time I had no idia of his ever being President therefore I did
not notice his course as close as I should of had."

The record of Lincoln's public activities is fuller after he moved to Springfield in 1837, but throughout his life he carefully guarded his feelings and kept his personal affairs out of the public gaze. Moreover, as a politician Lincoln rarely revealed what he was thinking until he had made up his mind, and in conversation often tested his ideas by arguing against positions he supported. Visitors frequently mistook his unpretentiousness for frankness, but as Republican Senator Lyman Trumbull of Illinois noted, he "communicated no more of his own thoughts and purposes than he thought would subserve the ends he had in view."

There are qualities of Lincoln's character and personality that simply cannot be fully explained without resorting to some dubious psychological theory. These include his burning ambition and desire to improve himself; his fear of intimacy and extraordinary private reserve (even his closest associates called him Lincoln, and his wife noted that he had trouble expressing what he felt most deeply); his estrangement from his father and family; his ability to draw other men to him while not being drawn to them; and the way he served as a father figure for a number of intensely admiring young men while he was a rather ineffective father himself. In some ways, his personality seems paradoxical, well captured by the juxtaposition of his hearty sense of humor and his deep-seated melancholy.

Lincoln himself had a limited view of the value of biography. Herndon recalled once handing his partner a biography that he was reading. After briefly leafing through it, Lincoln impatiently tossed it on the table with the comment, "It's like all the others. Biographies as generally written are not only misleading, but false. . . . In most instances they commemorate a lie, and cheat posterity out of the truth." He was especially critical of the tendency to praise a subject's every act and deny that he or she had made any mistakes.

I have not sought to deny that Lincoln made mistakes. Nor have I evaluated him in terms of how well he measured up to the values and ideals of our own times, for such a standard, though frequently invoked by modern critics, is fundamentally ahistorical. I have attempted to explain, however, why this man turned out to be such an extraordinary war leader. In analyzing his presidential leadership, I have woven together political and military developments, because these two concerns absorbed the bulk of his time and thought in the White House.

While the war presented an enormous military challenge to the United States government, it also unleashed forces that transformed the war into a social and political revolution. This revolution greatly expanded presidential power, dramatically stretched the meaning of the Constitution, and uprooted the two-hundred-year-old institution of racial slavery. It is one of the ironies of history that someone as conservative as Abraham Lincoln presided over the greatest revolution in American history. At the same time, the Union developed a new military strategy that incorporated economic and psychological dimensions and bore down on southern civilians with growing severity. As such, this strategy pointed directly toward the twentieth-century concept of total war.

As president, Lincoln had to manage both the political and military dimensions of the conflict, and his record of leadership depended on his ability to coordinate these two aspects of the war effort. That he never fully lost control over the revolution the war precipitated was testimony to his great leadership ability; that he led the nation to victory and succeeded in preserving the Union without destroying democracy assured his lasting place in American history.

Yet success did not come to him easily or quickly. In his early political career, the defeats and setbacks outweighed the victories and achievements. When he was suddenly thrust into the forefront by his election as president in 1860, he did not fully comprehend the nature of the crisis he would soon confront, and he learned how to meet the responsibilities of his new office only through trial and error. Throughout the war years, his basic character shone through: his good will and fundamental decency, his remarkable self-confidence encapsulated in genuine humility (he never liked to refer to himself as president and spoke of the office as "this place"), his immunity to the passions and hatreds the war spawned, his extraordinary patience and generosity of spirit. Even in the darkest days of the war, he never faltered in his commitment to persevere until the Union was restored. The personal and political qualities he brought to the challenge of waging a civil war are the major focus of this book.

This study synthesizes modern scholarship about Lincoln with my own ideas and interpretations of Lincoln and his age. My aim has been to write a short biography that is up-to-date in its scholarship. The notes at the back are limited to quotations in the text and have been kept to a minimum. The bibliography lists the most important studies I have drawn on in writing this book, but I have not attempted in either the notes or bibliography to list every book and article that has influenced my thinking about Lincoln and his times. The works listed in the bibliography will direct the interested reader to other relevant studies of Lincoln and the Civil War era.

When quoting from sources, I have followed several conventions to enhance the text's readability. I have sought to reproduce quotations accurately and have generally omitted the word *sic* to denote spelling and grammatical errors. In addition, I have replaced & with *and*, spelled out abbreviations, and changed terminal dashes to periods. In a few places, I have inserted a mark of punctuation, which is carefully indicated, to clarify the meaning of a phrase or sentence, but for the most part I have left punctuation unchanged. I have also omitted ellipses and silently modified capitalization at the opening of quotations.

During the course of writing this book, I have incurred many obligations that I wish to acknowledge. The idea for this book crystallized more than a decade ago in a conversation with Chris Rogers, who immediately signed the project for the history list he edited. Since then, both Chris and I have gone on to other positions, and the project suffered several major delays and had a complicated history, but it ended back on Chris's desk when he recruited it for Oxford University Press. I am grateful to Lyn Uhl for her generosity in making this outcome possible. At Oxford, I would particularly like to thank Peter Coveney and Joellyn Ausanka for adeptly guiding the book through the editorial and production process.

I did much of the research for this book in the various libraries at Harvard University. I am especially indebted to Nathaniel Bunker of Widener Library, who purchased many items on microfilm that were critical for my research. I would also like to thank the staffs at the Houghton Library and the Government Documents Library at Harvard for their many courtesies. In addition, the Inter-Library Loan office at Widener Library efficiently borrowed a number of items I requested, for which I am very appreciative.

A number of individuals have generously helped me over the years with sources and matters of interpretation. I am grateful for the assistance, suggestions, and critical commentary of Cullom Davis, David Donald, Mark Neely, John Simon, Michael Vorenberg, and Frank Williams. The outside readers for Oxford University Press made a number of helpful suggestions. In addition, I have benefited immensely from the observations of undergraduates who have taken my seminar on Lincoln at Harvard University.

Rodney Davis and Douglas Wilson, directors of the Lincoln Studies Center at Knox College, patiently answered my inquiries about the Herndon interviews concerning Lincoln's early life. I met Tom Schwartz, the Illinois state historian, two decades ago, and since then he has been a constant source of advice and assistance. He helped me sort through some of the complicated issues related to Lincoln's years in New Salem and Springfield. Michael Burlingame directed me to many less well known Lincoln sources, searched his files for information I needed, and patiently shared his ideas about Lincoln based on his research for the multivolume biography he is now writing. At a critical point James W. Davidson read the early chapters of the manuscript and offered some sage advice concerning style and content.

During the years I have been working on this book, my two sons, Bill and Jonathan, have grown from children to young adults. Their interest in the project, and in history more generally, has been immensely gratifying, and they provided countless hours of enjoyment separate from this book. The dedication recognizes the irreplaceable place they occupy in my life. My wife, Erica, offered encouragement without ever voicing concern about the time it took to complete the manuscript. Once it was finished, she gave it a thorough and careful reading and saved me from many errors and misstatements while greatly improving its clarity and style. As always, she was an unfailing source of support and encouragement.

To all of these individuals, I offer my sincere thanks. The book is much better for their efforts. Whatever errors and misinterpretations remain are because of my own stubbornness.

June 2001   William E. Gienapp

ABRAHAM LINCOLN AND CIVIL WAR AMERICA

Chapter 1

A SON OF THE FRONTIER

ABRAHAM LINCOLN rarely talked about his childhood. This silence stemmed from more than his well-developed sense of personal reserve, for while he was proud of his achievements, he was also embarrassed by his crude family background. In a brief autobiographical sketch he penned in 1859, when he was beginning to attract attention as a possible presidential candidate, he spent only a couple of lines on his parents, noted without elaboration that he did "farm work" as a youth, ignored his childhood social experiences entirely, and devoted the greatest attention—half a paragraph—to his limited education. "It is a great piece of folly to attempt to make anything out of my early life," he told a campaign biographer in 1860. "It can all be condensed into a single sentence . . . in Gray's Elegy: 'The short and simple annals of the poor.'"

DESCENDED FROM pioneer stock, Abraham knew little of his ancestry. The most vivid piece of family lore, which he had heard over and over again from his father Thomas, was how his grandfather had been killed by Indians while "laboring to open a farm" in the Kentucky forest. As a result, Thomas, who was eight years old at the time, had to make his own way in the world from an early age. He became "a wandering laboring boy, and grew up litterally without education." A capable carpenter in and around Elizabethtown, Kentucky, Thomas began to rise in the world and bought a farm, though he apparently never lived on it. In 1806, he married Nancy Hanks, who was probably illegitimate, and they set up housekeeping in Elizabethtown in a cabin that he had built. A daughter, Sarah, was born the following year.

Thomas soon displayed a wanderlust, however, that would repeatedly uproot the family. Devoting only part of his time to carpentry and cabinetmaking, he left Elizabethtown in 1808 and moved his family to a farm he purchased along Nolin Creek. It was here, on February 12, 1809, that Abraham (named for his grandfather) was born in the family's rude, one-room log cabin. When Abraham was two, his family moved to a more fertile farm on Knob Creek, which his father had rented, and Abraham's earliest memories were of this place. While living here his mother gave birth to another son, who died in infancy.

A man of above average height and powerful build, with straight black hair and leathery skin, Thomas worked hard but never seemed able to get very far ahead. An acquaintance later described him as "a tinker—a piddler—always doing but doing nothing great." Apparently he put limited stock in the value of education. Most likely he could not read, and according to his illustrious son, he "never did more in the way of writing than to bunglingly sign his own name." Still, the family's position was clearly improving, and Thomas was able to pay cash for the Knob Creek farm in 1815. He was also a respectable member of his frontier community: He owned property, performed several official duties, appeared a number of times in the local records, and enjoyed a reputation for scrupulous honesty and good morals. He was also renowned for his ability as a storyteller, a talent that he passed on to his son. Abraham remembered little of his mother, who has largely been lost in historical obscurity. Neighbors agreed that she was intelligent and deeply religious, and indeed, both she and Thomas belonged to the Baptist Church.

The labor of children was economically crucial on a farm, but when their duties allowed, Abraham and his sister attended local "A.B.C. schools" on two occasions for "short periods." His education was quite rudimentary, however, and when the family left Kentucky, Abraham, who was then seven, still could not write.

After a promising start, Thomas ran afoul of the maze of legal tangles that enveloped Kentucky land titles in these years. Rival claimants challenged the title to each of his farms, and lacking the resources for a prolonged legal fight, he simply sold out at a loss and in December 1816 moved to Indiana, where the federal government had surveyed the land. Indiana was a free state, and Thomas may also have wanted to get away from the institution of slavery. Hardin County, where the family had lived, had over a thousand slaves, who competed directly with white farmers and workers such as himself. Moreover, the Mount Separate Church, in which Thomas and Nancy were members, had seceded from the regular Baptist Church because of the latter's acceptance of slavery. Absorbing his parents' antislavery sentiments as he was growing up, Abraham later declared that he was "naturally anti-slavery" and added that he could not remember a time when he was not opposed to slavery.

The Lincolns settled on Little Pigeon Creek near Gentryville, in Spencer County, a sparsely populated, heavily wooded area near the Ohio River. After living several months in a crude shelter with one side open to a constantly roaring fire, they moved their meager possessions into a log cabin that Thomas had hastily constructed.

Life in Indiana was much more primitive than in Kentucky. Abraham remembered that it was "a wild region, with many bears and other wild animals still in the woods," and the family found conditions difficult. Perhaps Thomas had been beaten down by the loss of his Kentucky lands; perhaps he preferred hunting and did not pay sufficient attention to the difficult task of establishing a new farm; or perhaps his previously robust health declined. Whatever the reason, though Thomas continued to work as a cabinetmaker in the winter and at odd times, the family never entirely regained its earlier modest prosperity.

Abraham's life was that of a typical pioneer farm boy: doing chores, such as hauling water and chopping wood, and helping in the fields. The area was heavily wooded, and since he was remarkably strong for his age, the tall youngster was soon set to work clearing land with an axe. He later recalled that from then "till within his twentythird year, he was almost constantly handling that most useful instrument—less, of course, in plowing and harvesting seasons." For all his strength and prowess, however, he never enjoyed physical labor and once told a neighbor who hired him that "his father taught him to work but never learned him to love it." Nor did he cherish any romantic nostalgia for pioneer life, which he remembered as one of backbreaking labor and constant struggle with trees and grubs.

In 1817, after clearing and planting seventeen acres, Thomas Lincoln made the first payment on his farm. The arrival that fall of Nancy's aunt and uncle, Thomas and Elizabeth Sparrow, helped lessen the family's bleak isolation. Tagging along with them came eighteen-year-old Dennis Hanks, Abraham's easygoing, talkative cousin who, despite the difference in their ages, became his boon companion while growing up.

With the family's situation on the upswing, tragedy struck the little group the following year, when first the Sparrows and then Nancy Lincoln died from milk sickness (called "the puken" by pioneers), caused by cows grazing on the poisonous white snakeroot. With no minister available, family members held a brief service, and then Abraham's mother was buried near the cabin in a simple coffin Thomas had made. Abraham never said much about this loss, but it must have been a harsh blow to the nine-year-old boy and probably strengthened the melancholy streak in his personality.

Following Nancy Lincoln's death, living conditions at Pigeon Creek plummeted. Now alone, Dennis Hanks moved into the Lincoln cabin and shared the upstairs loft with Abe, as everyone called him, even though he hated the name. Thomas and Dennis spent most of their time hunting to provide food. Abraham's sister, Sarah, who was only twelve, did the cooking and tried to keep up the cabin, but she found the physical and emotional burden too much, and she and her brother became increasingly "wild—ragged and dirty." Thomas recognized that the family's situation was deteriorating, so late in 1819 he went to Kentucky and returned with a new wife, Sarah Bush Johnston, a widow, and her three children. Stepping out of the wagon, she beheld a ramshackle cabin without a suitable door or windows, a dirt floor, and a half-finished roof. Immediately taking charge, she soaped and scrubbed Abraham and Sarah, mended their clothes and dressed them up to make them appear "more human," instituted a new sense of order, and put her husband to work fixing up the cabin. Her energy, along with the furniture and household goods she brought with her, greatly improved the family's level of comfort.

A remarkable woman, Sarah Bush Lincoln exerted an enormous influence on Abraham. Though uneducated, she encouraged his interest in learning and loved and cared for him as if he were her own child. "Abe was the best boy I Ever Saw or Ever Expect to see," she

Lincoln's father, Thomas, and his stepmother, Sarah Bush Lincoln, as they appeared late in life. (Left: Abraham Lincoln Library and Museum, Lincoln Memorial University, Harrogate, TN; right: Illinois State Historical Library)

later declared, admitting that she liked him better than her own children. As the memory of his mother faded, a deep bond of affection developed between Abraham and his stepmother, who he called "Mama." He later said that "she had been his best Friend in this world and that no Son could love a Mother more than he loved her."

THROUGHOUT HIS LIFE, Abraham always keenly regretted the lack of educational opportunities in his youth. Schools were few, terms were short (two or three months in the winter), teachers were barely educated themselves, and as he later noted, "if a straggler supposed to understand latin, happened to sojourn in the neighborhood, he was looked upon as a wizzard." Most likely in the winter of 1819–20, when he was eleven years old, he attended a nearby "blab" school, in which students recited their lessons out loud all at once. The school was conducted by Andrew Crawford, whose most notable innovation was that he tried to teach the students manners. With his stepmother's backing, Abraham resumed his education two years later when a new school opened in the neighborhood. This school was more than four miles from the Lincoln cabin, however, so he was able to attend only sporadically. His last formal education came in 1824, when he was fifteen years old and he attended one term at a school closer to his home. A diligent student, he by now knew as much as his backwoods teachers, one of his classmates recalled, so "he went to school no more." By his calculation, his formal schooling did not total more than a year. "When I came of age," he confessed, "I did not know much. Still somehow, I could read, write, and cipher to the Rule of Three [proportions]; but that was all."

Concerning his Indiana boyhood, he contended that "there was absolutely nothing to excite ambition for education." Yet even at this early age, he displayed a burning desire for knowledge and self-improvement that set him apart from his surroundings. In his "Ambition," one of his Indiana acquaintances acknowledged, he "soared above us. . . ." His stepsister offered similar testimony: "Abe was not Energetic Except in one thing—he was active and persistant in learning —read Everything he Could—Ciphered on boards—on the walls." The well-entrenched image of the studious young lad reading by firelight is only a charming myth, for, like most farm boys, he went to bed early because he had to rise at daybreak to do his chores. His stepmother, though illiterate herself, valued knowledge and brought a few books with her, which Abraham read and reread. He also borrowed books from neighbors, often walking several miles to get a copy. Yet printed material was understandably scarce on the frontier, and his reading was predictably limited.

His reading included classic works such as *Robinson Crusoe*, *The Pilgrim's Progress*, and Aesop's *Fables*, plus Parson Weems's *Life of Washington*, which made a great impression on him and stimulated his interest in the country's founding; William Grimshaw's *History of the United States*; and William Scott's *Lessons in Elocution*, which heightened his attraction to public speaking at the same time that it introduced him to Shakespeare. The first law book he read was the *Revised Laws of Indiana*, which he borrowed from an employer sometime in his late teens. His later writings also establish that he carefully read the family Bible, despite his lack of religious inclinations.

In these early years, he developed the habit, which followed him through life, of reading slowly and carefully, pondering each point until satisfied that he understood it. His stepmother remembered that he had to "understand Every thing . . . Minutely and Exactly—: he would then repeat it over to himself again and again—some times in one form and then in another. . . ."

His father was less approving of Abraham's constant reading and noticeably favored his feckless stepson, John D. Johnston, in whom he found a kindred spirit. "Thos Lincoln never showed by his actions that he thought much of his son Abraham when a Boy," one Hanks family member noted, adding, "He treated him rather unkind than otherwise." Dennis Hanks admitted that Abraham's father sometimes "slash[ed] him for neglecting his work by reading." Indeed, like his father, neighbors considered him lazy because he preferred reading to farm work and often took a book to read between tasks. What Hanks termed Abraham's "Stubborn" reading was, in part, an act of rebellion against his father.

He stood apart from his environment in other ways as well. Although his father and stepmother were members of the local Baptist church, he was untouched by frontier revivalism and did not belong to any church. In a culture where masculinity was measured by fighting and drinking, he disapproved of violence and did not swear, drink, or use tobacco. Unusually sensitive, he was known for his kindness to animals, disliked fishing and hunting, and could not stand the sight of blood. Shortly before he was eight years old, he shot a wild turkey through a crack in the family cabin in Indiana. Deeply bothered by this act, he noted that "he has never since pulled a trigger on any larger game." And in a world where early marriage was common, he had little interest in girls. While they recognized his great kindness of heart, his homely looks, ill-fitting clothes, and lack of manners and social graces intensified his natural awkwardness in the presence of females.

In all-male company he was much more gregarious and at ease. Tall and sinewy, with large hands and exceptionally long arms, he was not especially coordinated, but he was a fast runner and powerful wrestler, feats which earned him a local reputation. He also attracted attention through his ability to tell stories. He "naturally assumed the leadership of the boys" and began to develop the skills that would be important in his subsequent political career. "When he appeared in Company the boys would gather and cluster around him to hear him talk," his playmate Nathaniel Grigsby stated. "He made fun and cracked his jokes making all happy. . . ." He also enjoyed a reputation for scrupulous honesty and truthfulness. "Men would Swear on his Simple word," insisted one Pigeon Creek pioneer.

As a teenager, he started giving speeches, using the elocution lessons he had studied as his guide. Taking a break from work that did not interest him, he would get up on a stump or fence and address his fellow workers, who would gather around and listen until his angry father "would come and make him quit—[and] send him to work." Even his early, unpolished speeches were notable for their clarity. "He argued much from Analogy and Explained things hard for us to understand by stories—maxims—tales and figures," one boyhood associate recounted. "He would almost always point his lesson or idea by some story that was plain and near as that we might instantly see the force and bearing of what he said."

Because he heartily disliked farm work, Abraham seized every opportunity to do something else: practicing his public speaking, regaling visitors at the local country store with his stories, participating in house raisings, competing in various athletic contests, observing sessions of the county court, and attending political meetings. To contribute to the family's income, he also did all sorts of odd jobs, including plowing and harvesting, daubing cabins, clearing land, splitting rails and building fences, packing pork, and clerking in a local store. As he ranged farther and farther from home, the tall, raw-boned lad— by age seventeen he already stood six feet two inches—became a familiar sight throughout the county. He never paid much attention to his appearance and normally traveled about in a shabby flax shirt, deerskin or linen britches that one schoolmate remembered stopped "6 or more inches" above his socks, and a coonskin cap. He was sixteen before he owned his first white shirt.

Newspapers provided another source of Abraham's education. He read all the papers he could get his hands on and became, in Dennis

Hanks's words, "a kind of news boy." Newspapers at this time were intensely partisan, and they stimulated Abraham's growing interest in politics. Nathaniel Grigsby said that as teenagers they went to political meetings and "heard questions discussed—talked Evry thing over and over and in fact wore it out—We learned much in this way." Abraham also frequently hung out at the store in Gentryville, a small settlement just down the road, where the local pundits incessantly discussed public affairs. Residents of more isolated backwoods areas were often supporters of Andrew Jackson, but, like his father, Abraham became a strong admirer of Henry Clay.

Increasingly, however, the nearby Ohio River, with its unique opportunities and experiences, beckoned him. When he was seventeen, he worked on a river ferry near the town of Troy, earning thirty-seven and a half cents a day for what he described as "the roughest work a young man could be made to do." One time, when he hastily rowed two passengers and their trunks out to a waiting steamboat in a small boat he had constructed, each man tossed the incredulous youth a silver half-dollar after boarding. "I could scarcely credit that I, a poor boy, had earned a dollar in less than a day," he recalled many years later. "The world seemed wider and fairer before me."

Two years later, in 1828, he and another companion were hired by a neighbor to take a load of produce by flatboat down the Ohio and Mississippi rivers to New Orleans, where they sold the boat and cargo and returned home on a steamboat. With its bustling river commerce, polyglot population, French architecture, and urban amusements, New Orleans was unlike anything the wide-eyed Indiana youth had ever seen before. It was also Abraham's first extended contact with the institution of slavery, although his reactions to this aspect of the trip are unknown. Since he was still a minor, he turned over to his father the twenty-four dollars he earned from the trip. Enchanted by the freedom and excitement of the river, he dreamed of becoming a steamboat pilot but was unable to find anyone who would take him on since he was underage.

This unsuccessful effort to get a river job was further evidence that his ties to his family were steadily weakening. Earlier that year he suffered another unsettling loss when his sister Sarah, one of the few people he was close to, died in childbirth. His life was further disrupted when Thomas Lincoln, hearing rumors of a new outbreak of milk sickness, pulled up stakes in 1830 and moved the family west again, this time to Illinois. When the group arrived at the new homestead, Abraham once again helped his father erect a primitive cabin, clear and fence ten acres, and plant corn, then hired himself out to split rails and do other odd jobs. But almost immediately his father decided the area was unhealthy, so the next spring the family moved once more, this time to Coles County.

Abraham was now of age, and instead of accompanying his family he agreed to make another trip to New Orleans in the employ of Denton Offutt, a local businessman whose grandiose plans outran his business acumen. Together with his stepbrother, John Johnston, and cousin John Hanks, Abraham journeyed to Springfield, where they learned that Offutt characteristically had failed to obtain a boat. After spending a month constructing a flatboat, they loaded it with Offutt's goods and started down the Sangamon River. When they reached New Salem, however, their boat got hung up on the milldam across the river, and they were unable to dislodge it. Finally, as Offutt and the curious residents watched, Abraham freed the flooded boat by drilling a hole in the bow, which protruded over the dam, to drain out the water. Impressed by the gangly young man's resourcefulness, Offutt, who intended to open a store in the town, agreed to hire him as a clerk when he got back from New Orleans. So upon his return in the summer of 1831, after a parting visit with his parents, Abraham set out for New Salem.

With his move to New Salem, Abraham left his father's world forever. Like his father, he was a product of the frontier, but they were very different in outlook and aspirations. During Abraham Lincoln's lifetime, the United States underwent a wrenching transformation from a rural, semisubsistence economy to a new commercial, market-oriented society. Thomas Lincoln, with his indifference to education, erratic work habits, limited ambition, agrarian outlook, and leisurely lifestyle, belonged to the premodern world. Rather than labor to produce a surplus for sale, the hallmark of an upwardly mobile farmer, he "lived Easy—and contented," a neighbor commented, since he "had but few wants and . . . Supplied them Easily." His ambitious, forward-looking son, in contrast, was very much part of the new modern world, with its emphasis on self-discipline, social mobility, and opportunity represented by commerce and industry. Abraham was anxious to rise in the world, and his negative image of his father served as a spur to drive him to greater intellectual and social distinction. By the time he left home a deep estrangement had developed between him and his father which would grow only stronger with time. Indeed, in all of his writings, there is not a single positive reference to his father.

Although he rejected the rural life of his boyhood, he had been inevitably shaped by it. He always spoke with a country twang and mispronounced certain words—much to the dismay of more refined listeners—and rustic references and images dotted his speeches and writings. Like many rural residents, he had a strong sense of fatalism and never could completely free himself from superstition. Abraham Lincoln was not a common man, but he knew how to effect a common touch, which his homespun stories reinforced, and throughout his life he displayed a great talent for communicating with ordinary citizens, from whose ranks he had risen.

Nevertheless, he had reached a turning point. When he left his family and set out on his own, he did not know what he wanted to do in the world. What he did know was that he wanted a different— and better—life than that of his father.

When Lincoln arrived in New Salem in July of 1831 carrying all his worldly possessions under his arm, he described himself as "a piece of floating driftwood" who had washed up on the town's shores. He did not lack for self-confidence—indeed, he had already developed a deeply rooted sense of intellectual superiority—but as a "penniless" and "friendless" stranger, he realized that whatever he achieved would have to be through the dint of his own labor. As a clerk, he made fifteen dollars a month and slept in the back room of Offutt's store.

The new arrival's crude, ill-fitting clothing, tousled hair, and uncouth looks made him seem every inch the traditional country bumpkin. When he came to New Salem he was, according to William Butler, a subsequent friend, "as ruff a specimen of humanity as could be found." Parthena Hill, the wife of a storeowner in New Salem, related that "he went about a good deal of the time without any hat. . . . His yellow tow-linen pants he usually wore rolled up one leg and down the other." The town's citizens quickly perceived, however, that his outward image was deceiving. "His external apperance was not prepossessing," conceded James Duncan, an educated physician who lived in New Salem, "but on cultivating an acquaintance with him," Duncan discovered that he possessed "intellegence far beyond the generality of youth of his age and opportunities."

New Salem was a raw pioneer village of about a hundred people located on a high bluff overlooking the Sangamon River. The community's future rested on the hope that steamboats could ply the river, thus connecting the village with the Mississippi valley. Its population was in constant flux, and it never numbered more than a couple of hundred inhabitants, most of whom, like Lincoln, were from the South. At various times the town contained a mill, wool-carding machine, several stores and taverns, some craftsmen, and a school.

Frontier culture placed a premium on manhood, and Lincoln's great physical strength inevitably attracted admiration and attention. His lean frame was all muscle, and he could lift incredible weights and was an expert wrestler. As they did with all new arrivals, local ruffians quickly tested Lincoln's mettle when he wrestled Jack Armstrong, head of a group of rowdies known as the Clary's Grove boys. Witnesses' recollections of this famous match differ substantially, but all agree that when it was over Lincoln had won the friendship and admiration of Armstrong and his associates. Major consequences sometimes arise from minor events, and their support would play an important role in Lincoln's early political career.

Lincoln's modest demeanor, affable manner, and rollicking sense of humor gained him many friends, and village loafers regularly congregated in the store to listen to his stories. "Geniel" and "fun loveing," he "was always the centre of the circle where ever he was" and "always had a story to tell." Reflective of his social background, the stories he regaled all-male audiences with were sometimes crude, although they generally did not deal with sexual matters (Lincoln was rather prudish where women were concerned).

One of the most famous of his stories from this period, which he told with dramatic gestures, comical facial expressions, and exagger-

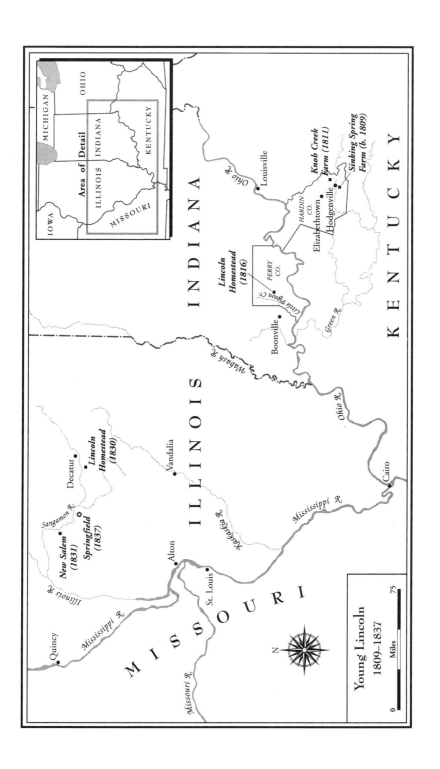

Area of Detail

MICHIGAN

OHIO

ILLINOIS   INDIANA

KENTUCKY

IOWA

MISSOURI

INDIANA

Louisville

Ohio R.

Knob Creek Farm (1811)

Sinking Spring Farm (b. 1809)

HARDIN CO.

Elizabethtown

Hodgenville

Lincoln Homestead (1816)

PERRY CO.

Little Pigeon Cr.

Green R.

Boonville

Wabash R.

KENTUCKY

ILLINOIS

Ohio R.

Decatur

Lincoln Homestead (1830)

Vandalia

Cairo

Sangamon R.

New Salem (1831)

Springfield (1837)

Kaskaskia R.

Mississippi R.

Alton

Illinois R.

Mississippi R.

St. Louis

Quincy

MISSOURI

Missouri R.

N

Young Lincoln
1809–1837

Miles

0   75

ated body movements, concerned an Indiana Baptist preacher who took as his text, "I am the Christ, whom I shall represent today." As the unfortunate minister began his sermon, a lizard ran up his leg. Rather than pausing, he continued his remarks, all the while slapping at his pants in a vain effort to dislodge the reptile. Failing to remove the intruder, the discomforted preacher unbuttoned his trousers and with a kick tossed them off, and as the lizard climbed higher, unfastened his collar and threw off his shirt. As the dazed congregation looked on in disbelief, an old woman rose in the back and shouted, "If you represent Christ then I'm done with the Bible."

The unpretentious newcomer quickly became part of the community. Attuned to the communal work patterns of frontier society by which neighbors helped one another, Lincoln readily participated in activities such as raising houses, harvesting crops, and repairing the milldam. His truthfulness and reputation for fair dealing invariably led residents to select him to judge races and other contests. Lincoln's judgment "was final," declared one inhabitant. "People relied implicitly on his honesty, integrity, and impartiality." While he was temperate— he complained that alcohol left him "flabby and undone"—he was no prig and did not either assume an air of moral superiority or seek to impose his values on others. Declining to judge people harshly, he made "great allowances for men's foibles," another associate asserted, and his conciliatory approach and obliging manner earned him additional friends. Thanks to his sociability and fondness for visiting, he soon "knew every man, woman and child for miles around."

Anxious to improve himself and get ahead, he was acutely sensitive to the deficiencies of his education, so in his spare time he embarked on a program of self-education. Lincoln probably was already thinking of trying his hand in politics or the law. In any event, he decided that he needed to improve his knowledge of grammar if he was to make something of himself. He somehow got hold of a book, probably Kirkham's *Grammar*, and "studied English grammar, imperfectly of course, but so as to speak and write as well as he now does." He also studied mathematics, which had always held a particular appeal for him because of its rigorous logic and precision. For assistance, he occasionally turned to Mentor Graham, who ran the school in town, and Jack Kelso, a village idler and proverbial cracker-barrel philosopher who was constantly spouting Burns and Shakespeare, but Lincoln was largely self-taught. As had been true in his boyhood, his preference for reading over manual labor and his fondness for swapping stories and telling jokes led some acquaintances to dismiss him as a loafer. Before long, however, the ambitious clerk was drafting simple legal documents for residents using a book of legal forms for guidance.

He also began to appear before Bowling Green, the local Justice of the Peace who took a liking to the shabby-looking young man. The corpulent Green often shook with laughter at Lincoln's stories and comments and initially allowed Lincoln to participate in court proceedings more for entertainment than anything else, but he soon recognized Lincoln's unusual intellectual ability. Though his legal knowledge was limited, Lincoln attended Green's court a number of times representing local citizens. Unlike most of Lincoln's friends, who scoffed at his ambition, Green encouraged him to continue his studies. A fellow store clerk testified that Lincoln "Used to say that he owed more to Mr Green for his advancement than any other Man."

Although small and unrefined, New Salem nevertheless offered intellectual outlets that far surpassed anything to which Lincoln had previously been exposed. It had a post office, local court, and even a debating society, and boasted at least six college graduates among its residents. He quickly joined the debating club and also hooked up with a group of free thinkers, whose views on religion were similar to his and who introduced him to several famous books attacking religion. In 1846, while a congressional candidate, he acknowledged that during this period of his life "I was inclined to believe in what I understand is called the 'Doctrine of Necessity'—that is, that the human mind is impelled to action, or held in rest by some power, over which the mind itself has no control," and "sometimes (with one, two, or three, but never publicly) tried to maintain this opinion in argument." In these years he apparently wrote an essay, which has not survived, denying that the Bible was divine revelation.

Even at this early age, Lincoln's real interest was politics. For an ambitious young man with oratorical skills, politics was a way to make a name and rise in the world. "Encouraged," as he put it, "by his great popularity among his immediate neighbors," Lincoln announced his candidacy for the state legislature in March 1832, less than a year since he had taken up residence in town. "Every man is said to have his peculiar ambition," he noted in a letter declaring his candidacy, but "I can say for one that I have no other so great as that of being truly esteemed of my fellow men, by rendering myself worthy of their esteem." His platform was improved transportation facilities (internal improvements), educational opportunity, and a law against excessive interest rates.

His statement declaring his candidacy, while characteristically modest, was shrewdly calculated to appeal to ordinary voters who, like himself, had not been born to privilege. "I am young and unknown to many of you," he wrote. "I was born and have ever remained in the most humble walks of life. I have no wealthy or popular relations to recommend me." Even after he had become a successful attorney, allusion to his humble origins was a campaign pitch that he would use over and over again in his political career. Promising to work ceaselessly for the people if elected, he assured his readers that if he was defeated, "I have been too familiar with disappointments to be very much chagrined."

This document advanced ideas that would remain central to Lincoln's career and thought throughout his life, in particular, his emphasis on education as a means of social and personal betterment, his belief that government should promote economic development, and his desire to create a modern system of sound credit. He devoted most of his letter announcing his candidacy to the importance of improving the navigation of the Sangamon River for steamboats (he ruled out the alternatives of a canal or railroad as too expensive). The call for improved transportation reflected the outlook of upwardly striving, commercially oriented people such as himself, who believed commerce was an agent of civilization and who wanted a market-driven society. Having grown up in the isolation of southern Indiana, Lincoln understood the importance of cheap transportation if residents were to increase their income and improve their standards of living by participating in a wider market. He also knew how much farmers and businessmen who wanted to pursue these economic opportunities depended on credit, and thus he called for elimination of usury. And like members of the more prosperous and respectable middle class, he linked education not only to social mobility but also to "morality, sobriety, enterprise and industry." He did not discuss national politics in his announcement, perhaps because his support for Henry Clay, who was running for president against Andrew Jackson, was not a popular position in the county.

Prior to the 1832 election, however, the Black Hawk War broke out in the spring when a band of Saux and Fox Indians crossed the Mississippi and reoccupied their old lands in Illinois. Offutt's store had failed in the meantime, and Lincoln, who was out of work, volunteered to serve in the militia. Backed by the Clary's Grove boys, who were in his company, he was elected captain. In an autobiographical statement written in 1860, he claimed that no subsequent success "gave him so much satisfaction." During the three months he served, he did no fighting—indeed, never even saw a hostile Indian—but the $124 he earned was, to him, a substantial and desperately needed sum. Later, while in Congress, he poked fun of his military career, but in fact he was proud of his service, which strengthened his sense of leadership and reinforced his political ambitions.

After he was mustered out in late July, Lincoln had only ten days to stump the county. There was not a shred of pretension about him. Having by now reached his full height of six feet four inches, he was a sight for sore eyes, wearing a straw hat to protect his sorrowful, sun-burned face, "a mixt Jeans Coat" with sleeves that were too short for his lanky arms, and "Flax and Tow linnen" pants that ended well above his rough shoes. His speeches were equally simple. "My politics are short and sweet, like the old woman's dance," he told one gathering. Explaining that he favored a national bank, internal improvements, and a protective tariff, he closed, "If elected I shall be thankful; if not it will be all the same." He was not well known outside his own community, and with only a short time to campaign he finished eighth, "the only time," he later proudly noted, that he was "ever beaten on a direct vote of the people." It was a very credible showing for a propertyless young man who had arrived in the county only a year ago. He was particularly encouraged by his standing in New Salem, where he received 277 out of 300 votes cast.

NEVERTHELESS, he was once again unemployed and needed a livelihood. He recalled that he "thought of learning the black-smith trade —thought of trying to study law—rather thought he could not succeed at that without a better education." Caught up in the boom mentality of the town, he became a partner with William F. Berry in a local store. Lacking any capital, they bought the goods of two local stores on credit. Neither of these would-be entrepreneurs was well suited for this business. Observers claimed that Berry drank up the profits and more from the store's whiskey barrel, and though Lincoln had already earned the appellation "Honest Abe" while clerking for Offutt, he spent more time joking with loafers who hung about the store than in minding the firm's business. Moreover, according to another storekeeper, Lincoln felt awkward around women and "allways disliked to wait on the Ladies" and "prefered trading with the Men and Boys as he used to Say." The partners, Lincoln later declared, "did nothing but get deeper and deeper in debt," and he finally sold out to Berry in April 1833. The store eventually "winked out," but Berry's subsequent death saddled Lincoln with the firm's debts totaling more than a thousand dollars, and it took him until the early 1840s to pay off what he termed his "national debt."

He received a stroke of good fortune in 1833 when he was appointed postmaster of the village. This office provided him a small salary for the next three years and also enabled him to become acquainted with virtually all the residents of the area, a vital aid to his political aspirations. Although postal regulations required people to pick up their mail at the office, if he had some business in the country, "he placed inside his hat all the letters belonging to people in the neighborhood and distributed them along the way," prompting residents to joke that "he carried the office around in his hat." When Lincoln received the appointment, one acquaintance reported that he "never saw a man better pleased . . . because, as he said, he would then have access to all the News papers—never yet being able to get the half that he wanted before." Since the mail arrived only twice a week, his duties as postmaster were light, giving him plenty of free time to read. But the salary was too small to support himself, so he took a variety of odd jobs. Offered the chance to become an assistant surveyor, he studied trigonometry and surveying and then "went at it" in order to keep "soul and body together." His horse, tools, and possessions were eventually seized for debt, however, a result of his ill-fated venture with William Berry, and only the assistance of his friends, who bought his belongings at auction in March 1835 and then returned them, allowed him to continue this work. Nothing he had tried had met with much success, and with no long-term prospects he seemed in danger of slipping permanently back into the ranks of ordinary laborers.

In the face of these setbacks, Lincoln persevered in his program of self-education. With more books and newspapers available than he had access to in Indiana, he became more selective in his reading. Even so, he "read a great deal, improving every opportunity, by day and by night." One New Salem resident remembered: "While clerking for Offatt [sic] as Post Master or in the pursuit of any avocation, An opportunity would offer, he would apply himself to his studies, if it was but five minutes time, would open his book, which he always kept at hand, and study, close it recite to himself, then entertain company or wait on a Customer in the Store or post office apparently without any interruption. When passing from business to boarding house for meals, he could usually be seen with his book under his arm, or open in his hand reading as he walked. . . ."

As the 1834 election neared, Lincoln again announced his candidacy for the legislature. Dark-complexioned with coarse, unruly black hair, he weighed only 180 pounds despite his great height. A local politician, who met Lincoln at this time, offered the following description: "His eyes were a bluish brown, his face was long and very angular, when at ease had nothing in his appearance that was marked or Striking, but when enlivened in conversation or engaged in telling, or hearing some mirth-inspiring Story, his countenance would brighten . . . up not in a flash, but rapidly. . . . his eyes would Sparkle, all terminating in an unrestrained Laugh in which every one present willing or unwilling were compelled to take part." His voice, while not entirely pleasant, was quite effective on the hustings. "He spooke [sic] in [a] . . . clear Shrill monotone Style of Speaking, that enabled his audience, however large, to hear distictly the lowest Sound of his voice."

Although running as a Whig, Lincoln enjoyed bipartisan support in New Salem, where he was immensely popular. Conspicuous among his champions were the Clary's Grove boys, Democrats to a man, who came to political meetings prepared to do battle, literally, with anyone who dared to criticize their townsman. In the era's democratic political culture, candidates had to be careful to avoid aristocratic pretensions and mix with the common people. Plunging into a field where thirty men were at work, Lincoln cut more grain than any of them—and thereby won their votes.

In August, Lincoln polled the second highest number of votes in the county and was elected. The office's salary promised at least temporary relief from his financial problems. John T. Stuart, a fellow Kentuckian and the Whig leader in the county, was impressed with Lincoln and encouraged him during the campaign to study law. Too poor to study in a law office, Lincoln undertook a program of self-study with some law books Stuart loaned him. He bought a copy of Blackstone's *Commentaries*, the standard text for lawyers, at a Springfield auction and "went at it in good earnest." After he took up the study of law, Lincoln displayed a new intensity and single-minded determination in his reading. His neighbors were both bewildered and amused at the sight of the rangy young man, sprawled out in some spot pondering a book, or reading late at night after business closed. "When he began to study law," one friend reported, "he would go day after day for weeks and sit under an oak tree on [a] hill near [New] Salem, and read—moved round [the] tree to keep in shade—was so absorbed that people said he was crazy."

Lincoln persisted in the face of constant scoffing by his companions. "The first time I Ever Saw him with a law book in his hands he was Sitting astraddle . . . [a] wood pile in New Salem," Russell Godbey recalled. Asked what he was doing, Lincoln replied, "Studying law," prompting Godbey to blurt out in amazement, "Great God Almighty."

WHEN IT WAS TIME to take his seat in the legislature, he borrowed $200 and used part of this sum to buy a new suit, the first decent clothing he had ever owned. Then hopping aboard a stagecoach, the twenty-three-year-old legislator traveled to Vandalia, the state capital, to take up his duties.

Lincoln was one of fifty-five representatives. As a Whig, he was in the minority, and as a newcomer, he was given only a minor committee assignment. The session, for which he received $258 in compensation, was essentially a learning experience. But it did confirm one thing in Lincoln's mind: His commitment to being a lawyer was strengthened, and when he returned to New Salem, he resumed his legal self-study, while continuing to work as postmaster and surveyor.

With a new sense of direction in his life, he became less shy and awkward around women (though never really at ease), and began to pay particular attention to Ann Rutledge, the young daughter of a New Salem tavernkeeper. Contemporaries, who were probably overly favorable, described the twenty-two-year-old Ann as pretty, with blue eyes and blond hair. Lincoln boarded at her father's tavern from time to time and got to know her quite well. Ann was engaged to John McNeil, but this fact probably facilitated their developing friendship, since Lincoln was always more at ease around unavailable women. In the fall of 1833, McNeil confessed to Ann that his real name was McNamar and explained that he had to go to New York to deal with some family matters. McNamar's story aroused suspicion among New Salem residents, and as Lincoln knew from his position as postmaster, he eventually ceased to write Ann.

With McNamar absent, Lincoln's friendship with Ann blossomed into romance. Their exact relationship is unclear, but it seems likely that in 1835 they became conditionally engaged. Apparently, Ann wanted to first gain a formal release from her engagement to Mc-Namar; moreover, Lincoln felt that marriage would be imprudent until he was admitted to the bar. Certainly when she suddenly died in August 1835, probably of typhoid fever, Lincoln was overcome with grief, and his erratic behavior was cause for concern among his friends. Ann's death produced the first significant references by associates to Lincoln's deep-seated melancholy, which verged on depression and continued to plague him throughout his life. Whatever the immediate emotional impact of Ann's death, however, he eventually recovered, and within a year was unsuccessfully courting another woman.

Lincoln had met Mary Owens in 1833 when she visited her sister in New Salem. She came from a prosperous Kentucky family and was educated, socially adept, and bright. When she returned in 1836, a year after Ann died, he began a less than ardent courtship which eventually led to an understanding that they might get married. Soon filled with doubts, Lincoln tried to get Mary to take the responsibility for ending the relationship and thereby preserve his sense of honor. When she failed to act on his not-so-subtle hints, he finally offered in 1837, in a remarkably dispassionate letter, to marry her if it would "add to your happiness." To his surprise, she rejected this proposal. Many years later, when recounting examples of Lincoln's inattentiveness, she explained that he "was deficient in those little links which make up the great chain of womans happiness. . . ." In a subsequent account lampooning the affair, Lincoln acknowledged, "My vanity was deeply wounded by the reflection . . . that she whom I had taught myself to believe no body else would have, had actually rejected me with all my fancied greatness; and to cap the whole, I then, for the first time, began to suspect that I was really a little in love with her."

Lincoln was still recovering from Ann Rutledge's death when a special legislative session was held in the winter of 1835–36. Perhaps for this reason, or perhaps because he was still learning the ways of the legislature, he did not assume a prominent role in the session. In the campaign in 1836, however, he emerged as a leading spokesman for the Whig cause and was easily reelected to a second term, outpolling all candidates in the county. As the new party system took shape, party lines were beginning to be drawn more tightly, as evidenced by the failure of his friend Jack Armstrong, a Democrat, to vote for him.

When the new legislature assembled in December 1836, Lincoln was selected as the Whigs' floor leader and, in another sign of his growing stature, though a member of the minority party, was made chairman of the finance committee. As the state's population grew, support to move the capital to a more central location increased, and Lincoln played the most important role in getting Springfield selected as the new capital. He also helped push through a bill to construct an ambitious (and ultimately economically ruinous) statewide system of internal improvements, and took the lead in defeating Democratic efforts to abolish the Illinois State Bank. During the debate over the bank, he offered his famous definition of politicians as "a set of men who have interests aside from the interests of the people, and who . . . are, taken as a mass, at least one long step removed from honest men." To take some of the sting out of his remarks, he added, "I say this with the greater freedom because, being a politician myself, none can regard it as personal." In only his third year of service, he had established himself as an important leader in the legislature.

This legislative session also marked Lincoln's first public endorsement of antislavery principles. Earlier, with Lincoln voting in the minority, the legislature had approved a set of resolutions condemning the abolitionist movement. Once the bills to relocate the state capital and construct a system of internal improvements, on which he placed first priority, had been approved, Lincoln and fellow Sangamon County representative Dan Stone entered a protest in the House Journal. While agreeing that Congress had no power to interfere with slavery in the states, they maintained that it could abolish the institution in the District of Columbia, but should do so only with the consent of its residents. Their protest also affirmed that "the institution of slavery is founded on both injustice and bad policy; but that the promulgation of abolition doctrines tends rather to increase than to abate its evils." While this statement fell far short of abolitionist ideals, it was, nevertheless, a courageous public act. Antislavery sentiment was weak in Illinois, and Lincoln had nothing to gain politically by taking such a stand.

By now Lincoln's ambitions had outgrown New Salem, and when the legislature adjourned, he returned simply to collect his belongings. The previous fall he had passed the bar exam with surprising ease and on September 9, 1836, received his license to practice law. John Stuart, a prominent attorney in Springfield as well as a fellow Whig legislator, had offered to take him on as a junior partner, and in any case New Salem did not have enough legal business to support him. Moreover, New Salem was now dying. The inability of steamboats to navigate the Sangamon River had doomed the once-thriving village, and its residents were now departing for more promising locales.

Unlike his years in Indiana, Lincoln always retained fond memories of New Salem and its inhabitants, who "treated him with so much generosity" during the six years he lived there. It was here that he first entered into serious public discussion of issues and launched his political career. It was here that he decided he wanted to be a lawyer and began his study of the law. And it was here that he deepened his understanding of the common people, which would be so crucial to his political career, by mixing with them, sharing stories and playing games, and helping them with their work. These experiences deepened his appreciation of democracy as both a political and a social system, and his self-confidence had steadily grown.

But greener pastures now beckoned. Having at last settled on a career, he stuffed his meager possessions into two saddlebags, said good-bye to his many friends, and then rode off on a borrowed horse to the new capital of Springfield. In marked contrast to his restless father, who had repeatedly uprooted the family, this move was the last one Lincoln would make until he went to Washington in 1861.

Chapter 2

THWARTED AMBITION

ON APRIL 15, 1837, at the age of twenty-eight, Lincoln arrived in Springfield to try his "experiment as a lawyer." Unable to afford a bed and bedding, he quickly accepted an offer from Joshua Speed to share a room and bed above Speed's store. Taking his saddlebags to the room, Lincoln soon returned and announced, "Well, Speed, I am moved!" Speed, who was four years younger than Lincoln, also came from Kentucky; in the four years they lived together, he became the only truly intimate friend Lincoln ever had.

Springfield was basically a frontier community where hogs still ran in the streets, but with 2000 inhabitants it was still a good sight larger and more cultivated than New Salem, and the rustic Lincoln felt badly out of place. "I am quite as lonesome here as [I] ever was anywhere in my life," he wrote a few weeks after his arrival. He soon found a circle of friends among young, upwardly mobile professional men in town, who regularly gathered at Speed's store in the evening to discuss politics and other matters. Lincoln was at ease in this male fraternity, regaling its members with his stories, but he remained woefully uncertain around women. "I have been spoken to by but one woman since I've been here," he reported, "and should not have been by her, if she could have avoided it."

᷾

WHEN HE RELOCATED to the new capital, a local paper announced that Lincoln would practice law with John T. Stuart. Stuart was a successful attorney with a large practice, but he devoted most of his time to politics and hence left much of the office work to the junior partner. While Lincoln's legal knowledge did not run deep, the practice of law in the state did not require extensive training or vast knowledge. Most cases involved basic legal points, and thus the ability to present a case clearly and sway a jury was more critical. Average fees were small, so to make a decent income he had to handle a large number of cases.

Since the court in Springfield met only a few weeks each year, Lincoln, like many of his fellow lawyers, rode the circuit, traveling to county seats to handle local cases, then moving on to the next county court session. As Stuart's partner, Lincoln practiced law throughout the Eighth Circuit, an especially large district of fourteen counties that covered over 10,000 square miles. Court sessions were held in each of the county seats according to a specified order in both the spring and the fall; attorneys traveling the circuit were on the road for ten weeks or more twice a year. One of his partners estimated that in some years Lincoln spent six months on the circuit. Travel was slow and arduous even under the best conditions, accommodations uncomfortable with two or three men sleeping in a single bed, and the food wretched.

Beyond the additional income and male camaraderie of his fellow lawyers that Lincoln so delighted in, such legal work also offered decided political benefits. Court week produced a beehive of activity in the town, as many farmers flocked to the county seat to watch the proceedings. On the frontier the courthouse "supplied the place of theatres, lecture and concert rooms, and other places of interest and amusement," one Illinois politician noted. "The leading lawyers and judges were the star actors," and when the county court session ended, their performances were discussed "at every cabin-raising, bee or horse-race, and at every log house and school in the county." Thus lawyers became well known outside their home county, which had great political advantages. They also built personal alliances with other lawyers, many of whom were politically active. And finally, in the fall after court adjourned for the day, they often participated in political debates and other campaign activities.

Lincoln's career in the circuit courts heightened his political skills at the same time it enhanced his public reputation. He met large numbers of ordinary people, discovered which issues concerned them, and sharpened his powers of political persuasion. Practicing on the circuit offered him an unrivaled opportunity to meet people and study human nature.

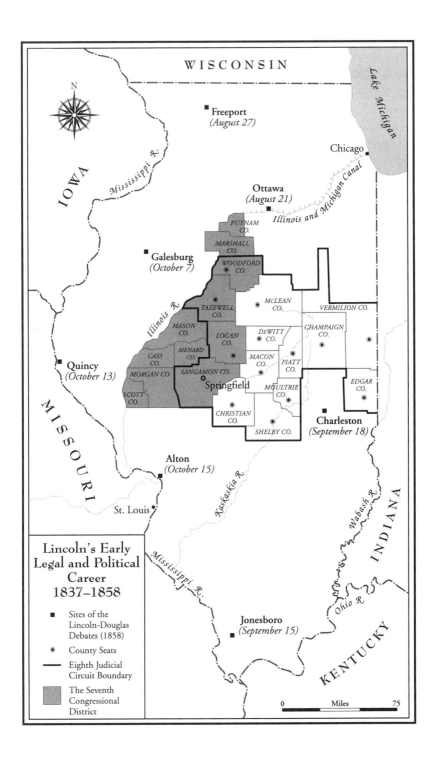

WISCONSIN

N

IOWA

Mississippi R.

MISSOURI

■ Freeport
(August 27)

Lake Michigan

Chicago ●

Ottawa
(August 21)

Illinois and Michigan Canal

PUTNAM
CO.

MARSHALL
CO.

■ Galesburg
(October 7)

WOODFORD
CO. ⊙

Illinois R.

TAZEWELL
CO. ⊙

MASON
CO.

MENARD
CO. ⊙

CASS
CO.

LOGAN
CO. ⊙

McLEAN
CO. ⊙

DeWITT
CO. ⊙

VERMILION CO.

CHAMPAIGN
CO. ⊙

⊙

■ Quincy
(October 13)

MORGAN CO.

SANGAMON CO. ⊕
Springfield

MACON
CO. ⊙

PIATT
CO. ⊙

SCOTT
CO.

CHRISTIAN
CO.

MOULTRIE
CO. ⊙

SHELBY CO. ⊙

EDGAR
CO. ⊙

■ Charleston
(September 18)

■ Alton
(October 15)

Kaskaskia R.

St. Louis ●

Lincoln's Early
Legal and Political
Career
1837–1858

Mississippi R.

INDIANA

Wabash R.

■ Sites of the
Lincoln-Douglas
Debates (1858)

⊙ County Seats

— Eighth Judicial
Circuit Boundary

The Seventh
Congressional
District

■ Jonesboro
(September 15)

Ohio R.

KENTUCKY

0   Miles   75

While his association with Stuart brought him instant recognition in the profession, Lincoln did not learn much from his partner, who was often absent or otherwise absorbed. After several years, he realized that he had to increase his legal knowledge in order to rise in the profession. Cases were becoming more complex, opposing lawyers more skilled, and larger fees could be had in the federal courts and in the state supreme court, which met in Springfield, but these cases involved more complicated legal matters. By mutual agreement, Lincoln and Stuart dissolved their partnership in 1841, and Lincoln became Stephen T. Logan's partner.

Logan, who was ten years older than Lincoln, was a fellow Kentuckian who dressed haphazardly and presented anything but an impressive figure in court. He was blessed with neither good looks nor a commanding voice and relied instead on hard work and thorough preparation. Lincoln's legal knowledge was "very small when I took him in," Logan subsequently observed. "I dont think he studied very much. I think he learned his law more in the study of cases." During their partnership he impressed upon Lincoln the necessity of applying himself to his profession, and for the first time Lincoln worked at becoming a better lawyer. As his technical command of the law expanded, his oratory and writing became less florid. "Don't shoot too high," he advised one young attorney. "Aim lower and the common people will understand you."

As his experience and reputation grew, however, he became increasingly dissatisfied with his secondary position in the firm. In 1844 the two men agreed to end their partnership, and in December of that year Lincoln took on William Herndon, who had just received his law license and was nine years younger, as his junior partner. The two continued to practice together until Lincoln became president.

DIVIDING HIS TIME between politics and the law, Lincoln's life now fell into a predictable pattern. In years when there was a state election, he devoted more attention to political matters, to the detriment of his professional income. In alternate years he concentrated on the law to restore his finances.

His main interest, however, was politics. Lincoln was a product of the intensely partisan world of the mid-nineteenth century. In these years parties were considered vital to the health of the Republic, mass interest was extraordinarily high, and partisanship was pronounced at all levels of government. Newspapers were openly partisan and regularly impaled the opposition, and party members reaffirmed their loyalty at countless parades, barbecues, and party rallies.

This was the political world that Abraham Lincoln came of age in and, more importantly, functioned in. Far from being alienated by this political system, he adopted its premises, formed his identity in conjunction with it, molded his outlook and behavior accordingly, and measured his accomplishments according to its standards. He made no apologies for being either a politician or a member of a political party. Indeed, to Lincoln, as to most of his male contemporaries, nothing seemed more natural than to be a political partisan. "The man who is of neither party," he contended, "is not—cannot be, of any consequence" in society.

As was true for others of his generation, Lincoln's party allegiance was not lightly assumed or easily discarded. He was, he proudly recalled, "always a whig in politics," and like most voters, Lincoln placed a high premium on party regularity and had a particular disdain for political turncoats. George Forquer, a onetime Whig who received a lucrative office after he switched to the Democratic party, was a particular object of Lincoln's scorn. Forquer owned the finest house in Springfield, on which he had erected a lightning rod. When Forquer replied to a speech he delivered at a political meeting, Lincoln retorted, "I desire to live—and I disire [sic] place and distinction as a politician —but I would rather die now than like the gentleman live to see the day that I would have to erect a lightning rod to protect a guilty Conscience from an offended God."

Politics in this period was largely an all-male concern, in which drinking and fighting were integral features, and in this environment Lincoln's courage and great physical strength were decided political assets. Once when a fight broke out while he was speaking, he strode into the crowd, grabbed one of the combatants by the neck and pants, and allegedly tossed him "10 or 12 feet, Easily." According to one witness, Lincoln's forceful intervention "made him many friends" that day. On another occasion, when a hostile crowd tried to prevent his friend Edward Baker from speaking at an 1839 meeting, Lincoln mounted the platform, lifted a stone pitcher, and threatened to clobber the first person who laid a hand on Baker.

Unlike some Whigs, Lincoln betrayed no doubts about the importance of party organization. He devoted great effort to perfecting the Whig organization for the 1840 campaign; and he promoted a similar enterprise in 1843. To his fellow Illinois Whigs, he stressed that organization was a "necessity," and whatever its abstract merits, adoption of the convention system for making nominations was essential: "While our opponents use it, it is madness in us not to defend ourselves with it." He wrote letters, gave speeches, promoted party papers, and supervised a thousand campaign details, all the while urging the Whigs on to victory. "Our intention," he proclaimed, "is to organize the whole State, so that every Whig can be brought to the polls. . . ." His plan envisioned nothing less than personal contact with every Whig and undecided voter in the county.

The political culture of Lincoln's America was also stridently democratic. Whigs and Democrats alike extolled the wisdom of the common people, believed that government should be responsive to their needs, and fiercely battled for popular favor.

From its inception, Lincoln's partisanship grew out of his belief in democracy. "I go for sharing the privileges of the government, who assist in bearing its burthens," he wrote in announcing his candidacy for the legislature in 1836. "Consequently I go for admitting all whites to the right of suffrage, who pay taxes or bear arms, (by no means excluding females)." He also accepted the idea that representatives should be guided by the will of their constituents rather than exercise any independent judgment. While a member of Congress in 1848, he asserted that "the primary, the cardinal, the one great living principle of all Democratic representative government . . . [is] the principle, that the representative is bound to carry out the known will of his constituents."

As he honed his speaking skills at countless mass rallies during these years, he became a particularly effective stump speaker. He laced his speeches with humorous anecdotes, often drawn from his frontier upbringing, to illustrate his points, a tactic that drew ordinary farmers and workers to him. A participant in a huge rally the Whigs held in Springfield in 1840 described Lincoln addressing a large crowd from a wagon. "At times he discussed the questions of the time in a logical way, but much time was devoted to telling stories to illustrate some phase of his argument, though more often the telling of these stories was resorted to for the purpose of rendering his opponents ridiculous."

Even a Democratic reporter conceded that he was a good "public debater" who displayed "much urbanity and suavity of manner." He also had a thick skin, which was essential in the rough-and-tumble world of frontier democracy. He "always replies jacosely and in good humor," this reporter continued, "the evident marks of disapprobation which greet many of his assertions, do not discompose him, and he is therefore hard to foil." Still, he had to struggle to control his temper and keep his biting ridicule within bounds.

Like many other Whigs who had not started out with life's advantages, Lincoln resented the Democratic strategy, well adapted to this political culture, of labeling their opponents as aristocrats. At an 1840 meeting, when Dick Taylor, a local Democratic leader who liked fine clothes, began denouncing the aristocratic principles of the Whigs, Lincoln pulled on his opponent's vest, which popped open to reveal a ruffled shirt, gold watch, and chain, to the immense laughter of the crowd.

Lincoln constantly invoked his hardscrabble early life to validate his democratic principles. At this same meeting, he noted that while Taylor "was riding in a fine carriage, wore his kid gloves and had a gold headed cane, he was a poor boy hired on a flat boat at eight dollars a month, and had only one pair of breeches and they were of buckskin. . . . If you call this aristocracy," he concluded, "I plead guilty to the charge."

BY THE TIME he moved to Springfield, Lincoln was an important party leader and, therefore, was invited to deliver an address in January 1838 to the Young Men's Lyceum in Springfield. In recent months several mob actions had attracted widespread attention, and Lincoln took as his theme reverence for the laws. Portraying uncontrolled passion as now the enemy of the Republic, he argued that the proper defense was to rely on "cold, calculating, unimpassioned reason." Lincoln's speech reflected his own inner turmoil in these years, as he struggled to impose self-control on his emotions, discipline his ambition, and improve himself intellectually and socially.

His famous "skinning" of Jesse Thomas illustrated Lincoln's power to hurt people when he lost self-control. When Thomas, who was a local Democratic leader, poked fun of Lincoln in an 1840 campaign speech, Lincoln strode to the stage and made an uncharacteristically caustic reply in which he used his unrivaled ability at mimicry to caricature Thomas's speech, gesture, and walk. So piercing was his ridicule that Thomas finally broke into tears. Those in the audience remembered the incident for years, but Lincoln admitted that his conduct "filled him with the deepest chagrin," and he subsequently apologized to Thomas.

In 1838 and again in 1840 Lincoln was elected to another term in the legislature. As the Whigs' floor leader, he focused his energies on preserving the party's economic program, particularly the statewide internal improvements program and the State Bank at Springfield. A depression that had begun in the summer of 1837 severely reduced state revenues, and the internal improvements program under way threatened to bankrupt the state. Ignoring fiscal reality, Lincoln fought all efforts to halt or scale down the extensive construction program. His stance was further testimony to his belief that public transportation projects, by expanding opportunity, would increase the income of workers and farmers. Lincoln fought equally hard to protect the State Bank, which under the pressure of hard times had ceased redeeming its notes (paper money) in specie (gold and silver), from Democratic assaults. Despite Lincoln's efforts, including on one occasion jumping out of a window in the legislative hall to prevent a quorum, the bank eventually was forced to close.

But the problems of the State Bank ultimately got Lincoln into a different kind of trouble. In September 1842 he published an anonymous letter in the *Sangamo Journal* skewering James Shields, the Democratic state auditor, for his policies toward the State Bank's badly depreciated currency. After the volatile Shields learned that Lincoln had written the letter, yet another anonymous letter lampooning him appeared. This letter had been secretly written by two female acquaintances, Julia Jayne and Mary Todd, but Lincoln gallantly assumed responsibility for both letters in order to protect them. Seething with outrage, Shields challenged Lincoln to a duel. Lincoln offered to apologize but was unwilling to have his courage impugned or his reputation degraded. When the hot-tempered Shields persisted in his challenge, Lincoln chose as weapons cavalry broadswords, with the combatants to be separated by a wooden plank. This arrangement would have put Shields at a serious disadvantage, for there was no possibility that the auditor, who was much shorter, could reach and injure his long-armed opponent. Friends finally managed to settle the matter peacefully.

The affair was a permanent embarrassment to Lincoln, and he refused to ever discuss it. He was chagrined that he had broken the law and allowed his emotions to override his reason, on which he prided himself. But the incident taught him a valuable lesson by demonstrating the stinging power of his satiric prose, and he learned to soften it in the future. In addition, he was not so quick to judge his adversaries' motives or take offense at what others said, and he began to display the incredible patience and fundamental good will that would characterize his later political career.

During his four terms in the legislature, Lincoln was guided by a vision that was fundamentally economic. Envisioning a society in which all had the right to improve their station in life, Lincoln argued that it was the responsibility of government to promote economic development, which, he believed, would enhance opportunity and reward the ambitious. "The legitimate object of government," he succinctly explained, "is to do for the people what needs to be done, but which they can not, by individual effort, do at all, or do so well, for themselves." As a sound Whig, he embraced Henry Clay's American System and advocated a protective tariff, a national bank and paper currency, and a national program of internal improvements.

His Whiggery also reflected his identification with the moral perspective of the rising middle class, with its emphasis on hard work, self-discipline, education, and social respectability. His fascination with technology and inventions, which he believed would improve people's lives, underscored his modern outlook; he even patented a device to lift steamboats over shoals. Upwardly mobile, forward looking, and intensely ambitious, he found a congenial home in the Whig party.

WHEN HE FIRST arrived in town, the uncouth Lincoln was excluded from the social world of Springfield's aristocracy. An acquaintance from this period described him as "awkward, homely, and badly dressed," and added that "although he then had considerable ambition to rise in the world, he had . . . done very little to improve his manners, or appearance, or conversation." These shortcomings notwithstanding, his political prominence and growing stature in the legal profession soon gained him entry into the town's elite society, which brought him into contact with young unmarried ladies of the upper crust. Lincoln was as uncertain of himself in social matters as he was self-assured in political and intellectual endeavors. While physically attracted to women, he feared the intimacy of marriage and believed he could never make a woman happy. Deeply conflicted, he was ill at ease in social gatherings: He lacked finished manners, was ungraceful in his movements, had no gift for small talk, and often sat in complete silence in mixed company.

Among the young unmarried ladies he met at these affairs was Mary Todd, who was a member of a prosperous Lexington, Kentucky, family. She had come to Springfield in 1839 to live with her sister, and she and Lincoln began a difficult courtship. Mary was bright and intelligent, had a keen interest in politics (as her involvement in the Shields affair demonstrated), and was very ambitious to gain public recognition. A loyal Whig, she was obviously attracted to Lincoln's ambition and political importance (she once boasted that she intended to marry a future president), but beyond that it is difficult to say what drew her to the young attorney. They were complete emotional, physical, and social opposites. Her short, plump stature contrasted sharply with his tall, slender frame, and she was cultivated and polished, having been raised in high society and attended exclusive schools. Although she had a volcanic temper and was subject to hysterical outbursts, she was a witty conversationalist who absolutely sparkled in social gatherings, loved to flirt, and was one of the town's belles.

Lincoln was attracted by her intelligence, her social grace, and her cultured background. Mary's older sister said that when the two were sitting together, "Mary led the Conversation—Lincoln would listen and gaze on her as if drawn by some Superior power, irresistably So: he listened—never Scarcely Said a word." Orville Browning, who served in the legislature with Lincoln, was probably correct when he maintained that Mary "did most of the courting" and earnestly set out to catch him. Sometime late in 1840 they became engaged.

Almost as soon as he made this commitment, Lincoln began to have second thoughts. He fell into a depression, uncertain of his true feelings and worried that he was unsuited for marriage. When he sought to break the engagement a few days later, Mary released him, but fearing that he had behaved dishonorably, he failed to regain his emotional balance. Soon he was too sick to leave his bed and was so gloomy his friends feared he might commit suicide. Guilt-stricken, he wrote to Stuart: "I am now the most miserable man living. If what I feel were equally distributed to the whole human family, there would not be one cheerful face on the earth."

Lincoln slowly recovered but did not resume his former place in Springfield society. After more than a year, friends contrived to bring Mary and him together again, and they resumed their courtship. Lincoln was pained by the belief that he had not acted honorably in backing out of their original engagement, for prior to this incident he considered his ability "to keep my resolves when they are made" to be "the chief gem, of my character." When he asked his old friend Joshua Speed, who had recently moved to Kentucky and married, for advice, Speed encouraged him to consider marriage again.

On November 4, 1842, with virtually no notice, Mary Todd and Abraham Lincoln were married. He was thirty-three years old, and she was ten years younger. While he had genuine feelings for her, Lincoln's decision apparently stemmed more from a sense of obligation—of keeping his commitment—than from any emotional sentiment. When asking James Matheny to be his best man, he remarked, "I shall have to marry that girl." As he blacked his boots for the ceremony, a young boy asked the groom where he was going. "To hell I reckon," was Lincoln's response. A few days later, he informed a friend, "Nothing new here, except my marrying, which to me, is [a] matter of profound wonder."

A woman of aristocratic tastes accustomed to having servants and slaves wait on her, Mary made sacrifices so they could get ahead. The

These are the earliest known photographs of Abraham Lincoln and Mary Todd Lincoln, probably made just after Lincoln was elected to Congress in 1846. (Library of Congress)

couple took lodgings at the Globe Tavern, hardly plush accommodations, and then rented a house after their first son, Robert Todd Lincoln, was born in August 1843. The following year, Lincoln bought a house at the corner of Eighth and Jackson for $1500. It remained the Lincolns' home until they left for Washington in 1861. In 1846 a second son, Eddie, arrived.

Mary Lincoln set out to upgrade her husband's wardrobe and make it more appropriate for a professional man. She struggled to lengthen his pants, match his socks, and coordinate the colors of his outfits, but met with only limited success. Lincoln remained indifferent to his appearance and seemed oblivious to style and color, causing her on more than one occasion to blurt out in frustration, "Why don't you dress up and look like somebody?"

She also undertook to polish his manners. She lectured him about letting servants answer the door, wearing his coat when receiving callers, and not coming to dinner in his shirt-sleeves. Sometimes shocked guests found Lincoln lying on the floor reading, with no regard for Victorian decorum. She was furious when she overhead him inelegantly tell visitors that he would "trot [the] women folks out." Lincoln irked her by failing to observe proper etiquette at the dinner table, and Herndon reported that "she played merry war when he persisted in using his knife in the butter rather instead of the special silver-handled one." A niece who lived with the Lincolns for a time complained that, unlike her plebian husband, Mary Lincoln "loved to put on *Style*."

THOUGH ASSURED of reelection, Lincoln decided not to run in 1842 for another term in the legislature. He had come under mounting attack, much of it personal, for his steadfast support of the state's internal improvements program, which had finally driven the state into bankruptcy, and the prospect of being once again the leader of a legislative minority held no particular charm for him. Indeed, with the Whigs a hopeless minority in the state, there were few political avenues open to him. The only attractive possibility was Congress, but since the single seat the Whigs controlled in the state was the Springfield district, competition for the nomination was keen. Unable to win the nomination in 1843, Lincoln persuaded the convention to endorse the principle of rotating the nomination among the leading aspirants, which put him in line for the nomination in 1846.

In that year Lincoln finally won the Whig nomination for Congress in the Seventh District. His Democratic opponent was Peter Cartwright, the famous Methodist preacher. The campaign was notable for producing the most elaborate statement Lincoln ever offered regarding his religious views. When Cartwright accused his opponent of religious infidelity, Lincoln printed a statement in the *Lacon Illinois Gazette* (August 15, 1846) which acknowledged that he was not a member of any church, but added, not entirely accurately, "I have never denied the truth of the Scriptures; and I have never spoken with intentional disrespect of religion in general, or of any denomination of Christians in particular." He concluded, "I do not think I could myself, be brought to support a man for office, whom I knew to be an open enemy of, and scoffer at, religion." Ironically, Cartwright, for all his skill as a revivalist, was an inept campaigner, and Lincoln easily swept to victory. Befitting his new prominence, he had his first photograph taken around this time decked out in a carefully tailored suit and satin vest.

Under the era's political calendar, Lincoln did not take his seat in Congress for more than a year after he was elected. During the period between his nomination in May 1846 and the opening of Congress in December 1847, the political situation in the country dramatically changed. President James K. Polk's vigorous defense of the annexation of Texas led to war with Mexico in the summer of 1846. Polk was a committed expansionist, and his goal was to add the Mexican provinces of New Mexico and California to the national domain. By the time Lincoln arrived in Washington, the United States army had won a series of decisive victories and the fighting was over, although a peace treaty had not yet been negotiated.

The war, however, thrust the issue of slavery's expansion into national politics. In August 1846, dissident northern congressmen had introduced the Wilmot Proviso, which sought to prohibit slavery from any territory acquired from Mexico. The proviso gained wide support in the North, especially among Whigs, who were more strongly antislavery and who believed that Polk had deliberately provoked a war with Mexico in order to acquire additional slave territory. When Lincoln took his seat in Congress as the sole Whig representative from Illinois, the slavery issue had assumed greater importance in national politics than had previously been the case.

Lincoln was slow to grasp the significance of this development. In 1845 he confessed, "I never was much interested in the Texas question. I never could see much good to come of annexation; inasmuch, as they were already a free republican people on our own model; on the other hand, I never could very clearly see how the annexation would augment the evil of slavery. It always seemed to me that slaves would be taken there in about equal numbers, with or without annexation." Nor did he express concern about adding a slave state to the Union.

Influenced by Whig opinion, however, Lincoln concluded that Polk was responsible for the outbreak of hostilities with Mexico. Seeking to embarrass the president, he introduced a series of resolutions in December 1847 designed to demonstrate that the "spot" on which the war began was not American soil. Three weeks later he gave his first important speech, rehashing the standard Whig line about the war's origins. Democrats back home denounced "Spotty" Lincoln's position, but like most Whigs he was always careful to vote for military supply bills while condemning Polk's war policies.

Blaming Polk for the war was the conventional Whig view, but on related questions Lincoln stood apart from the dominant opinion in his party. For one thing, he "did not believe . . . that this war was originated for the purpose of extending slave territory." He thought it was simply a political move by Polk to increase his popularity. Moreover, Lincoln was far less opposed to geographic expansion than many eastern Whigs, and he recognized that taking some Mexican territory was "a sort of necessity." Believing the acquisition of territory inevitable, he hoped to limit it to Mexico's northern provinces, and he consistently voted to apply the Wilmot Proviso to this territory.

Nevertheless, Lincoln continued to view slavery as a "distracting question" and focused his attention instead on traditional economic issues. With the banking issue now dead, he considered internal improvements the most crucial matter confronting the country. He voted with the Whig majority on the tariff and internal improvements, and he delivered no less than three speeches urging federal assistance for internal improvement projects in the states. He faithfully attended sessions, worked hard on the committees to which he was assigned, and answered most roll calls. Even so, as a newcomer, he made little impression on experienced members.

Lincoln had a greater impact on President-making, an activity that always dominated Congress in a national election year. He joined a group of younger Whig members in promoting the candidacy of Zachary Taylor, a hero of the Mexican War, who won the Whig nomination in June. Lincoln worked hard for the national ticket, including making a campaign swing through New England, and was pleased when Taylor was elected in November, though as expected he failed to carry Illinois.

The second session of the Thirtieth Congress was unusually contentious, as members struggled to deal with the status of slavery in the region acquired from Mexico as a result of the 1848 peace treaty. Lincoln said nothing in the charged debates but voted consistently to establish free territorial governments in California and New Mexico.

While other northern Whigs were scurrying from the slavery issue and seeking federal office, Lincoln boldly announced his intention to introduce a bill to enact a program of gradual emancipation in the District of Columbia, subject to the approval of its residents. When it became clear that the bill would not pass, he decided not to present it and contented himself with voting for another bill to abolish the slave trade in the district, which was defeated.

Despite his early and strong support for Taylor, Lincoln had little influence with the new administration. The most important federal appointment Illinois received went to a candidate he opposed, and he turned down an appointment as territorial governor of Oregon.

LINCOLN WAS ONLY forty years old when his congressional term ended, and his political career seemingly had come to a dead end. Democrats' control of Illinois blocked any aspirations for state office, and the rotation policy in his congressional district ruled out further national service. His ambition for political distinction remained unquenched, but with no outlet available to fulfill that ambition, he largely withdrew from public life and turned his attention to his legal career. For the next five years, he "practiced law more assiduously than ever before." Along with an expanding legal practice, he also commenced a program of personal self-improvement. These years were a time of intellectual growth that laid the basis for his eventual return to politics in 1854.

Lincoln's political activities after 1849 were quite limited compared with earlier years. He did not participate in local meetings to endorse Henry Clay's compromise package, which passed Congress in 1850. Two years later he served as Whig national committeeman from Illinois, but deeming the party's chances hopeless, his participation in the election was half-hearted. He declined to run again for the legislature and discouraged talk of nominating him for governor, which would have entailed considerable time and expense with no likelihood of victory.

While he continued to read newspapers, which were the major source of political information at that time, he also resumed his earlier program of self-study. Herndon indicated that in these years Lincoln undertook to remedy what he perceived as "a certain lack of discipline —a want of mental training and method." Always intrigued by mathematics, he now studied Euclid's geometry, and proudly noted that he "nearly mastered" all six books.

He remained a fatalist, convinced that human beings were controlled by some independent force, but his melancholy now became a persistent part of his personality. "Melancholy dripped from him as he walked," Herndon declared, and he continued to seek relief through humor, which he used, as Judge David Davis remarked, "to whistle off sadness." Outwardly sociable, he remained a very private individual, remote and reserved. Davis, who knew Lincoln well from their days together on the circuit, bitingly observed that he had "no Strong Emotional feelings for any person—Mankind or thing." Acquaintances, including longtime friends, did not assume any familiarity with him, and even his best friends called him "Lincoln." The nickname "Abe" was strictly for political purposes.

Firmly ensconced in respectable Springfield society, Lincoln's separation from his own family became almost complete. He rarely visited his parents and did not keep up social relations with his relatives. Although his political and legal travels sometimes brought him back in contact with family members, they did not visit him in his Springfield home, and his father and stepmother never met Mary Lincoln or their grandchildren. To make sure his father could support himself, Lincoln bought his father's farm and deeded it back to him for life, but otherwise he did not extend himself financially to aid his parents.

In 1851 John Johnston, his stepbrother, wrote informing him that his father was dying and wanted to see his son one last time. Lincoln's estrangement from his father had not lessened with time, and he declined to come. "Say to him that if we could meet now, it is doubtful whether it would not be more painful than pleasant," he wrote, "but that if it be his lot to go now, he will soon have a joyous [meeting] with many loved ones gone before." When Thomas passed away five days later, in January 1851, Lincoln did not attend the funeral, and he took no steps during his lifetime to mark his father's grave. Dennis Hanks, who was quite fond of Thomas Lincoln, wondered whether "Abe Loved his farther Very well or Not," and concluded, "I Dont think he Did."

Dennis Hanks felt the sting of Lincoln's conscious separation from his relatives, noting that "when he was with us he Seemed to think a great Deal of us but I thought Sum times it was hipocritical But I am Not Shore."

꙰

LINCOLN, WHO CONTINUED to practice with William Herndon, was by now a well-established lawyer earning a good income. Despite temperamental differences—the impulsive Herndon was much more pompous and windy—the two men worked well together. Each handled his cases separately, although Lincoln generally conducted the cases in federal court. After the state was divided into two federal judicial districts, Lincoln began trying cases in Chicago as well as Springfield. Unable to keep track of accounts, they simply divided the fees equally. There was never any doubt, however, of their relative position. To Lincoln, his associate was "Billy," whereas Herndon always referred to his partner as "Mr. Lincoln."

Their sparsely furnished office across the street from the capitol was a chaotic mess of books, newspapers, and papers which were scattered everywhere. Neither partner had any aptitude for organization. Lincoln carried letters and memoranda on which he had jotted down ideas in the lining of his hat, which Herndon designated "his desk and his memorandum-book." (Indeed, he once informed an attorney that the purchase of a new hat accounted for his delay in answering a letter.) On the desk was a bundle of papers, tied with a string, with the notation, "When you can't find it anywhere else, look in this."

Often sprawled on the dingy couch, Lincoln drove his partner to distraction with his habit of reading out loud. "When I read aloud," he explained, "two senses catch the idea: first, I see what I read; second, I hear it, and therefore I can remember it better." For his part, Herndon was constantly frustrated in his attempts to broaden Lincoln intellectually by interesting him in philosophical works and other books, which his partner soon tossed aside out of boredom.

Springfield had grown considerably since Lincoln's arrival; by 1850 it boasted a population of 4500, and that total would double in the next decade. As a result, the town had more legal business, but despite his prominence in the bar and his growing federal practice, Lincoln continued to travel the Eighth Judicial Circuit in search of clients and business. His extensive experience, many acquaintances, and reputation for scrupulous honesty, which he consciously cultivated, secured him a large number of cases.

Lincoln liked life on the circuit. Now one of the senior attorneys, he had a large circle of friends among his fellow lawyers, and because of his indifference to food and physical surroundings, he endured circuit practice better than most of his colleagues. David Davis believed that Lincoln was "as happy as *he* could be, when on this Circuit—and happy no other place. This was his place of Enjoyment." As his fellow itinerants noted, whereas other lawyers on the circuit went home each weekend, Lincoln remained on the road. Being left alone on the weekends in distant towns gave him the solitude he craved. When Lincoln was on the circuit, Herndon managed the office in Springfield.

Before the advent of railroads, attorneys and judges usually traveled together by horseback or occasionally in a buggy on the prairie roads from one county to the next, sometimes stopping at a farmhouse for dinner. When they reached the county seat, they slept together in a local hotel or tavern, where at times lawyers, jurors, witnesses, and prisoners all took their meals at the same table. At the end of the day, Lincoln often entertained those lounging about the tavern with his repertory of stories. According to Herndon, "As he neared the pith or point of the joke or story every vestige of seriousness disappeared from his face. His . . . eyes sparked; a smile seemed to gather up, curtain like, the corners of his mouth;" and when he reached the punch line, "no one's laugh was heartier than his."

In spite of his wife's efforts to outfit him properly, Lincoln continued to dress carelessly. "He probably had as little taste about dress and attire as anybody that ever was born," one colleague on the circuit recounted. In chilly weather he wore "a short circular blue cloak, which he got in Washington in 1849, and kept for ten years," while on warm days he put on a soiled linen duster. "His trousers were always too short," and his hat was "faded and had no *nap.*" He carried under his arm a worn green umbrella, which lacked a nob and was tied with a string, along with a battered striped carpet bag, in which he stuffed his possessions.

His negligent appearance was deceiving, for veteran court watchers recognized that despite gaps in his legal knowledge, Lincoln was one of the best jury lawyers in the state. He knew how to present evidence simply and logically, was unmatched in examining witnesses, spoke in a way that the jury could understand, and used his famous sense of humor to great advantage. Moreover, his unpretentious manner and unfashionable attire were an asset in the unrefined world of county courts. He also quickly grasped the key points of a case. Leonard Swett, a skilled attorney who practiced with Lincoln on the circuit, explained that in a trial Lincoln often beguiled opposing attorneys by yielding a number of minor points while carefully retaining the one crucial for his case. "What he was so blanly giving away was simply what he couldnt get and Keep. By giving away 6 points and carrying the 7th he carried his case and the whole case hanging on the 7th. . . ." From close observation Swett realized that "any man who took Lincoln for a simple minded man would very soon wake [up] with his back in a ditch."

Lincoln's most famous criminal case occurred in 1858, when he defended Duff Armstrong, who was accused of murder. Duff was the son of Jack Armstrong, with whom Lincoln had the famous wrestling match at New Salem and who had been a good friend and supporter until his recent death. Taking the case without fee, Lincoln displayed little zeal to discover what happened. Instead, he concentrated on discrediting the testimony of the chief prosecution witness, who claimed that he had clearly seen the accused hit the deceased, though he was some 150 feet away and it was near midnight, because the moon was full and bright. Producing an almanac, Lincoln established that on the night in question, the moon had already set, skirting the fact that even so there was ample light. In his summation Lincoln uncharacteristically played on the jurors' emotions, speaking of the many kindnesses the family of the accused extended to him as a young, poor boy. In tears, the jurors acquitted the defendant. One of the reporters covering the trial declared afterward that Lincoln's brilliant defense put him "at the head of the [legal] profession in this state."

Lincoln's legal practice was shifting, however, in response to the state's economic growth. More and more he represented railroad corporations in cases that offered much larger fees. In one of his most important cases, he successfully defended the Illinois Central Railroad from having to pay county property taxes, for which he received the largest fee ($5000) of his career. In another case that attracted wide attention, he defended the right of a railroad to construct a bridge across the Mississippi River, after a steamboat struck one of the pilings and caught fire. In his presentation, Lincoln, who had always been an advocate of internal improvements, argued for the necessity of bridges to create an east–west transportation network that would foster economic growth.

In addition to navigation and transportation, Lincoln had long been interested in inventions and patents. He was hired in 1855 by the defense to participate in a patent infringement case brought by Cyrus McCormick, the inventor of the reaper, against one of his competitors, John Manny. After Lincoln had been retained, however, Manny's famous eastern attorneys proceeded to completely ignore him and refused to let him participate in the case. One of them, Edwin Stanton, who ironically would one day be Lincoln's Secretary of War, sneeringly referred to him as "that d——d long armed Ape." Lincoln, who went to Cincinnati for the trial, was shunted to the sidelines by the other attorneys and allowed only to observe the proceedings. Although he was by now accustomed to snide remarks prompted by his ungainly physique and disheveled clothing, Lincoln nevertheless felt that he had been "roughly handled."

AWAY FROM HOME for three months or more every year, Lincoln found his circuit practice a welcome break from his troubled domestic situation, as his marriage was fraught with deep strains and tensions. Neither Lincoln nor his wife was blameless. Lincoln was undemonstrative and often self-absorbed, and spent long periods quietly reading or thinking. He suffered repeated periods of melancholy that produced intense mood swings, and he did not always give his wife the emotional support and comfort she needed. As Mary Lincoln noted, her husband "was *not*, a demonstrative man, when he felt most deeply, he expressed, the least." Accustomed to place and deference, Mary liked to put on airs, and was irritated by her husband's studied indifference to social propriety.

She was sociable and gregarious, worried constantly about what others thought of her, and demanded flattery. Afflicted by throbbing headaches, which may have been partly caused by allergies, and severe monthly cramps, Mary was easily provoked and would explode in a rage. Servants were never able to satisfy her and quickly came and went, and she often clashed with neighbors, who also heard her tongue-lash her husband. Moreover, with Lincoln away a good part of the time, either campaigning or practicing on the judicial circuit, she was left with the care of the children. She confessed to a friend that if her husband were home more "She could love him better." When she erupted in a fury, a neighbor recalled that "Lincoln paid no attention" or, if her anger was unusually fierce, "would pick up one of his Children and walked off," leaving the house until the storm blew over. His difficult marriage sharpened his political skills by strengthening his forbearance and teaching him ways to deal with contentious personalities. Yet the two also shared moments of tenderness and affection, and the ambitious Mary was intensely proud of her husband's accomplishments.

They suffered a deep loss when their son Eddie, who had always been sickly, died in 1850. As if to replace him, Mary became pregnant immediately, and William Wallace Lincoln was born at the end of the year. So that he would have a playmate, they had a fourth son, Thomas (nicknamed by his father Tad), born in 1853. The emerging ethos of the middle class viewed family size as a reflection of moral self-restraint and financial responsibility, and as the spacing of their childrens' births indicates, the Lincolns, like other middle-class couples, practiced some form of birth control.

Eddie's death brought about a complete change in Lincoln's parental attitude. His own father had not provided him with an example of paternal affection, and because of his frequent absences and absorption in his career, Lincoln was not close to either of his first two sons. Now he became an overindulgent parent, lavishing attention on his younger children and, along with his wife, abandoning any effort to discipline or control them. Robert was smug and aloof, Tad had a speech impediment and learning disability, and only Willie manifested his father's sense of humor, keen intelligence, and kindly disposition.

Herndon was particularly infuriated by Lincoln's younger sons, whom his partner often brought to the office on Sunday mornings while Mary was at church. Herndon complained that they "soon gutted the room—gutted the shelves of books—rifled the drawers and riddled boxes—battered the points . . . of gold pens against the stove—turned over the ink stands on the papers—scattered letters over the office and danced over them." While Herndon fumed, their father either ignored their antics as he worked or simply laughed.

Lincoln's time on the circuit, which continued until his election as president, was made less difficult by the construction of railroads in the 1850s. Now he found it possible to return home on weekends and still practice in the various county seats. His more frequent presence at home was important, because Mary's instability was becoming more serious, and she was especially flighty when he was away. Her mood swings—she could be vivacious and charming, or cross and censorious—became more pronounced, and as one of Lincoln's longtime friends, Orville H. Browning, commented, she was always "either in the garret or cellar."

Lincoln's law practice brought him a comfortable income, totaling $2000 or more a year. Never a speculator, he handled his money conservatively, yet in 1860 he was worth $17,000. With a larger family and more money, the Lincolns remodeled their house in 1856 by adding a second story. For the first time, they had sufficient room and, equally important in Mary's eyes, possessed a home more in keeping with her husband's prominence. It was done in the Greek Revival style, and like many respectable couples, they now had separate bedrooms. In what would become a frequent problem in the White House, Mary's remodeling expenditures exceeded what her husband believed was justified.

In the years after his return from Congress, Lincoln was a well-respected member of his community. With a very successful legal practice, a socially prominent wife, and a tasteful, comfortable home, he had entered the ranks of social respectability. In an 1860 campaign biography, William Dean Howells, the famous novelist, portrayed Lincoln during these years as "successful in his profession, happy in his home, secure in the affection of his neighbors." He was sufficiently content and at ease with himself that "ambition could not tempt him."

In reality, he was deeply frustrated and unhappy, which was manifested by his growing moodiness. His thirst for distinction had not slackened, and his driving ambition remained unfulfilled. Believing that he had done nothing of lasting significance, he exclaimed to Herndon, "How hard, oh, how hard it is to die and leave one's country no better than if one had never lived for it!"

His bouts of depression, while less acute than earlier in his life, were nevertheless a recurring phenomenon. At the law office, Herndon often found him in "a sad terribly gloomy state." Starting to write, Lincoln would stop and "become abstracted," staring out the window and saying nothing for long periods of time. On some days, his partner was so depressed that Herndon simply locked the office, drew the shade, and left, leaving him to the solitude he desired. When Herndon returned an hour or two later, the spell had passed, and he would find Lincoln talking to a client or telling a joke.

On the circuit, he could be the center of merriment and mirth one hour, and by himself the next, leaning his chair against the wall with his hands clasped around his knees, "the very picture of dejection and gloom." Absorbed in his thoughts, he might "sit for hours at a time, defying the interruption of even his closest friends . . . for by his moody silence and abstraction he had thrown about him a barrier so dense and impenetrable no one dared to break through." When they got up in the morning, his colleagues often discovered him sitting by himself, dejectedly staring into the fire, saying nothing, far away in his thoughts, until the breakfast bell rang.

For Lincoln, the race of life appeared over. He had reached the top rung of his profession in Illinois, and he had established himself as a respectable member of his community. Fulfilling the quest that he began as an adult, he had disciplined his emotions, honed his knowledge, and fashioned a mature identity. But he was depressed and unhappy, for his first love had always been politics, and the avenue of political distinction remained closed to him. When the political situation in Illinois suddenly changed in 1854, however, his long-smoldering ambition blazed forth again in a bright, searing flame.

Chapter 3

RISE TO POWER

ABRAHAM LINCOLN'S withdrawal from politics abruptly ceased in 1854. In a later autobiographical sketch, he acknowledged that "in 1854, his profession had almost superseded the thought of politics in his mind, when the repeal of the Missouri compromise aroused him as he had never been before." His return to the political hustings following passage of the Kansas–Nebraska Act launched him on the path that would—amazingly—take him to the White House in just a few years.

ORIGINALLY INTRODUCED by Senator Stephen A. Douglas of Illinois, the Kansas–Nebraska Act organized the region immediately west of Iowa and Missouri. Under terms of the Missouri Compromise of 1820, slavery had been forever prohibited from this region of the Louisiana Purchase, but in response to southern pressure the new bill repealed this prohibition and substituted the doctrine of popular sovereignty, by which the residents of a territory were to decide the status of slavery. On May 30, President Franklin Pierce signed the Kansas–Nebraska Act into law.

As Douglas had correctly predicted, the repeal of the Missouri Compromise raised "a hell of a storm." Across the North, indignant Whigs joined Democrats and Free Soilers in protesting Congress's unexpected action. Pondering Douglas's motivations and the significance of this legislation, Lincoln seemed more withdrawn than usual on the circuit. Back home in Springfield, he began reading the congressional debates on slavery, taking notes at the State Library for future use.

When Lincoln resumed his political career in 1854, he had changed in important ways from when, as a young man, he had served in the legislature. While the years had done nothing to slake his thirst for public distinction, his moral passion now ran deeper as he shifted his primary focus from economic issues to slavery. Moreover, his prose was more crisp and lean, like the man himself. Gone were the partisan hyperbole and extravagant flourishes of his earlier speeches. His power as a public speaker now grew, aided by his moral commitment, his hard logic, and his reputation for honest purpose. It was easy for listeners, as it has been for historians, to lose sight of Lincoln's partisanship in these years and to speak of him as a statesman.

The popular protest against the Kansas–Nebraska Act precipitated a movement to form a new antislavery, sectional Republican party combining Whigs, anti-Nebraska Democrats, and Free Soilers. Efforts to organize the Republican party, however, met with little success in most northern states, including Illinois. In addition, the sudden emergence of the anti-Catholic, anti-immigrant Know Nothing, or American, party greatly complicated matters in many northern states, as did the growing strength of prohibition sentiment.

In the prevailing political confusion, Lincoln characteristically acted with great caution. He still thought of himself as a Whig, and therefore he declined to attend the 1854 Republican state convention and held aloof from the new party. Urging cooperation among the groups opposed to the repeal of the Missouri Compromise, he avoided any discussion in his speeches of nativism, prohibition, or even economic issues, all of which divided the anti-Nebraska forces. Instead, he focused exclusively on the Kansas–Nebraska Act and the slavery issue.

The strength of the anti-Nebraska movement, which threatened the Democratic party's dominance in the state, rekindled Lincoln's political ambition, and he threw himself into the 1854 contest with his accustomed former vigor. His speeches attracted great attention in the prevailing supercharged political atmosphere, and he soon began to receive invitations to speak outside the congressional district. His three-hour speech at Peoria in reply to Douglas was Lincoln's first great speech against slavery.

In this address, Lincoln developed several points that would dominate his thinking on slavery during the rest of the decade. These points were not original with him—they had been developed earlier by antislavery leaders such as Salmon P. Chase—but Lincoln presented them in an unusually effective manner. The true intent of the Kansas–Nebraska Act, he contended, was to allow slavery to expand, and he dismissed as "a *lullaby*" the idea that climate, soil, or anything but statutory prohibition would keep slavery out of Kansas. He placed great emphasis on the idea that Douglas's law overturned the policy of the Founding Fathers, who, he maintained, had intended for slavery to gradually die out. "Let no one be deceived. The spirit of seventy-six and the spirit of Nebraska, are utter antagonisms; and the former is being rapidly displaced by the latter." In advancing this proposition, designed to link the anti-Nebraska cause to the ideals of the Founders and make it seem conservative, Lincoln simplified the Founders' record concerning slavery, which was much more mixed than he suggested. It was at this point in his career that the Declaration of Independence became a significant component of Lincoln's thought. Hailing it as the "first precept of our ancient faith," he henceforth designated it (rather than the Constitution) as the nation's founding charter.

He also offered a powerful moral indictment of slavery, invoking the Declaration of Independence for his authority: "There can be no moral right in connection with one man's making a slave of another." While Lincoln had long thought slavery a moral evil, he had never spoken so forthrightly on this issue before. In condemning Douglas's professed indifference to the expansion of slavery, Lincoln proclaimed: "I hate it because of the monstrous injustice of slavery itself. I hate it because it deprives our republican example of its just influence in the world—enables the enemies of free institutions, with plausibility, to taunt us as hypocrites—causes the real friends of freedom to doubt our sincerity, and especially because it forces so many really good men amongst ourselves into an open war with the very fundamental principles of civil liberty—criticising the Declaration of Independence, and insisting that there is no right principle of action but *self-interest*." Invoking the idea that the United States was to be an example to the world, he charged that "our republican robe is soiled, and trailed in the dust" by the presence of slavery in the Republic.

Lincoln was careful, however, to deny that he had any intention of interfering with slavery in the southern states, acknowledging that there was no power under the Constitution to do so. Instead, he focused on stopping the spread of slavery into the western territories, which would preserve opportunity for white workers and farmers. Restricting slavery would lead to its eventual demise as the Fathers intended, Lincoln insisted, though he ventured no explanation as to how or when slavery would end. "If all earthly power were given me," he candidly confessed, "I should not know what to do, as to the existing institution."

One obstacle the antislavery movement had always confronted was Northerners' widespread hostility to blacks. For personal and strategic reasons, Lincoln devoted little attention to the racial consequences of emancipation. As an ambitious politician, he was sensitive to the power of antiblack sentiment in Illinois and frankly conceded that most whites, including himself, would not accept former slaves as political and social equals. "Whether this feeling accords with justice and sound judgment, is not the sole question. . . . A universal feeling, whether well or ill-founded, can not be safely disregarded." He took refuge, politically and psychologically, in the policy of colonization, an utterly unrealistic program to transport ex-slaves back to Africa. Instead of taking his usual hardheaded look at this scheme, he clung to it as a way to avoid confronting the consequences of emancipation, for which he had no solution.

The other major handicap the antislavery cause labored under in northern society was the belief that the movement threatened the Union. Lincoln addressed this issue more forthrightly. "Much as I hate slavery," he declared, "I would consent to the extension of it rather than see the Union dissolved, just as I would consent to any GREAT evil, to avoid a GREATER one." But he dismissed the possibility that the South would secede over this issue and argued that restoration of the Missouri Compromise would, on the contrary, restore sectional concord. Yet he refrained from the harsh condemnation of Southerners that many antislavery leaders indulged in. "I have no prejudice against the Southern people," he avowed. "They are just what we would be in their situation. If slavery did not exist amongst them, they would not introduce it. If it did exist amongst us, we should not instantly give it up." Lincoln's tolerance and fair-mindedness, evident in passages like this one, gave the Peoria speech great power and helped mask his partisan intentions.

Lincoln later claimed that he had no more immediate purpose in taking the stump than to help Richard Yates, the Whig congressman from the Seventh Congressional District who was running for reelection. But the fact he agreed to run for the state legislature, which held no attraction for him, belied this statement. The next legislature would elect a U.S. Senator to succeed James Shields, Lincoln's old dueling adversary and a Nebraska Democrat. Lincoln's greatest ambition had always been to serve in the Senate, where his idol Henry Clay had been such a distinguished member, and he now had his sights firmly set on this goal as he maneuvered for political advantage in the swirling eddies of Illinois politics. At the same time that he bolstered his standing in the Whig party, he carefully tried to avoid giving offense to other anti-Nebraska groups in the state, including immigrants, Know Nothings, abolitionists, and dissident Democrats. When Republicans placed his name on their state central committee without his consent, he made no reply until after the election, for he could not afford either to alienate radical antislavery elements or to be identified with their principles. Even then, he did not formally decline the appointment. "That man who thinks Lincoln calmly sat down and gathered his robes about him, waiting for the people to call him, has a very erroneous knowledge of Lincoln," his law partner William Herndon commented. "He was always calculating, and always planning ahead. His ambition was a little engine that knew no rest."

The November election produced a political earthquake in Illinois that toppled the long-invincible Democratic party. The anti-Nebraska forces scored a stunning victory, electing five of nine congressmen and gaining control of the new legislature. The opposition was deeply divided among Whigs, Free Soilers, anti-Nebraska Democrats, and Know Nothings, but if they were able to unite, the anti-Douglas forces could elect the next senator. The Illinois constitution prohibited members of the legislature from being elected senator, so Lincoln quickly resigned from the legislative seat he had just won and began actively soliciting support for senator with "his characteristic activity and vigilance."

When the balloting began in early February, Lincoln led all contenders on the initial tally with forty-four votes, seven short of a majority. Four anti-Nebraska Democrats, however, adamantly refused to support him because he was a Whig. When it seemed that the Douglas forces were on the verge of prevailing, Lincoln instructed his die-hard supporters to switch to Lyman Trumbull, an anti-Nebraska Democrat, who was elected. "I regret my defeat moderately," Lincoln wrote afterward as he tried to soothe the anger of his Whig supporters over the outcome. Trumbull's election was a severe defeat for the Douglasites, and he could not "let the whole political result go to ruin, on a point merely personal to myself." Lincoln's restrained response to his defeat paid subsequent political dividends; several of the anti-Nebraska Democrats who prevented his election became important political supporters, and Trumbull soon pledged to support Lincoln against Douglas for the senate in 1858.

FOLLOWING HIS USUAL CUSTOM, Lincoln focused on his legal profession in 1855 in order to "pick up my lost crumbs of last year." National politics remained muddled. The collapse of the northern Whig party accelerated, as countless supporters abandoned it for either the Republican party or, in greater numbers, the Know Nothings. Indeed, in most northern states, including Illinois, the Know Nothings were the strongest party opposed to the Democrats. Since Illinois did not have a major statewide contest in 1855, Lincoln could hold back and wait to see how these diverse elements sorted themselves out. He was reluctant, however, to abandon the Whig party, with which he had identified since its founding, and he recognized that although the anti-Douglas forces were a majority in the state, the basic problem was how to get old-line Whigs, Know Nothings, German immigrants, anti-Nebraska Democrats, and political abolitionists to unite.

Adding fuel to the political fire was the deteriorating situation in Kansas. Contrary to Douglas's assurances that popular sovereignty would peacefully resolve the slavery issue, Kansas was soon the scene of chaos, fraud, and violence. Aided by the numerous illegal votes of Missouri residents, proslavery forces controlled the territorial government, which the Pierce administration legally recognized. Antislavery forces, on the other hand, organized their own government and applied for admission to the Union as a free state. Sporadic fighting soon broke out between the two factions in the territory.

Lincoln's mood darkened as he pondered the growing sectional crisis. In response to a letter from his friend Joshua Speed complaining about antislavery activity in Kansas, Lincoln made clear his political uncertainty. "I think I am a whig," he wrote, "but others say there are no whigs, and that I am an abolitionist," even though "I now do no more than oppose the *extension* of slavery." Passing over the Republican party in silence, he avowed his opposition to the Know Nothings. "I am not a Know-Nothing. That is certain. How could I be? How can any one who abhors the oppression of negroes, be in favor of degrading classes of white people?" Bemoaning the country's degeneracy, he concluded: "As a nation, we began by declaring that '*all men are created equal.*' We now practically read it 'all men are created equal, *except negroes.*' When the Know-Nothings get control, it will read 'all men are created equal, except negroes, *and foreigners, and catholics.*' When it comes to this I should prefer emigrating to some country where they make no pretense of loving liberty. . . ."

Publicly, however, Lincoln said nothing against the Know Nothings, who were too powerful to antagonize, and many of whom were his "old political and personal friends." (Even his wife, tired of battling Irish servants, supported them.) Lincoln's unwillingness to speak out against the Know Nothings at this time, despite his strong feelings, would be a crucial factor in his successful bid for the Republican nomination in 1860.

It was obvious that the Whig party was moribund, and with the national Know Nothing organization increasingly split along sectional lines over the slavery issue, Lincoln decided that the prospects for uniting the various anti-Democratic factions in the state had improved. Early in 1856, he cast his lot with the Republican party. On February 22, he attended a meeting of anti-Nebraska editors at Decatur to urge the importance of moderation on the slavery issue in order to promote unity. He warned the more advanced antislavery people that a radical antislavery program would drive away potential supporters in the central and southern parts of the state and cripple the movement. After adopting a statement of principles crafted to appeal to a broad antislavery coalition, those in attendance called for a state convention to meet in Bloomington on May 29.

Lincoln went to Bloomington as a delegate to keep the Republican movement on track. In the week before the convention assembled, two shocking events electrified northern public opinion. On May 22, a proslavery mob had raided the free state town of Lawrence, Kansas, and terrorized the inhabitants. The next day, Preston Brooks, a South Carolina congressman, attacked Republican Senator Charles Sumner of Massachusetts in the Senate chamber and beat the antislavery leader unconscious with his cane. With popular emotions running high, leaders worried that antislavery radicals would stampede the convention, but in the end the delegates adopted a moderate platform that focused on the issue of slavery's expansion and nominated a state ticket representing all the factions in the Republican coalition. The climax of the convention was a powerful speech Lincoln delivered to the cheering assembly in which he urged unity and maintained that "the Union must be preserved in the purity of its principles as well as in the integrity of its territorial parts."

Two weeks later the Republicans' first national nominating convention assembled in Philadelphia. The delegates nominated John C. Frémont, the famous western explorer, for president. At the last minute, the Illinois delegation mounted an unsuccessful drive to nominate Lincoln for vice-president, and despite his lack of a national reputation, he received a very respectable 110 votes on the first ballot.

Illinois was one of the battleground states in the election. Northern Illinois, where antislavery sentiment was strongest, was certain to go for Frémont, while the southern part of the state, largely settled by Southerners, was equally certain for James Buchanan, the Democratic candidate. Lincoln concentrated his efforts in the central counties, which would decide the election, working feverishly to keep conservative Whigs from voting for former president Millard Fillmore on the American ticket. He delivered over fifty speeches in what observers agreed was the most exciting election yet in the state's history.

In the end, Buchanan carried Illinois and also the nation. Nevertheless, Illinois Republicans were optimistic about the future. Not only had the Republican state ticket triumphed, but, combined, Frémont and Fillmore's vote exceeded that for Buchanan by a comfortable margin. Equally important, the Republicans had displaced the dying Know Nothing movement, which had ridden the crest of victory just two years earlier, as the major opposition party to the Democrats. Finally, the 1856 election established Lincoln as one of the major leaders of the Republican party in Illinois, and he received a number of invitations, most of which he declined, to speak in neighboring states.

JAMES BUCHANAN assumed the presidency determined to dampen sectional tensions and check the growth of the Republican party. His program of sectional conciliation got off to a rocky start, however, when the Supreme Court issued the Dred Scott decision on March 6, 1857, two days after his inauguration. In this decision, the Court majority, led by Chief Justice Roger Taney, ruled that blacks could not be citizens of the United States and that Congress had no power to prohibit slavery in a territory. The decision was a direct blow at the Republican party, whose most important principle (and the only one all party members could agree upon) was that Congress should prohibit slavery from all the territories.

The only important political speech Lincoln delivered in 1857 dealt with the Dred Scott decision. Speaking in Springfield on June 26, Lincoln deprecated any resistance to the Court's ruling but vowed that Republicans would work to get the decision reversed. Lincoln elaborated on his view that the Declaration of Independence had erected equality as the nation's guiding principle. By proclaiming the ideal of human equality, the Founders had "meant to set up a standard maxim for free society, which should be familiar to all, and revered by all; constantly looked to, constantly labored for, and even though never perfectly attained, constantly approximated, and thereby constantly spreading and deepening its influence, and augmenting the happiness and value of life to all people of all colors everywhere."

In criticizing the Court's ruling, Lincoln homed in on Taney's assertion that blacks were not included in the Declaration of Independence's promise of equality. In what had by now become a standard theme in his writings and speeches, Lincoln protested that in order to protect slavery, the once revered Declaration "is assailed, and sneered at, and construed, and hawked at, and torn, till, if its framers could rise from their graves, they could not at all recognize it." Lincoln argued that the Declaration's authors "did not intend to declare all men equal *in all respects*. They did not mean to say all were equal in color, size, intellect, moral development, or social capacity," but they "did consider all men created equal—equal in 'certain inalienable rights, among which are life, liberty, and the pursuit of happiness.'"

At the same time, Lincoln tried to tarnish Douglas, who had delivered a speech two weeks earlier defending the Court, by lumping Taney and Douglas together in a desire to make slavery a permanent institution. Armed with the Court's decision, Democratic leaders were riveting ever more tightly the shackles that bound the oppressed slave. "All the powers of earth seem rapidly combining against him . . . ," he observed. "They have him in his prison house; they have searched his person, and left no prying instrument with him. One after another they have closed the heavy iron doors upon him, and now they have him, as it were, bolted in with a lock of a hundred keys, which can never be unlocked without the concurrence of every key; the keys in the hands of a hundred different men, and they scattered to a hundred different and distant places; and they stand musing as to what invention, in all the dominions of mind and matter, can be produced to make the impossiblity of his escape more complete than it is." In making this charge, Lincoln ignored the ways in which the Dred Scott decision also undercut Douglas's doctrine of popular sovereignty. The kernels of Lincoln's emerging belief in a Democratic conspiracy to spread slavery were clearly visible in this address.

Lincoln devoted most of his attention in 1857 to his legal profession, but he was already looking ahead to 1858, when Douglas's seat in the Senate would be up for grabs. He had had his eye on this contest since his narrow defeat for the senate in 1855, and he began planning for the race as early as 1857. As he traveled the judicial circuit that fall, Lincoln ceaselessly promoted his senatorial ambitions.

In devising his campaign plans, Lincoln had not anticipated the personal rupture between Douglas and Buchanan over the Kansas issue. In the summer of 1857, a constitutional convention, which met in the town of Lecompton, Kansas, drafted a proposed state constitution that recognized the legality of slavery. Because proslavery leaders feared that voters would reject the constitution, they refused to submit it for popular ratification. Instead, voters could decide only whether they wanted to authorize the importation of new slaves into the state. With free state men boycotting what they considered to be a rigged election, the Lecompton constitution easily won approval, as did a separate provision allowing the importation of additional slaves. Offended by this procedure, Buchanan's territorial governor warned that the Lecompton constitution represented the wishes of only a small minority of the residents of Kansas. Nevertheless, the president, ignoring the gathering storm clouds, urged Congress to admit Kansas under the Lecompton constitution as a slave state.

This action was too much for Douglas, who argued that the Lecompton constitution made a mockery of the Democratic principle of popular sovereignty. Believing that the very survival of the Democratic party in the free states was at stake, Douglas broke with the administration and southern Democrats and opposed the Lecompton constitution. After the House and Senate deadlocked, Congress, through indirect means, sent the constitution back to Kansas for a new vote, and in August 1858 the territory's electors overwhelmingly rejected the Lecompton constitution.

Douglas's dramatic break with Buchanan put Illinois Republicans in a difficult position. The senator's opposition to the Lecompton bill undercut the Republicans' traditional accusation that Douglas and northern Democrats favored the expansion of slavery, and that popular sovereignty was merely a device to accomplish this end. Moreover, a number of eastern Republicans, led by Horace Greeley, the editor of the vastly influential *New York Tribune*, urged Illinois Republicans to support Douglas's reelection to the Senate.

Such advice deeply angered Lincoln and other Illinois Republicans, many of whom had spent years battling the haughty Douglas and who sensed that at long last they had a good chance to defeat their hated adversary. In a calculated repudiation of the advice of eastern Republicans, the delegates to the state Republican convention in Springfield in June unanimously passed a resolution declaring that "Abraham Lincoln is the first and only choice of the Republicans of Illinois for the United States Senate, as the successor of Stephen A. Douglas." At this time senators were elected by state legislatures, not by the voters, and it was highly unusual for a party to designate a senatorial candidate in advance. The action of the state convention unambiguously narrowed the choice to Lincoln or Douglas. It had an added significance, for without Lincoln's nomination his famous debates with Douglas would never have occurred.

That evening, in a stiflingly hot legislative chamber, Lincoln delivered an address to the delegates that laid out the main themes of his upcoming senatorial campaign. He had carefully drafted the speech over a period of several weeks, jotting down ideas as they occurred to him. His advisers thought it too radical, but Lincoln, who always relied on his own political judgment, decided not to change it.

The speech's title derived from the Biblical quotation, "A house divided against itself cannot stand," which Lincoln recited at the beginning of his remarks. He had first used the Biblical image of a house divided in 1843, and had returned to it several times in 1856 and 1857, but he now gave this idea full scope and development. "I believe this government cannot endure, permanently half *slave* and half *free*," the Republican nominee proclaimed. "I do not expect the Union to be *dissolved*—I do not expect the house to *fall*—but I *do* expect it will cease to be divided. It will become *all* one thing, or *all* the other. Either the *opponents* of slavery, will arrest the further spread of it, and place it where the public mind shall rest in the belief that it is in course of ultimate extinction; or its *advocates* will push it forward, till it shall become alike lawful in *all* the States, *old* as well as *new—North* as well as *South*."

And then, in a sentence that historians usually ignore but which in fact was the transition to the body of his speech, he asked, "Have we no *tendency* to the latter condition?" Although the phrases "house divided" and "ultimate extinction" attracted the most attention in the press, the thrust of Lincoln's argument was that a conspiracy existed among Democratic leaders to make slavery a national institution. Chief Justice Roger Taney, who wrote the Dred Scott decision, along with Franklin Pierce, James Buchanan, and Stephen A. Douglas, were all involved in this plot. Another Dred Scott decision was coming, Lincoln warned, that would decree no state could prohibit slavery, and then slavery would be a national institution. "Welcome or unwelcome, such decision *is* probably coming, and will soon be upon us, unless the power of the present political dynasty shall be met and overthrown." Douglas's contribution to the plan, Lincoln explained, was to mold northern public opinion "to not *care* whether slavery is voted *down* or voted *up*." He prophesied: "We shall *lie down* pleasantly dreaming that the people of *Missouri* are on the verge of making their State *free;* and we shall *awake* to the *reality,* instead, that the *Supreme* Court has made *Illinois* a *slave* State."

Lincoln's allegation of a plan to spread slavery contained more substance than historians have acknowledged, but his insistence that Douglas was implicated in this plot was partisan propaganda. By this time Douglas was under harsh attack in the South for his opposition to the Lecompton constitution, and he was engaged in a bitter personal feud with Buchanan. Lincoln, however, believed Douglas's motives in repealing the Missouri Compromise were selfish, and he resented Douglas's "assumption of superiority on account of his elevated position," his scorn for his opponents, and his unscrupulousness as evidenced by his persistent resort to race baiting. But he also envied Douglas and the Little Giant's great political success. Reviewing their long acquaintance and respective careers, he noted, "With *me*, the race of ambition has been a failure—a flat failure; with *him* it has been one of splendid success."

To sharpen the differences between himself and Douglas, Lincoln focused on the moral issue of slavery. Beginning with his first public statement on slavery in 1837, Lincoln had always opposed the institution on moral grounds, but Douglas's opposition to the Lecompton constitution forced Lincoln to emphasize the moral issue in order to discredit his opponent's credentials as an antislavery leader.

Douglas knew he faced the greatest challenge of his political career. "I shall have my hands full," the combative senator said when informed of Lincoln's nomination. "He is the strong man of his party— full of wit, facts, dates, and the best stump-speaker, with his droll ways and dry jokes, in the West. He is as honest as he is shrewd; and if I beat him, my victory will be hardly won."

No sooner had he returned to Illinois than Douglas took the offensive and charged that Lincoln's House Divided speech was a radical document that advocated "a war of the North against the South." He also laid heavy emphasis on the race issue, which had long been the

Democrats' trump card in Illinois politics, and insisted that Lincoln, with his talk about the extinction of slavery, was preaching racial equality. "This government of ours is founded on the white basis," he affirmed in Chicago. "It was made by the white man, for the benefit of the white man, to be administered by white men." Finally, he repeated his view that popular sovereignty was based on the American principle of democracy, the right of the people to govern themselves.

Hoping to attract the largest audience possible, Lincoln hit upon the strategy of following Douglas around the state, delivering a speech after the senator had spoken. This tactic clearly irritated Douglas, and Democratic papers charged that it was the only way Lincoln could assemble a crowd. When Lincoln responded by challenging Douglas to debate him, Douglas hesitated, since his presence would assure Lincoln a large audience, and since, as the more famous leader, he had little to gain and much to lose in any confrontation. Lincoln had envisioned the two men campaigning together, but in the end Douglas agreed to only seven debates, one in each of the remaining congressional districts where they had not already spoken together, in order to get Lincoln to stop following him all over the state. Under the agreed-upon rules, the opening speaker would have one hour, the second man an hour and a half, and then the first speaker would have thirty minutes for rebuttal.

The underdog Lincoln threw himself into the canvass, traveling 4,350 miles and delivering sixty-three major speeches, only to be outdone by Douglas, who made 130 speeches of various lengths and traveled over a thousand miles farther. As the two candidates criss-crossed the state, their respective traveling accommodations bespoke their relative reputations. Douglas and his vivacious wife rode in a private railroad car, accompanied by a number of supporters and an ever-present corps of reporters. No such retinue followed Lincoln, who traveled as a regular passenger, often alone, with only a bag containing a change of clothing. This mode of travel reinforced Lincoln's carefully cultivated image as a humble, self-made man, as did his decision to keep his aristocratic wife out of sight. His plain, well-worn clothing fostered this image as well. Taken aback by Lincoln's rumpled appearance, a member of the audience at Freeport reported that he wore an "old high stovepipe hat with a coarse looking coat with sleeves far too short, and baggy looking trousers that were so short that they showed his rough boots."

The Lincoln–Douglas debates occupy an honored place in American political folklore. Arriving by foot, on horseback and in wagons, or on special trains, thousands of ordinary citizens gathered to hear the debates. All the usual campaign pageantry was evident: blaring brass bands, flags and banners, glee clubs, processions honoring the two candidates, fireworks, and thundering cannons. Countless reporters were present, and each party hired a stenographer to take down what Lincoln and Douglas said so that party newspapers could publish their exchanges. The contest received unusual attention outside the state, for as the *New York Times* observed, Illinois in 1858 was "the most interesting political battle-ground in the Union."

The two men were blessed with keen intellects and tenacious memories, but in many ways they were a study in contrasts. Unlike the tall, angular Lincoln, who moved and spoke deliberately, Douglas was short (five feet four inches), stocky, and bursting with energy. He was also the better extemporaneous speaker and had the more graceful platform manner. A natty dresser with a white hat to set off his carefully tailored dark coat and contrasting pants, he played to the audience, "clenching his fists," shaking his black mane, "stamping his feet," and defiantly scowling at his opponents, all the while booming out points in his rich baritone voice.

Uncertain what to do with his oversized hands, Lincoln never seemed entirely at ease on the platform. One newspaperman wrote that "he used singularly awkward, almost absurd, up-and-down and sidewise movements of his body to give emphasis to his arguments." To make an important point, he had the odd habit of bending his knees and then springing upward when he reached the concluding phrase. His high-pitched voice, for all its great carrying power, sounded harsh and unpleasant, but as he continued speaking, Lincoln became more and more effective, carrying his listeners along by his earnestness, plain style, clear logic, and occasional jokes. After a hesitant performance in the first debate at Ottawa, he hit his stride during the second debate at Freeport, in which he was much more aggressive.

Like modern candidates, both Douglas and Lincoln had a standard speech which they delivered with variations throughout the campaign.

Stephen A. Douglas (left) and Abraham Lincoln as they appeared about the time of their joint debates in 1858. Despite quite different speaking styles, both were formidable debaters. (Left: The National Portrait Gallery, Washington, DC/Art Resource, NY; right: Library of Congress)

While Lincoln's speeches varied more than Douglas's, he often read long passages from his earlier addresses. As a result, the debates quickly became repetitious and at times extremely tedious, with the two candidates often merely rehashing points that they had made in speeches opening their campaigns. Douglas stressed the radicalism of the House Divided doctrine, labeled Lincoln an abolitionist, constantly brought up the race issue, and defended popular sovereignty as a democratic principle. Lincoln charged Douglas with seeking to extend slavery, denounced slavery as a moral evil, and tried as much as possible to dodge the race question.

Lincoln spent most of the campaign on the defensive on the issues of abolitionism and race. Antiblack feeling was strong in Illinois (in 1848 a provision of the new state constitution to exclude free blacks from entering the state won approval by a 4 to 1 margin). Fully imbibing this racial animosity, Douglas repeatedly sought to tarnish Lincoln and the Republicans with a belief in black equality. Lincoln tried to ignore the issue, since he could hardly outbid Douglas for racist support, but finally in exasperation he outlined his views on race at the Charleston debate. "I am not, nor ever have been, in favor of bringing about in any way the social and political equality of the white and black races," the Republican candidate began, "—that I am not nor ever have been in favor of making voters or jurors of negroes, nor of qualifying them to hold office, nor to intermarry with white people; and I will say in addition to this that there is a physical difference between the white and black races which I believe will forever forbid the two races living together on terms of social and political equality. And inasmuch as they cannot so live, while they do remain together there must be the position of superior and inferior, and I as much as any other man am in favor of having the superior position assigned to the white race." While he would change his mind on some of these issues by the end of his life, this statement was the most extensive one Abraham Lincoln ever made concerning his views on race and equality.

That being said, Lincoln nevertheless insisted that "there is no reason in the world why the negro is not entitled to all the natural rights enumerated in the Declaration of Independence, the right to life, liberty, and the pursuit of happiness. I hold that he is as much entitled to these as the white man." Linking this point to his belief in opportunity as one of the defining principles of the Republic, he concluded, "In the right to eat the bread . . . which his own hand earns, *he is my equal . . . and the equal of every living man.*"

As the campaign continued, Lincoln devoted more and more attention to the moral issue of slavery. In the final debate at Alton, in the southern part of the state, Lincoln affirmed, "The real issue in this controversy—the one pressing upon every mind—is the sentiment on the part of one class that looks upon the institution of slavery *as a wrong*, and of another class that *does not* look upon it as a wrong. The sentiment that contemplates the institution of slavery in this country as a wrong is the sentiment of the Republican party. . . . They look upon it as being a moral, social and political wrong." He was careful to disassociate himself from abolitionism, insisting that Republicans had no intention of interfering with slavery in the states, which he argued would violate the Constitution, and he refused to specify precisely either how or when ultimate extinction would be achieved.

Republicans believed that Lincoln had acquitted himself quite well in the debates. In the end, however, it was not enough. Although legislative candidates pledged to Lincoln outpolled those who favored Douglas, both the apportionment of the legislature, in which the rapidly growing, heavily Republican northern counties were underrepresented, and the holdovers in the Senate favored the Democrats. When the new legislature convened, Douglas was reelected by a vote of 54 to 46.

"I am glad I made the . . . race," Lincoln declared afterward. "It gave me a hearing on the great and durable question of the age, which I could have had in no other way." Still, the outcome was a bitter disappointment. Twice now he had come close to attaining his dream of serving in the Senate, and he could not help thinking that his political career was over. The antislavery cause would continue, he wrote a friend, but he expected to "sink out of view."

THE 1858 SENATORIAL contest was the turning point in Abraham Lincoln's political career. He had solidified his hold on the Illinois Republican party by his vigorous canvass. He had skillfully staked out a moderate position designed to hold the divergent Republican coalition together. He had held his own against the most popular and charismatic Democratic leader in the country. And for the first time in his career, he had attracted national attention.

Lincoln's immediate problem, however, was to restore his finances. When Republican party chairman Norman Judd asked for a contribution to pay off the party's campaign debt, he replied, "I have been on expences so long without earning any thing that I am absolutely without money now for even household purposes." He lost no time in again turning his attention to his law practice.

Nonetheless, there were already signs of the impression Lincoln had made in his recent campaign. Urging him to toss his hat into the presidential ring, Jesse Fell, a political friend, solicited an autobiographical sketch for use in promoting his candidacy. Lincoln demurred. When a Rock Island editor indicated he wanted to endorse him, he replied, "I must, in candor, say I do not think myself fit for the Presidency." Some of this newspaper talk was merely intended to make him the favorite son of Illinois, or to push him for the second spot on the national ticket, but Lincoln, who was not given to flights of fancy, adopted a sober view. More prominent party leaders, such as Senator William Henry Seward of New York and Governor Salmon P. Chase of Ohio, were seeking the Republican nomination, and Lincoln, who had been out of office for a decade and who had just been defeated for senator, realistically did not see how he could challenge them.

Bolstered by his newly won reputation, he carried on a wide correspondence with party leaders in other states, urging unity in the upcoming national contest. Moreover, he received a number of invitations in 1859 from Republicans to speak in other states. He declined most, but he did speak in Iowa, Wisconsin, Ohio, Indiana, and Kansas.

The presidential talk continued in spite of Lincoln's attempts to brush it aside. His friends argued that he was a more available candidate than any of the front-runners, and Lincoln, though not convinced, decided to keep his options open. He sent Fell the sketch that he had requested the previous year, and authorized the Illinois delegation to give him a complementary vote at the national convention. He also took steps to publish his recent debates with Douglas. In February 1860, the *Chicago Tribune*, the most important Republican paper in the West, endorsed Lincoln for president.

That same month, Lincoln traveled to New York to deliver an address at the Cooper Union. He worked especially hard on this speech, which would introduce him to Republicans in the East, where he was not well known. He spent hours in the State Library, poring over the records of the Constitutional convention and the early Congresses to determine the Founders' policy on slavery. The time he invested in preparing his remarks provides clear evidence that he was seriously considering making a bid for the Republican nomination. He even spent $100 on a new black suit, trying (without complete success) to look more respectable.

A snowstorm failed to deter those who were curious to see this western Republican, and they packed the hall on the evening of February 27. His unkempt appearance and Kentucky drawl were greater handicaps before an eastern audience than they were back home, and as was usually the case, his high-pitched voice bothered listeners until he got warmed up. Carefully reading his address, Lincoln skillfully used the occasion to enhance his reputation as a sound, conservative leader, not given to wild-eyed causes and inflammatory rhetoric.

In his speech he portrayed the Republican party as a conservative organization that sought to restore the policies of the Founders by restricting the spread of slavery. He once again stressed the moral issue of slavery, contending that Southerners' belief that slavery was right, and Republicans' belief that it was wrong, constituted "the precise fact upon which depends the whole controversy." Urging Republicans not to be intimidated by southern threats of disunion, he called on them to stand by the old policy of restricting slavery from the territories and limiting it to the states. "Let us have faith that right makes might," he affirmed in closing, "and in that faith, let us, to the end, dare to do our duty as we understand it." The overflow crowd burst into applause, and the anti-Seward press of the city, led by the *New York Tribune*, was lavish in its praise. He followed up this exhilarating success with a series of speeches in New England. By the time Lincoln returned home, he had decided to mount a serious effort to win the Republican presidential nomination.

"The taste *is* in my mouth a little," he confessed to Trumbull at the end of April in reference to the presidential nomination. The Republican state convention in May endorsed him and bound the state's delegation to vote for him at the upcoming national convention. On the first day of the proceedings, Lincoln's cousin John Hanks entered carrying two rails that he claimed were from a batch that Lincoln and he had split in 1830, when Lincoln first came to Illinois. Thus was born the symbol of "The Railsplitter," which emphasized Lincoln's humble beginnings.

The Republican convention assembled in Chicago in May. Directing the Lincoln forces was David Davis, who had known Lincoln for years from his service as Judge of the Eighth Circuit. He was assisted by a number of prominent Illinois Republicans, many of whom were acquaintances from his circuit court days, and all of whom had been key advisers in his 1858 senatorial campaign. Often hostile to each other, they were united only by their personal loyalty to Lincoln. It was always one of Lincoln's great political talents that he could get men of diverse viewpoints to work together in a common cause and usually also keep them personally loyal to him. Establishing their headquarters in the Tremont House, members of this inner circle mixed with various delegations, soliciting support for Lincoln.

Lincoln had earlier outlined his basic convention strategy. "I suppose I am not the *first* choice of a very great many," he observed. "Our policy, then, is to give no offence to others—leave them in a mood to come to us, if they shall be compelled to give up their first [choice]." Accordingly, Lincoln's managers sought to prevent Senator William Henry Seward of New York, who was the front-runner, from winning the nomination on the first ballot, while seeking commitments from supporters of other candidates to go for Lincoln as their second choice. They argued that because of his radical antislavery reputation, Seward could not be elected, whereas Lincoln, as a moderate from a crucial battleground state, was the strongest candidate the Republicans could run. Strengthening Lincoln's chances was the fact that he was the one possible nominee who was acceptable to all factions of the party, particularly former Know Nothings and German immigrants, who hated one another. The night before the balloting, aided by unauthorized patronage pledges his managers made, Lincoln picked up vital support in the delegations from Indiana, Pennsylvania, and New Jersey, all closely contested states where the Republicans faced a hard fight in November.

As expected, Seward led on the first ballot with 173½ votes, but Lincoln surprised experienced observers by finishing second with 102 votes. On the second ballot, as more anti-Seward votes swung to Lincoln, he pulled nearly even with the New Yorker. The choice was now narrowed to Seward or Lincoln, and on the third ballot most of the remaining anti-Seward votes went to Lincoln, and he was nominated. His selection was purely a triumph of availability. In making this choice, the delegates simply concluded that he had the best chance of winning; they gave little thought to Lincoln's character or qualifications for office. Like the candidate, the Republican platform was also moderate and emphasized opposition to the expansion of slavery rather than its existence in the southern states.

Republicans' prospects received a further boost when Democrats could not agree on a presidential candidate. In the end, the northern wing of the party nominated Douglas, while southern Democrats selected Vice President John C. Breckinridge of Kentucky. Also in the race was Senator John Bell of Tennessee, who had been nominated by the new Constitutional Union party, a national conservative organization.

With their opponents divided, Republicans seemed destined to win in November, so they opted to conduct a campaign that featured pageantry and hoopla and focused on the candidate rather than the issues. Republican campaign literature drew heavily on the symbols of "Honest Abe" and "The Railsplitter," emphasizing Lincoln's moral character and his undistinguished origins, in order to portray him as a symbol of democracy. Confident of victory, Republicans generally avoided any serious discussion of the issues confronting the country.

Outwardly Lincoln took no part in the campaign. "By the lessons of the past, and the united voice of all discreet friends," he advised, "I am neither [to] write or speak a word for the public. . . ." He remained in Springfield and did not electioneer, occupying his time receiving visitors in the governor's room on the second floor of the capitol. His good friend Orville H. Browning reported that "Lincoln bears his honors meekly. As soon as other company had retired after I went in he fell into his old habit of telling amusing stories, and we had a free and easy talk of an hour or two." Privately, Lincoln kept a close watch on political developments and corresponded with Republican leaders in other states, urging, in particular, careful attention to the "dry, and irksome labor" required for "thorough organization," but Herndon sensed that his partner was *bored badly.*" Lincoln's unchanged demeanor contrasted sharply with that of his wife; one critical Springfield minister was of the opinion that since her husband's nomination, she "ought to be sent to the cooper's and well secured against bursting by iron hoops."

In October, as the campaign neared its climax, Lincoln received a letter from eleven-year-old Grace Bedell of Westfield, New York. His young admirer informed him that he would look "a good deal better" with a beard. Besides, "all the ladies like whiskers" and thus would get "their husband's to vote for you." Even with all that was on his mind, Lincoln took the time to reply that he worried people would consider it "a piece of silly affect[at]ion" if he now let his whiskers grow. Shortly after the election, however, he began to grow a beard.

Republican victories in the October state elections in key northern states made Lincoln's election a foregone conclusion and rendered the balloting in November anticlimatic. Sweeping the northern states except for New Jersey, which he divided with Douglas, Lincoln won an easy victory in the Electoral College, with 180 electoral votes, 27 more than were necessary to win. He ran almost 900,000 votes ahead of Douglas, his nearest competitor, in the popular tally; virtually all of Lincoln's votes were cast in the free states. Yet he won less than 40 percent of the ballots cast, making him a minority president. Because he had absolute majorities in all but three of the states he carried, however, even if the votes for Bell, Breckinridge, and Douglas had been combined on a single candidate, Lincoln would still have been elected, though with a reduced margin in the Electoral College.

Lincoln spent most of election day in his campaign office in the capitol, but in the afternoon, during a temporary lull, he walked over to the polls amidst enthusiastic cheers and voted. Later that evening, as the results began to clatter in over the telegraph, he went down to the office of the *Illinois State Journal* to study the returns. When word finally arrived after midnight that the Republican ticket had carried New York, his victory was assured. As he walked home to tell his wife the news, jubilant Republicans back at the courthouse square were singing one of the most popular songs of the just concluded campaign, "Ain't you glad you joined the Republicans?"

Chapter 4

A PEOPLE'S CONTEST

WHILE IMMENSELY GRATIFIED by his victory, Abraham Lincoln couldn't help wishing that he had been elected senator instead. "The Presidency, even to the most experienced politicians, is no bed of roses," he had accurately observed a decade earlier. "No human being can fill that station and escape censure." He was especially conscious that his lack of administrative experience was a handicap. The morning after his election, he allegedly joked to reporters in Springfield, "Well, boys, your troubles are over now, but mine have just commenced." In reality, he had no conception of the magnitude of the crisis he would soon confront as president.

LINCOLN WAS ONLY fifty-one years old when he was elected, one of the youngest presidents up to that time and the first to be born in a western state. Following his election, Lincoln continued to greet visitors in the governor's room at the state capitol (when the legislature convened in January, he rented an office in a nearby building). The number of callers greatly increased, however, as did the volume of mail, which soon overwhelmed his secretary, John Nicolay. Nicolay therefore recruited John Hay, a socially ambitious law student in Springfield, to help. These two young men would serve as Lincoln's secretaries throughout his presidency.

During the recently concluded campaign, Republicans had dismissed southern threats of secession, but as soon as Lincoln's election was certain, the South Carolina legislature summoned a popular convention to consider this move. In the next weeks, a number of other southern states did likewise. Yet Lincoln, convinced that a majority of

In this 1863 photograph, Lincoln is flanked by his two private secretaries, John Nicolay (seated) and John Hay (standing). They were unabashed admirers and defenders of the president. (The Lincoln Museum, Fort Wayne, IN # 0–76)

white Southerners were Unionists, was slow to grasp the depth of this crisis and viewed the threat to break up the Union as merely a southern "trick" to extort concessions from the North.

As it became clear that the secession movement was far more serious than Northerners had previously acknowledged, Lincoln came under heavy pressure to say something to conciliate Southerners and defuse the crisis. But Lincoln, who would not assume office for four months, lacked any power to deal with the situation. Moreover, he believed such a statement would do no good, since his views—which southern editors and politicians had consistently distorted—were already on the record. "I could say nothing which I have not already said, and which is in print and accessible to the public," he replied to one correspondent. In private, he was somewhat more forthcoming, but he told a southern Unionist that he could not act "as if I repented for the crime of having been elected, and was anxious to apologize and beg forgiveness." When reporters or visitors sought his opinion on secession, he often resorted to his familiar practice of telling a funny story to avoid saying anything meaningful.

On December 20, South Carolina became the first southern state to secede. The remaining states of the Deep South followed suit, and in early February, 1861, they established the Confederate States of America and elected Jefferson Davis the Confederacy's first president. In the Upper South and the border states, however, secession was defeated—at least for the time being.

When Congress assembled at the beginning of December, a number of compromise proposals were introduced to resolve the crisis. From the start, Lincoln took a hard line on secession and compromise, and privately he threw all of his influence behind the effort to defeat compromise. He was particularly inflexible on the issue of extending slavery. "Let there be no compromise on the question of *extending* slavery," he wrote Senator Lyman Trumbull almost as soon as Congress convened. "If there be, all our labor is lost, and, ere long, must be done again. . . . The tug has to come, and better now, than any time hereafter." In the end, Congress could agree on almost nothing. Only a proposed unamendable amendment protecting slavery in the southern states won approval, and the outbreak of war a few weeks later ended any chance it would be ratified.

In the first weeks of the secession crisis, Lincoln embraced the strategy of doing nothing provocative in order to give southern Unionists time to regain control of the seceded states and bring them back into the Union. This strategy was based on the idea, which Lincoln clung to even after he adopted a more vigorous approach, that only a minority of southern whites supported secession. Once the seceded states seized federal property, however, Lincoln began to think that perhaps some limited show of force might be required to put down secession.

Come what may, he was adamant about preserving the Union. "No state can, in any way lawfully, get out of the Union, without the consent of the others," he insisted in response to the developing secession movement. Built on the Declaration of Independence, which formed the bedrock of his political ideals, the Union symbolized the American example of self-government in the world. "The central idea pervading this struggle," he would repeatedly affirm over the next four years, "is the necessity . . . of proving that popular government is not an absurdity. . . . If we fail it will go far to prove the incapability of the people to govern themselves."

Most of Lincoln's time in Springfield as president-elect was spent dealing with office-seekers and forming his cabinet. Like other politicians, Lincoln considered patronage the cement of parties, and as a minority president, he was particularly sensitive to the need to maintain party unity. The deepest divisions in the Republican ranks were between former Whigs and ex-Democrats, who jealously eyed each other, and between radical antislavery proponents and moderates and conservatives, who advocated widely divergent approaches to the problem of slavery. Lincoln's skill in holding the Republican party together would be a major factor in his success as president.

He quickly decided to offer the secretary of stateship to William Henry Seward, the foremost Republican leader in Congress. A former Whig, Seward, who was short and disheveled with a sharp nose and tousled hair, was determined to keep his enemies, especially ex-Democrats, out of the cabinet in order to assure his dominance over the inexperienced Lincoln. Lincoln, however, recognized that he had to include former Democrats in his official family. Once Seward had accepted, Lincoln offered the post of the secretary of treasury to Governor Salmon P. Chase of Ohio, who, like Seward, had sought the 1860 Republican presidential nomination. The most prominent Democratic-Republican in the country, the tall and dignified Chase was a radical on the slavery question. Insufferably self-righteous and inordinately ambitious, he would become increasingly jealous of his cabinet rival, Seward.

Other cabinet members included Edward Bates of Missouri (attorney general) and Gideon Welles of Connecticut (secretary of the navy). The reserved, plodding Bates was a former Whig, whereas the waspish Welles was an ex-Democrat, yet both were extremely conservative. For Secretary of the Interior, he named Caleb Smith of Indiana, a party wheelhorse who lacked much stature. Realizing the necessity of including a Southerner in the cabinet, Lincoln finally selected Montgomery Blair of Maryland, a member of a famous political family known for its ferocious combativeness, as Postmaster General.

Lincoln's greatest dilemma was what to do with Senator Simon Cameron of Pennsylvania, a skilled political operator with an unsavory reputation for corruption. A former Democrat, Cameron sought control of the treasury department as a reward for his support of Lincoln at the Chicago convention, but in the end Lincoln named the Pennsylvania leader, whose beguiling, unpretentious nature masked his ingrained deviousness, secretary of war. Of all his cabinet selections, Cameron proved to be the poorest; indeed, Lincoln's placement of Cameron in such a key position was good evidence that he did not anticipate a war.

While the cabinet was carefully balanced between Whigs and Democrats, its most striking feature was that it contained all of Lincoln's main rivals for the 1860 Republican nomination: Seward, Chase, Bates, and Cameron. Lincoln's decision to include these men in his cabinet reflected his great self-confidence, as well as the fact that he intended to be the leader of his administration, a lesson several members would absorb only with difficulty. Yet these selections also meant that the cabinet would not be a harmonious body, nor its members particularly loyal to him.

On his last full day in Springfield, Lincoln went to his old law office to see his partner, William Herndon. In a cheerful mood, he spent some time reminiscing about their years together. Finally gathering some books and papers to take with him, he told Herndon to leave the sign "Lincoln and Herndon" hanging outside. "Give our clients to understand that the election of a President makes no change . . . ," he said as he left. "If I live I'm coming back some time, and then we'll go right on practicing law as if nothing had ever happened."

The next day, February 11, he boarded the special train that was to

take him to the nation's capital. Standing at the rear of the car in a
light drizzle, Lincoln said a few parting words to his fellow towns-
people. "No one, not in my situation, can appreciate my feeling of
sadness at this parting," he began with visible emotion. "To this place,
and the kindness of these people, I owe every thing. Here I have lived
a quarter of a century, and have passed from a young to an old man.
. . . I now leave, not knowing when, or whether ever, I may return,
with a task before me greater than that which rested upon Washington. Without the assistance of that Divine Being, who ever attended
him, I cannot succeed. . . . Trusting in Him, . . . let us confidently hope
that all will yet be well. To His care commending you, as I hope in
your prayers you will commend me, I bid you an affectionate farewell." Then the train pulled out of the station.

LINCOLN'S JOURNEY to Washington, which followed a circuitous
route so that more people could see the president-elect, took almost
two weeks. In each community, crowds gathered to greet him, and at
many stops he made a few brief remarks. These impromptu utterances
were the first public evidence of Lincoln's thoughts concerning the
secession crisis. Although he denied any purpose to coerce the seceded
states, he also indicated that he would not accept disunion, and that
he intended to enforce the laws and protect federal property. In a
speech to the New Jersey legislature, he affirmed his devotion to
peace, but added that "it may be necessary to put the foot down
firmly."

When he reached Philadelphia, Lincoln received warnings of a plot
to assassinate him in Baltimore as he drove across the city to change
trains. Uncertain that these reports were authentic, Lincoln finally
decided to "run no risk where no risk was necessary" and agreed to
leave for Washington on the night train. He arrived in the capital
unannounced at six in the morning, wearing an overcoat, muffler, and
a soft wool hat. When critics circulated the story that he had entered
the city in disguise, he was subjected to unmerciful ridicule, and even
supporters were troubled by his sneaking into Washington. This em-
barrassing incident hardly enhanced his prestige.

His prestige was further damaged by his less-than-presidential demeanor. Critics sneered at his unattractive features, his physical awkwardness, his lack of social graces, and his affinity for telling stories. Even William Howard Russell, the war correspondent for the *London Times*, who immediately discerned Lincoln's inner strength of character, nevertheless could not resist recording that no one would "take him to be . . . a 'gentleman.'"

Staying at Willard's Hotel, Lincoln spent the next ten days until his inauguration formalizing plans for his administration. He had written his inaugural address in Springfield, and he now showed it to Seward and several others, including Orville H. Browning, a longtime Illinois colleague. They suggested several changes designed to tone down the language and make the speech more conciliatory, most of which he adopted.

March 4, inauguration day, was overcast, but by noon, when outgoing President James Buchanan arrived in a carriage to take Lincoln to the ceremonies, the sun had broken through. As the two men traveled to the Capitol, its new dome still under construction, heavy security precautions were apparent. Dressed in a new black suit, Lincoln delivered his inaugural address in a clear voice audible throughout the crowd. He then took the oath of office administered by Chief Justice Roger Taney, whom Lincoln had assailed for the Dred Scott decision.

In his inaugural address, Lincoln sought to reassure white Southerners. Quoting from his earlier speeches, he reaffirmed that he had no intention of interfering with slavery in the southern states, and added that he had no power to do so under the Constitution. He pledged to enforce the fugitive slave law, and he endorsed the proposed constitutional amendment protecting slavery in the states that had just passed Congress. But having made these points, Lincoln pronounced secession "the essence of anarchy" and insisted that under the Constitution no state had the right to secede from the Union. He also proclaimed that he intended to "hold, occupy, and possess" federal property in the South, and to collect the tariff duties at southern ports. In a democracy, the will of the majority must prevail, and thus there could be no appeal from the ballot box. "In *your* hands, my dissatisfied fellow countrymen, and not in *mine*, is the momentous issue of civil war," he continued. "The government will not assail *you*. You can have no conflict, without being yourselves the aggressors."

Adopting Seward's suggestion that he close with "words of affection," he added a final, eloquent paragraph appealing to Southerners: "We are not enemies, but friends. We must not be enemies. Though passion may have strained, it must not break our bonds of affection. The mystic chords of memory, stretching from every battle-field, and patriot grave, to every living heart and hearthstone, all over this broad land, will yet swell the chorus of the Union, when again touched, as surely they will be, by the better angels of our nature."

IN OUTLINING his policy to deal with secession, Lincoln assumed that he would have time to work out some solution to the problem of federal forts in the Deep South, only four of which still remained in federal hands. The most critical situation existed at Fort Sumter, in Charleston harbor, which was occupied by a small federal garrison under the command of Major Robert Anderson. On his first day in office, however, Lincoln learned that Anderson had just sent a letter indicating that he was nearly out of food. Anderson estimated that he could hold out for at most six weeks, after which he would have no alternative but to surrender.

By now the American flag flying over Fort Sumter had become a symbol of the North's—and Lincoln's—claim that the Union remained unbroken. Uncertain of his options, Lincoln consulted General Winfield Scott, the army's commander, who concurred with Anderson's assessment that it was impossible to reinforce the fort. The cabinet convened on March 9, and again on the 15th, to discuss the situation. At the second meeting, only Montgomery Blair unambiguously favored holding Fort Sumter. Seward, in particular, urged that it be abandoned.

But Lincoln, who was under growing popular pressure to take action, could not bring himself to abandon the fort, a move which, he later contended, "would be our national destruction consummated." Instead, he sought other ways to deal with the crisis. He ordered that troops be landed at Fort Pickens, off Pensacola harbor, Florida, in a display of federal determination (only later did he learn that this order and a subsequent one were not carried out). When Gustavus V. Fox, a former naval officer and brother-in-law of Blair, proposed trying to resupply Anderson using a small fleet, Lincoln withheld judgment and sent Fox to Charleston to survey the situation.

Despite the importance of the situation in the South, Lincoln could not give it his full attention during this period. Most of his time was taken up with organizing his administration and dealing with the horde of office-seekers who flocked to Washington seeking federal jobs. To the reporter Henry Villard, Lincoln groaned, "It was bad enough in Springfield, but it was child's play compared with this tussle here. I hardly have a chance to eat or sleep. I am fair game for everybody of that hungry lot."

In a new office and surrounded by advisors he barely knew, he was feeling his way, trying to learn the art of executive leadership. Only with time would he grow into the office and display firm leadership. He later explained to a friend that when he entered the presidency, "he was entirely ignorant not only of the duties, but of the manner of doing the business" of the office. Temperamentally cautious, he was slow to make up his mind, and thus outwardly seemed to be doing nothing to deal with the crisis. Even supporters began to wonder out loud if the administration had a policy.

Fox returned to Washington convinced that his plan would work. The time had come for a decision, and, after a sleepless night, Lincoln assembled the cabinet on March 29 to consider the situation at Fort Sumter. This time, all the members except Seward recommended trying Fox's plan to resupply the fort. Later that day, Lincoln ordered Fox to assemble a fleet in New York City and be ready to sail no later than April 6.

Seward was now desperate, for he had already promised Confederate diplomatic emissaries through intermediaries that Fort Sumter would be abandoned. In reaction, he sent the president a truly remarkable letter dated April 1. In this letter, the secretary of state recommended that the United States provoke a war with either Spain or France or both. The seceded states, Seward blithely predicted, would quickly return to the Union so they could share the war's spoils. Or if this gambit did not work, he recommended surrendering Fort Sumter and making a stand at Fort Pickens instead. Finally, Seward observed that the administration needed a leader, and if the president wished, he was willing to assume this burden.

That Lincoln was able to reply to this letter without offending the secretary or losing his support was testimony to his extraordinary tact. Passing over in silence Seward's fantastic scheme for a foreign war, he noted that his policy did not differ much from Seward's, except that he did not propose to surrender Fort Sumter. In addition, Lincoln agreed that leadership was necessary and that as president, "*I* must do it." This exchange marked the end of Seward's pretensions to be the premier of the Lincoln administration, and before long Seward was writing to his wife, "Executive skill and vigor are rare qualities. The President is the best of us." Indeed, after a rocky beginning, Seward would become Lincoln's closest adviser in the cabinet.

By now Lincoln was physically exhausted. Feeling the weight of responsibility, he commented that "all the troubles and anxieties of his life had not equalled those" he had confronted since assuming the presidency. He dispatched a messenger to South Carolina on April 6 to inform the governor that a relief expedition was being sent to Fort Sumter, and if it was not resisted only provisions would be landed. Seeking an alternative to war, Lincoln, in effect, was offering the Confederate authorities a continuation of the existing stalemate in Charleston harbor. But he had little hope now that war could be averted. After a fumbling start, and in spite of internal divisions in his administration, Lincoln had maneuvered the situation so that if war ensued, the Confederates would have to fire the first shot. On April 9, Fox's fleet departed from New York.

Quickly informed of Lincoln's action by South Carolina's governor, Jefferson Davis and the Confederate cabinet decided to demand the immediate surrender of Fort Sumter. When Anderson refused, Confederate batteries opened fire at 4:30 in the morning on April 12. Fox's fleet, which arrived after the battle had started, could only watch helplessly off shore. After thirty-six hours of bombardment, Anderson finally surrendered. The Civil War had begun.

FOLLOWING THE SURRENDER of Fort Sumter, the administration lurched into action. The next day, April 15, Lincoln issued a proclamation for 75,000 troops to put down "combinations" in the seceded states "too powerful to be suppressed by the ordinary course of judicial proceedings." In the same proclamation, he also called a special session of Congress, to assemble on July 4, 1861.

The popular response to Lincoln's call for troops was overwhelming. Northerners, like Southerners, were relieved that the stalemate, which had gone on now almost six months, was finally over, and they hailed the decision for war without comprehending its consequences. Indeed, the War Department was inundated with volunteers and, unable to equip them all, had to turn thousands away. In this heady atmosphere, both sides expected the war would last only a few months at most.

But Lincoln's decision to use force also galvanized white Southerners. The next day Virginia, the largest and most heavily populated southern state, seceded. In the next few weeks, the remaining states of the Upper South—North Carolina, Tennessee, and Arkansas—followed suit, enlarging the Confederacy to eleven states. And in a decision of far-reaching significance, Robert E. Lee declined Lincoln's offer to command the Union army and soon became a Confederate general. In all, approximately one third of the army's officers resigned to serve the Confederacy.

When the war began, Washington was virtually unprotected. Only a handful of troops guarded the capital, rumors of disloyalty among government officials were rampant, and countless residents of the city sported secessionist badges. "Disaffection lurked, if it did not openly avow itself, in every department, and in every bureau, in every regiment and in every ship of war, in the postoffice and in the custom house," claimed Seward. Lincoln's first priority was to protect the capital from a Confederate attack by rushing troops to Washington. On April 19 members of the Sixth Massachusetts, on their way to Washington, were attacked by a pro-Confederate mob in Baltimore. At this point, the Governor of Maryland requested that no more troops be sent across Maryland soil. "I must have troops," Lincoln tersely replied to a delegation from the state. "Our men are not moles, and can't dig under the earth; they are not birds, and can't fly through the air. There is no way but to march across, and that they must do." With rail traffic through Baltimore temporarily halted after the authorities burned the railroad bridges, the War Department devised an alternate route via Annapolis, and after a tense week sufficient troops had finally arrived to secure the capital.

Backed by his cabinet, Lincoln moved decisively to deal with the crisis he now confronted. On April 19 and 27 he instituted a blockade of the southern coast from Virginia to Texas. Without any clear constitutional authority, he increased the size of both the regular army and the navy, as well as called for 40,000 three-year volunteers. He instructed the navy to purchase ships, spent money without congressional authorization, and delegated private citizens to oversee defensive preparations in various communities.

But his most controversial action was a proclamation issued on April 27 suspending the writ of habeas corpus along the railroad line from Philadelphia to Washington (on July 2 he extended it to New York City). This decision, in effect, authorized army commanders to arrest and hold without trial civilians suspected of disloyalty. Chief Justice Taney, sitting on the circuit court, argued that only Congress could suspend the writ and ruled Lincoln's action illegal. Convinced that the suspension of the writ was necessary to preserve Union control of the crucial state of Maryland, Lincoln ignored Taney's ruling. "Are all the laws, *but one*, to go unexecuted, and the government itself go to pieces," he pointedly asked, "lest that one be violated?"

In taking these steps, many of which clearly exceeded his constitutional authority, Lincoln cited the gravity of the situation and the fact that Congress was not in session. But Lincoln also understood that once Congress assembled, it would have no choice but to ratify his actions. "These measures," he subsequently informed Congress, "whether strictly legal or not, were ventured upon, under what appeared to be a popular demand, and a public necessity; trusting, then as now, that Congress would readily ratify them." Indeed, he had delayed the date for the special session as long as possible in order to give himself a free hand to deal with the emergency without congressional interference. The hardheaded Seward believed that these actions taken at the beginning of the conflict, which, he bluntly noted, could have "brought them all to the scaffold," were the most crucial ones of Lincoln's entire presidency. Certainly Lincoln's vigorous response during the opening days of the conflict was the first sign that he would assume extraordinary powers in waging this war.

Lincoln faced the added difficulty of fighting a war that was not really a war. Denying that secession was legal, Lincoln held that the southern states had never left the Union and that the Confederate government had no legal existence. The war was, in his view, an "insurrection" or a "rebellion." Feeling his way in an uncertain situation, he argued that it was his duty, as commander-in-chief, to put down these illegal "insurrectionary combinations" and restore national authority over the southern states. Lincoln's proclamation of a blockade was the closest the government came to issuing a declaration of war.

Whatever the Union's theory of the conflict, the United States government in practice conducted it as a war. Southern soldiers and sailors were treated as prisoners-of-war, not as criminals and pirates. Moreover, Lincoln's proclamation of a blockade was tantamount to recognizing the Confederacy as a belligerent, since a nation legally cannot blockade itself. In the many documents he wrote as president, however, Lincoln was always careful to avoid anything that implied the Confederacy was a legitimate government.

In his message to Congress in July, Lincoln explained the nature of the struggle the country now confronted. "This is essentially a People's contest," he declared. "On the side of the Union, it is a struggle for maintaining in the world, that form, and substance of government, whose leading object is, to elevate the condition of men—to lift artificial weights from all shoulders—to clear the paths of laudable pursuit for all—to afford all, an unfettered start, and a fair chance, in the race of life." Putting the conflict in a worldwide context, he saw the war as part of the struggle to save democracy, not just in this country, but for future generations in other parts of the globe. "It presents to the whole family of man, the question, whether . . . a democracy . . . can, or cannot, maintain its territorial integrity, against its own domestic foes."

Struck by the power of Lincoln's language, George W. Curtis, the editor of *Harper's Weekly*, considered the message "wonderfully acute, simple, sagacious, and of antique honesty!" He apologetically added: "I can forgive the jokes and the big hands, and the inability to make bows. Some of us who doubted were wrong."

LINCOLN'S MOST PRESSING problem when the war began was to keep the border slave states in the Union. Support for secession posed no threat in Delaware, but in the other border states—Maryland, Kentucky, and Missouri—substantial Confederate sentiment existed. Although slavery was weak in each of these states, the institution was strongly supported by public opinion, rendering the political situation quite delicate. Lincoln demonstrated enormous political skill in dealing with the border states.

Lincoln was determined to hold Maryland in the Union at all costs, since the secession of that state would make retention of Washington impossible. As soon as sufficient troops had arrived to protect the capital, Lincoln moved forcefully to suppress disunion sentiment in Maryland. The army seized the railroads in the state, arrested prominent disunionists, and fortified Federal hill overlooking Baltimore. Bolstered by these actions, Unionists won control of the state's congressional delegation in a special election in June, and in the fall carried the state election as well, ending any possibility Maryland would secede.

Kentucky and Missouri, on the other hand, were too large and too far away simply to be militarily occupied. Each state had a pro-Confederate governor who refused to provide any troops for the Union war effort. Moreover, the Kentucky state legislature endorsed the governor's proclamation of neutrality. Ignoring this provocation, Lincoln refused to allow his generals to invade the state in order to allow Union sentiment to develop. Lincoln's hands-off policy paid immediate dividends in Kentucky's special congressional election, when Unionists won all but one seat. Lincoln's policy proved less successful in Missouri, where fighting soon broke out between civilians loyal to the two governments. With greater resources, the Union was able to commit more troops to Missouri and maintain control of the reorganized state government, though civil disorder continued to plague the state throughout the war.

While Lincoln was struggling to keep Kentucky and Missouri in the Union, northern public opinion clamored for a decisive military movement against the Confederacy. The influential *New York Tribune* emblazoned its masthead with "On to Richmond!" soon after the war began, while its rival, the *New York Times*, demanded swift action against rebels: "By no government in the wide world other than this of ours," it snorted, "is treason treated so kindly or rebellion sprinkled with so much rosewater." Lincoln knew very little about military strategy, but he understood that in a democracy, military decisions had to take public opinion into account. For this reason, he rejected General Winfield Scott's "anaconda plan" designed to strangle the Confederacy into submission by encircling it on land and blockading its coast. Lincoln realized that even if successful, this strategy would take too long, and that northern public opinion would never sustain a prolonged war.

As president, Lincoln was the focal point of the demand for action. Predicting a short war, *Harper's Weekly* bluntly announced that "if this war be not brought to a speedy close, and the supremacy of the Government forcibly asserted throughout the country, it will be the fault of ABRAHAM LINCOLN." Sensitive to this pressure, and believing that further delay would deflate northern morale, Lincoln ordered General Irvin McDowell to attack the Confederate forces at Manassas, Virginia, some twenty-five miles from Washington. When McDowell protested that his troops needed more training, he was told, "You are green, it is true, but they are green also; you are all green alike."

On July 21, 1861, the Union army clashed with Confederate forces along the stream Bull Run in the war's first significant battle. Union troops did well in the early fighting, but late in the afternoon their line broke and what began as a disorderly retreat quickly degenerated into panic and chaos. Learning of the disaster when he returned from his customary drive, Lincoln stayed up all night listening to reports and calmly analyzing the situation.

A sobered North now recognized that the struggle would take more time and require many more troops. The *Chicago Tribune*, which had earlier predicted a short war, declared, "If this is to be a war of years instead of months, so let it be." A new determination was apparent, both in the administration and in public opinion. "The fat is all in the fire now," Nicolay commented after the defeat at Bull Run. "The preparations for the war will be continued with increased vigor by the Government." The very next day, Lincoln signed a bill authorizing half a million three-year volunteers, and a few days later he approved another 500,000 enlistments.

MORE THAN ANYONE else, Lincoln bore responsibility for having pushed the army into battle. Rather than faltering, however, he buckled down to deal with the task in front of him. The luckless McDowell had come within an ace of winning, but the defeat had so thoroughly discredited him in the public mind that on July 22, Lincoln summoned General George McClellan, who had won several minor victories in western Virginia, to take charge of the army at Washington. He also drew up a memorandum on military policy that evidenced a growing understanding of military matters. Long-term volunteers were needed, he noted, and they had to be drilled and trained. Lincoln also proposed tightening the blockade and, when ready, launching a three-pronged offensive in Virginia, eastern Tennessee, and down the Mississippi River. Already Lincoln grasped the critical importance of the western theater in the war.

Chastened by the defeat, Lincoln checked out several books on war from the Library of Congress and began studying military strategy. William Russell, who seriously underestimated Lincoln's military ability, disdainfully reported that the "poor President" was "trying with all his might to understand strategy, naval warfare, big guns, the movements of troops, military maps, reconnaissances, occupations, interior and exterior lines, and all the technical details" of war. "He runs from one house to another, armed with plans, papers, reports, recommendations, sometimes good humoured, never angry, occasionally dejected, and always a little fussy." Time would demonstrate that Lincoln had a natural aptitude for strategic thinking.

With his hopes for a quick war ended, Lincoln, on the advice of Scott and other military leaders, adopted the strategy of a limited war.

This strategy, which envisioned respecting the rights of southern civilians, was based on the belief that a majority of southern whites were basically loyal, a view Lincoln clung to throughout the first year of the conflict. In his message to Congress on July 4, he asserted: "It may well be questioned whether there is, to-day, a majority of the legally qualified voters of any State, except perhaps South Carolina, in favor of disunion." In his initial call for troops, Lincoln pledged that "the utmost care will be observed . . . to avoid any devastation, any destruction of, or interference with, property, or any disturbance of peaceful citizens in any part of the country." In waging a restrained war, the government sought only to suppress the insurrection and thereby induce southern whites to reaffirm their loyalty to the Union.

The situation in the border states, however, particularly Kentucky and Missouri, remained precarious. Fearful that the Union defeat at Bull Run might tip the balance in these states in favor of the Confederacy, Congress in late July passed a resolution offered by John J. Crittenden declaring that the war was being waged solely to save the Union and not to destroy slavery. Lincoln heartily endorsed this resolution, which was intended to reassure the residents of the border states.

In his message to Congress in July, Lincoln repeated his inaugural pledge that he did not intend to interfere with slavery in the South. Earlier, however, when Union General Benjamin F. Butler in late May designated runaway slaves in Virginia as contraband of war and refused to return them to their disloyal masters, Lincoln let the policy stand. In the absence of any Union military advances, antislavery sentiment continued to build, and Congress soon sanctioned Butler's approach. On August 6 it passed the First Confiscation Act, which provided that slaves used by the Confederacy for military purposes could be confiscated and freed. Despite strong opposition from Democrats and border state congressmen, Lincoln signed the bill. It was his first concession to the radical antislavery members of his party.

Shortly thereafter, the actions of another one of his generals seriously jeopardized the cause of the Union in the border states. The Union military commander in Missouri was John C. Frémont, the Republican presidential candidate in 1856. Unable to control the state's civilian population, Frémont, acting on his own authority, issued a proclamation on August 30 imposing martial law and emancipating the slaves of disloyal residents.

News of Frémont's emancipation edict elated antislavery radicals but horrified border state Unionists, who admonished Lincoln that it would have a disastrous effect on public opinion in these states. "There is not a day to lose in disavowing emancipation or Kentucky is gone over the mill dam," one wire from Kentucky Unionists warned. "I think to lose Kentucky is nearly . . . to lose the whole game," Lincoln told a Republican senator during this crisis. "Kentucky gone, we can not hold Missouri, nor, as I think, Maryland. These all against us, and the job on our hands is too large for us. We would as well consent to separation at once, including the surrender of this capitol." Unwilling to allow his generals to determine policy, and aware of the great stakes involved, Lincoln instructed Frémont to revoke his proclamation, and when the general refused, the president did so on his own authority.

A howl of protest greeted Lincoln's action throughout the North. Even some conservatives, like his old friend Orville H. Browning, criticized the president's action. But one of the qualities that made Lincoln a successful president was that he could not be pressured into adopting a policy that he believed mistaken. Frémont's action was *"purely political*, and not within the range of *military* law, or necessity," he patiently explained, and to allow a commander to institute emancipation, contrary to the laws of Congress, was "itself the surrender of the government." Shortly thereafter, he removed Frémont from command in Missouri.

By this point, Unionist sentiment was in the ascendancy in all the border states, including Kentucky. When the Confederate army, trying to get the jump on Union forces, invaded Kentucky in September, the Union-controlled legislature requested the assistance of the federal government. This was the opening Lincoln had been waiting for, and he sent Union troops pouring into the state. Abandoning its proclaimed neutrality, Kentucky had cast its lot with the Union. The Union army soon drove Confederate forces out of Missouri as well, rendering that state safe for the Union as well. By early 1862, thanks to Lincoln's skillful leadership, the four original border states, along with the new border state of West Virginia, which was created during the war, were in the Union to stay. The decision of the border states for the Union was the first major turning point of the Civil War.

Lincoln faced another crisis, this time in foreign affairs, when at the end of the year a U.S. navy ship, commanded by Captain Charles Wilkes, stopped the British steamer *Trent* in the Atlantic on November 8 and seized James M. Mason and John Slidell, two Confederate diplomats who were on their way to Europe. Northern papers hailed Wilkes's action, but the British government, which had earlier declared its neutrality, protested the American action as a violation of neutral rights. In the ensuing diplomatic crisis, Lincoln, who normally did not involve himself with foreign affairs, moderated Seward's language and, following a cabinet discussion on December 25, concluded that the envoys had to be released. "One war at a time," he counseled his secretary of state.

NEVERTHELESS, political observers still questioned Lincoln's leadership ability. The government seemed overwhelmed by the problem of raising such a large army, and Lincoln was too unsystematic to be an effective administrator. The result, Chase complained, was that "everything goes in confused disorder." Lincoln's secretaries, John Nicolay and John Hay, tried to bring some sort of system to Lincoln's activities, but they soon gave up in despair. He filed letters in a haphazard fashion in marked pigeonholes in his desk, and sometimes wandered the corridor greeting people. After observing Lincoln at work, a longtime acquaintance noted, "He adopted no hours for business, but did business at all hours, rising early in the morning, and retiring late at night, making appointments at very early, and very late hours."

His secretaries screened the incoming correspondence and passed only the most important letters to the president. Hay later estimated that he saw only one in fifty that arrived. Hay also prepared answers to routine correspondence, which Lincoln signed. When Lincoln first assumed office, he attempted to look over the morning papers, but he soon found he did not have time to do this, so his secretaries began preparing a daily digest of the press. Before long, he ceased to look at even this summary and paid little attention to newspaper articles, saying, "I know more about that than any of them." From his office next door, Nicolay controlled access to the president and tried to head off as many visitors as possible. Privately Nicolay and Hay referred to Lincoln, whom they idolized, as "the Tycoon," after the Emperor of Japan.

Official and unofficial callers took up a good part of Lincoln's time; indeed, he was so pestered by office-seekers that he remarked to an old friend from Illinois that he "was Surprised any body would want the office." Nicolay and Hay eventually tried to limit the hours he received visitors, only to complain that Lincoln proceeded to "break through every Regulation as fast as it was made." Cabinet members and congressmen had priority, yet a large number of ordinary citizens managed to gain entry. His secretaries perceived the strain these interviews exerted, which left him almost exhausted by their conclusion.

The stream of visitors was unending: congressmen requesting favors, self-serving politicians seeking office, mothers pleading for clemency for their soldier sons, wives seeking an army promotion for their husbands, inventors promoting some new weapon, critics demanding a change in policy, and citizens just wanting to meet the president. He quickly learned how to say no without giving offense, and he often drew upon his large fund of stories to divert a caller whose request could not be honored. Supporters urged him to devote less time to petitioners, but Lincoln responded that "they dont want much and dont get but Little, and I must see them." He disapproved of "anything that kept the people themselves away from him," and used meetings with ordinary citizens, which he termed his "public-opinion baths," to gauge the public pulse. His accessibility enhanced his popularity with the people, who affectionately called him Father Abraham.

By the time Congress adjourned in August, Lincoln had largely developed his style of presidential leadership. On matters that he believed were the responsibility of Congress, such as economic legislation, he played only a limited role. He was also relatively passive on matters distant from his interest, such as the conduct of foreign relations, which he largely left up to Seward. But on questions of war policy, which he considered his responsibility, he was much more forceful and did not hesitate to assume new executive powers even when they were not sanctioned by the law. On these problems, he sometimes sought Congressional approval afterward, but he generally made his own decisions and did not work with Congress, as his handling of the border states illustrates. As a result, his most important decisions were often made when Congress was not in session. Only on military matters, where he initially deferred to his generals, would Lincoln's leadership significantly change from the pattern of these early months.

Slow and deliberate, Lincoln carefully thought through problems, weighing alternatives in his mind, before reaching a decision. Nicolay reported that "he would sometimes sit for an hour in complete silence, his eyes almost shut," pondering some question. Even in the early months of the war, his leadership demonstrated the combination of resolute ends and flexible means that would be the hallmark of his presidency. Determined to control his own administration, he was self-confident without being arrogant and had the unusual ability to delegate authority without surrendering it. His personal involvement varied depending on the situation, but cabinet members soon learned, as the Sumter crisis demonstrated, that he reserved the final decision to himself.

While Lincoln wrestled with his position as war leader, his wife, Mary, devoted her energies to redecorating the White House. Congress had appropriated $20,000, to be spent over the next four years, to repair the building and buy new furnishings. Indulging in lavish shopping sprees in New York and Philadelphia, Mary overspent the entire four-year appropriation in the summer of 1861. Desperate to hide her expenditures from her husband, she padded expense accounts and clashed repeatedly with Nicolay and Hay over control of White House funds.

When Lincoln learned of her extravagant spending, he was furious. The White House was "better than any house *they* had ever lived in," and he vowed that he would never ask Congress to pay "for *flub dubs for that damned old house.*" Unlike his self-centered wife, he was sensitive to appearances in the midst of war. "It would stink in the land," he fumed, "to have it said that an appropriation of $20,000 for furnishing the house had been overrun by the President when the poor

This photograph of Mary Todd Lincoln, taken late in 1861 by Mathew Brady, is one of the few formal portraits of her as first lady. (National Archives)

freezing soldiers could not have blankets." In the end, Congress appropriated additional funds and the scandal was hushed up, but this was not the last time his wife would cause him embarrassment.

His children, on the other hand, offered welcome diversion from the daily pressures of the job. Robert was a student at Harvard and rarely with the family, but Willie and Tad were always around and full of fun and mischief. With great glee they manipulated the executive mansion's bell system, which was used to signal servants, and sent the staff scurrying in all directions; Tad especially was prone to interrupt meetings and receptions. Taking a break from his mountain

This wartime photograph, one of the most famous from his presidency, shows Lincoln with his youngest son, Tad. While Lincoln seems to be reading to his son, they are actually looking at a photograph album. (National Archives)

of work, Lincoln would tussle with his sons and their playmates, carry them around on his shoulders, or entertain them with stories. According to one teenage visitor, the motto of the Lincoln White House in these early months was, "Let the children have a good time."

LINCOLN'S POLITICAL and diplomatic successes, however, were overshadowed by the army's inactivity. He desperately needed decisive military action in order to reinvigorate northern morale, forestall European recognition of the Confederacy, and sustain northern volunteering. His hopes rested on the broad shoulders of thirty-four-year-old George McClellan, a West Point graduate who had been a railroad executive when the war began. Of average height, with auburn hair and a large mustache, McClellan was strong and muscular, with an erect figure, and was an excellent horseman. He looked like a general and radiated confidence. After visiting him, Henry W. Bellows of the U.S. Sanitary Commission declared, "There is an indefinable *air of success* about him. . . ."

McClellan possessed considerable organizational skills and was a dynamo of energy. Upon arriving in Washington, he immediately took charge of reorganizing and training the Army of the Potomac, the Union's main army. The troops displayed great affection for their commander, whom they dubbed "Little Mac," and he also impressed political leaders, including Lincoln, who normally was not easily humbugged. "I find myself in a new and strange position here," the Union commander was soon writing to his wife. "President, Cabinet, General Scott and all deferring to me. By some strange operation of magic I seem to have become *the* power of the land."

Such acclaim merely pumped up higher McClellan's already colossal ego. Envisioning himself as the savior of the country, he boasted to his wife that he could become a dictator if he wished (modestly, he declined). To senators and other leaders, he promised that he would "crush the rebels in one campaign." McClellan's bravado and arrogance, however, masked a deep-seated insecurity. A brilliant parade ground general, he loved the pomp of the military and the adulation of his troops. But he had an overriding fear of failure, and therefore formulated no plans to launch a military offensive or use the massive forces under his control. As the favorable fall weather ebbed away, McClellan was content to merely drill his troops.

The army's failure to take the field caused Republican leaders to become increasingly critical of McClellan's generalship. That McClellan was a Democrat unconcerned about slavery only heightened the suspicion of radical Republicans in Congress that he did not really want to destroy the rebellion. Having prematurely pushed the army into battle at Bull Run, Lincoln promised McClellan that he would not be hurried and would have his "own way," but even as the president resisted mounting pressure from Republicans in Congress, he tried to impress upon his obtuse commander that the popular demand for action was "a reality and should be taken into the account." With Confederate outposts within sight of Washington, Senator Zachariah Chandler of Michigan, a prominent radical, stormed that if McClellan did not fight before winter ended campaigning, he "was in favor of sending for Jeff Davis *at once.*"

McClellan tried to deflect this criticism by blaming Scott, who was seventy-five years old and well past his prime, for thwarting his plans and demanded his removal. Finally, on November 1, Lincoln accepted Scott's resignation and placed McClellan in charge of all Union armies. When the president expressed concern about the magnitude of the responsibilities McClellan now faced, the general confidently replied, "I can do it all."

In reality, McClellan did nothing. The call for a forward movement was no longer limited to radicals. His former congressional defenders became openly hostile, and McClellan's support in the cabinet declined as well. Speaking of the growing exasperation with McClellan, General James B. Fry, the army's Provost Marshal, recalled that by the fall of 1861 "the offensive was demanded from all quarters, and in all ways." Yet McClellan refused to move. He took no action to eliminate Confederate batteries from the lower Potomac, and when he dispatched an ineptly planned demonstration to Ball's Bluff in late October, it produced another Union military debacle.

McClellan responded to this growing criticism by sneering at the political leaders in Washington, headed by the president, whom he dismissed as "the *original gorrilla*" and "nothing more than a well meaning baboon." Despite the time and attention Lincoln patiently expended on him, the patrician McClellan never developed the slightest understanding of the relationship between democracy and the war effort. He ignored politicians, whom he considered guilty of "venality and bad faith"; paid no heed to public opinion, which he deemed irrelevant; and believed he stood above the government, which he was convinced would fail if it thwarted his wishes since he was indispensable. These attitudes did not bode well for the future, even had McClellan displayed greater military ability.

A remarkable incident in mid-November revealed McClellan's condescending attitude and also Lincoln's enormous strength of character. Lincoln called at McClellan's house in Washington one evening, accompanied by Seward and John Hay, his private secretary. McClellan was out when they arrived, and upon his return went to bed without seeing the president, who was waiting in the parlor. As they walked back to the White House, Hay commented on McClellan's insolence, but Lincoln quietly responded that it was "better at this time not to be making points of etiquette and personal dignity." One of Lincoln's strengths as a war leader was that he always kept his focus on the larger questions, rather than becoming embroiled in personal disputes. "I will hold McClellan's horse, if he will only bring us success," he remarked on another occasion. Hay noted, however, that Lincoln ceased calling on the general and began summoning him to come to the White House. Lincoln was beginning to grow into the job.

Still, the time and attention Lincoln lavished on McClellan backfired. In deferring to McClellan's judgment, accepting his excuses, and protecting him from congressional critics, Lincoln intended to instill some military vigor in his commander. Instead, by placing McClellan on the same level with him, Lincoln merely stoked the general's vanity and fostered his contemptuous attitude toward the president.

As the end of 1861 approached, McClellan became ill with typhoid and took to his bed. What plans, if any, he had to prosecute the war once winter ended, nobody knew. When Congress convened in December, frustration over McClellan's inactivity led to the establishment of the Joint Committee on the Conduct of the War to press Lincoln and Union generals for a more vigorous military effort. Republicans on the committee, led by Senators Benjamin F. Wade and Zachariah

Chandler, both antislavery radicals, were especially hostile to McClellan. Lincoln parried the committee members' criticism, but he was privately discouraged. The war was going poorly, the Republican party was increasingly divided, northern morale was steadily declining, northern banks had suspended specie payments, and the federal treasury was empty. In a meeting in early January with Montgomery Meigs, the Quartermaster General, Lincoln fretted: "General, what shall I do? The people are impatient; Chase has no money and he tells me he can raise no more; the General of the Army has typhoid fever. The bottom is out of the tub. What shall I do?"

Meanwhile, the president urged his main western generals, Don Carlos Buell and Henry Halleck, to coordinate their movements. Feeling free to ignore the president, both generals reported that they were not ready to advance. "It is exceedingly discouraging," Lincoln lamented. "As everywhere else, nothing can be done." To Buell, he tersely observed, "Delay is ruining us."

With his spirits at low ebb as the new year opened, Lincoln contemplated the possibility that the cause of the Union could actually fail. After talking to him while on a visit to the Navy Yard on January 2, the commander, John Dahlgren, recorded in his diary, "For the first time I heard the President speak of the bare possibility of our being two nations."

Chapter 5

FROM LIMITED WAR TO REVOLUTION

WARS OFTEN TAKE on a momentum of their own that defeats the purposes of leaders. Throughout 1861, Lincoln had struggled to keep the war against the Confederacy within clearly defined bounds. As part of this limited war strategy, he resisted demands from radicals to make emancipation a Union war aim. "In considering the policy to be adopted for suppressing the insurrection," he explained in his annual message in December, "I have been anxious and careful that the inevitable conflict for this purpose shall not degenerate into a violent and remorseless revolutionary struggle." But with northern impatience growing, this strategy had to end the war quickly if it was to retain popular support. Thus the Union's 1862 military offensive would be the acid test of the concept of a limited war.

STRATEGY IN WARTIME is two-fold. It combines national strategy (war aims and a nation's political goals) with military strategy (the use of armed forces to achieve these goals). In a democracy, military strategy cannot be separated from politics or public opinion, since the support of the home front is both crucial and, ultimately, voluntary. It is the responsibility of the president to keep these two strategies— national and military—in harmony so that they reinforce one another.

Initially, the Union planned to conduct a limited war that would not fundamentally reshape southern society. Proponents of this strategy, led by Generals George McClellan and Don Carlos Buell, who were both proslavery Democrats, argued plausibly that a harsh, vindictive war would inflame southern resistance and make reunion difficult if not impossible. Maintaining that "the precise issue for which we are fighting . . . is the preservation of the Union and the restoration of the full authority of the General Government over all portions of our territory," McClellan instructed Buell in Kentucky, "We shall most readily suppress this rebellion and restore the authority of the Government by religiously respecting the Constitutional rights of all," including slaveholders. Thus both generals prohibited their troops from foraging for food, which they believed hurt discipline, placed guards over southern civilians' property, and forbade any interference with slavery.

They also clung to the idea of a war of maneuver to occupy southern territory. "The object is not to fight great battles, and storm impregnable fortifications," Buell forthrightly explained, "but by demonstrations and maneuvering to prevent the enemy from concentrating his scattered forces." Blind to the nature of this war, they separated politics from military considerations and believed that the war should be humanely conducted by professionals according to a set of scientific rules without regard to public opinion. In their eyes, war was a gigantic chess game.

This concept of war ran counter to the views of many Union officers and men, a number of whom favored a more punitive approach, but the real test was military success. The burden of demonstrating that the Confederacy could be defeated by this strategy fell most heavily on its primary proponent, George McClellan.

In a meeting with congressmen in early January, Lincoln indicated that since he was not a military man, "it was his duty to defer to General McClellan." Actually, he was losing patience with his sluggish commander, and at a meeting with McClellan's division commanders, he stressed that "if something was not done soon," support for the war would cease, and if McClellan did not intend to use the army "he would like to *borrow it*." Rousing himself from his sickbed, McClellan attended a subsequent conference but petulantly refused to divulge his plans for a spring offensive. The president professed himself satisfied, but in fact this meeting produced a fundamental change in Lincoln's attitude. Finally convinced, as he told Gustavus Fox, that he had no choice but to "take these army matters into his own hands," he from then on gave more forceful direction to the military effort.

At the same time, Lincoln also took steps to energize the War Department. Secretary of War Simon Cameron, who Lincoln had reluctantly appointed and who proved lax and inefficient, came under censure even from fellow Republicans for corruption and fraud in administering war contracts. In unusually harsh language, Lincoln privately complained that Cameron was "selfish and openly discourteous," "obnoxious to the Country," and "incapable of either organizing details or conceiving and advising general plans."

In mid-January 1862, Lincoln forced Cameron to resign and replaced him with Edwin Stanton, a Democrat. Stanton had snubbed Lincoln when they were cocounsels in the McCormick reaper case, but Lincoln was always able to overlook personal slights. Heavyset, with short legs and thick glasses, Stanton possessed keen intellectual power and an unbending will, was incredibly hardworking and scrupulously honest, and exhibited enormous energy and great efficiency. As secretary he quickly imposed a sense of order on the Union war effort.

Although Stanton could be curt and harsh, Lincoln had a special talent for dealing with difficult individuals, and he soon developed a good working relationship with his unpleasant cabinet minister. He often used the secretary's gruff personality to shield himself from unwanted demands, disingenuously claiming that he dare not brook his irascible war secretary. Yet when he wanted something done, Lincoln did not hesitate to overrule Stanton.

Frustrated by his generals' unending excuses, Lincoln finally issued General War Order Number One on January 27, 1862, an utterly impractical directive which ordered all Union armies to advance on or before February 22. Lincoln had already arrived at one of the most fundamental strategic insights of the war when he disclosed to Senator Orville Browning that his plan was to "threaten all their positions at the same time with superior force, and if they weakened one to strengthen another seize and hold the one weakened." Lincoln withdrew his order after McClellan finally revealed his plan to take his army by sea to Virginia's coast and operate against Richmond from the east.

Lincoln, however, preferred a more direct advance against the Confederate army at Manassas and worried that McClellan's plan would

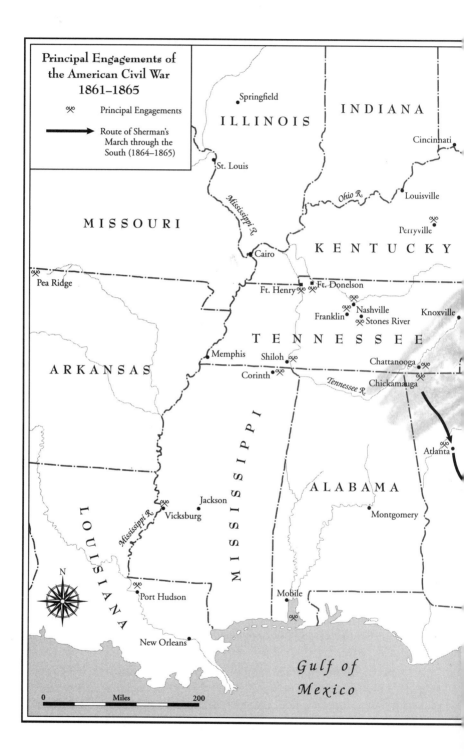

Principal Engagements of the American Civil War 1861–1865

⚔ Principal Engagements

➡ Route of Sherman's March through the South (1864–1865)

Springfield

ILLINOIS

INDIANA

Cincinnati

St. Louis

MISSOURI

Mississippi R.

Ohio R.

Louisville

KENTUCKY

Perryville ⚔

Cairo

Pea Ridge ⚔

Ft. Henry ⚔ ⚔ Ft. Donelson

Nashville ⚔
Franklin ⚔ Stones River

Knoxville

TENNESSEE

Memphis

Shiloh ⚔

Corinth ⚔

Chattanooga ⚔

Tennessee R.

Chickamauga

ARKANSAS

MISSISSIPPI

Atlanta ⚔

ALABAMA

Jackson

Vicksburg ⚔

Mississippi R.

Montgomery

LOUISIANA

N

Port Hudson ⚔

Mobile

⚔

New Orleans

Gulf of
Mexico

0   Miles   200

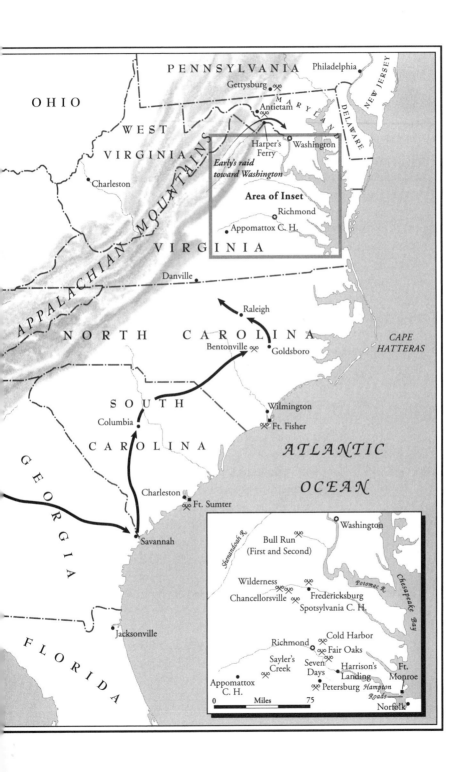

OHIO

PENNSYLVANIA

Philadelphia

Gettysburg

MARYLAND

Antietam

NEW JERSEY

DELAWARE

WEST
VIRGINIA

Harper's
Ferry

Washington

Charleston

*Early's raid
toward Washington*

Area of Inset

Richmond

Appomattox C. H.

VIRGINIA

APPALACHIAN MOUNTAINS

Danville

NORTH CAROLINA

Raleigh

Bentonville

Goldsboro

CAPE
HATTERAS

SOUTH

Wilmington

Columbia

Ft. Fisher

CAROLINA

ATLANTIC

Charleston

Ft. Sumter

OCEAN

GEORGIA

Savannah

Shenandoah R.

Bull Run
(First and Second)

Washington

Wilderness

Potomac R.

Chancellorsville

Fredericksburg

Chesapeake Bay

Spotsylvania C. H.

Jacksonville

Cold Harbor

Richmond

Fair Oaks

Sayler's
Creek

Seven
Days

Harrison's
Landing

Ft.
Monroe

FLORIDA

Appomattox
C. H.

Petersburg

Hampton
Roads

0   Miles   75

Norfolk

leave Washington vulnerable to a Confederate attack. He should have insisted that his plan be adopted instead, but he was still not completely sure of himself on military matters. In the end, he reluctantly acquiesced but stipulated that an adequate force remain to protect Washington. He also restricted McClellan's command to the Army of the Potomac, and his failure to name a new commanding general indicated that he intended to exercise overall control himself, in consultation with Stanton and generals in Washington.

In the meantime, a different kind of general finally provided the president with some cheering news. In early February, Ulysses S. Grant, aided by a flotilla of gunboats, captured Forts Henry and Donelson in Tennessee, along with 14,000 prisoners. The taciturn Grant was a physically unremarkable man of medium height, with brown hair and a close-cropped beard, and only his piercing gray eyes gave any hint of his inner determination. Unlike most Union generals, however, he moved quickly and aggressively. Nashville fell to Union forces, the first Confederate state capital to be captured, followed by the major river port of Memphis. Northern papers, desperate for favorable military news, made Grant an instant hero.

More heartening news followed. Union forces were victorious at Pea Ridge, Arkansas (March 6–8), securing Missouri from a Confederate threat, and an amphibious operation captured Roanoke Island off North Carolina. "The cause of the Union now marches on in every section of the country," trumpeted the *New York Tribune*. "It now requires no very far-reaching prophet to predict the end of this struggle."

With the Union war effort finally underway, however, Lincoln's son Willie came down with typhoid. Both parents spent long hours at his bedside, but on February 20, the eleven-year-old boy died. Quietly entering John Nicolay's office, the president blurted out, "My boy is gone—he is actually gone!" and burst into tears. Overcome with grief and hysteria, Mary Lincoln remained in mourning for months and ended all but the most crucial social activities at the White House for the next two years. Mentally unstable herself, she could provide no solace for her harried husband. With momentous events now in the offing, he did not have the luxury of withdrawing into his private grief.

◦🦅◦

WHEN CONGRESS ASSEMBLED in December 1861, the radicals kept up a constant clamor on the issue of slavery. It was clear that public opinion in the North was shifting. When John Crittenden of Kentucky reintroduced his resolution declaring that the war was being waged solely to save the Union, a resolution that had passed almost unanimously a few months earlier, it was defeated. Republicans voted overwhelmingly against it, clear evidence that sentiment within Lincoln's party was hardening against slavery.

As a result, Lincoln was increasingly criticized by both radicals and moderates in his party. Calling for a vigorous war against the Confederacy, radicals advocated emancipation and confiscation of rebels' property as part of the war effort. Moderates, on the other hand, shrank from such a revolutionary step as emancipation. One attitude the two groups shared in common, however, was a growing lack of faith in Lincoln and what they considered his weak and indecisive leadership. In addition, neither group accepted Lincoln's view that war policy was solely a presidential responsibility.

In the early stages of the war, Lincoln had let stand General Benjamin F. Butler's refusal to return runaway slaves to disloyal masters. Butler's designation of these slaves as "contraband" neatly sidestepped a difficult legal problem, but the question of what to do with these runaways persisted. In his annual message, Lincoln coupled state emancipation with colonization of blacks outside the country as the way to deal with the problem of slavery. He followed up this statement in March 1862 with a special message calling for the federal government to provide funds to any state that adopted a program of gradual, compensated emancipation. "The general government," he affirmed, "sets up no claim of a right, by federal authority, to interfere with slavery within state limits. . . ." A congressional resolution pledging financial aid won easy approval.

Still, Lincoln resisted the pressure to make emancipation a Union war aim. In the absence of presidential action, the Thirty-seventh Congress passed a series of laws designed to chip away at the institution. These laws forbade the army from returning runaway slaves (even to loyal owners), abolished slavery in all the territories (in violation of the Dred Scott decision), and enacted a program of compensated emancipation in the District of Columbia.

Lincoln, however, believed that emancipation should occur under state auspices, since the federal government had no power over slavery. He was also convinced that if the border states adopted emancipation, their action would shorten the war. Therefore, he summoned the representatives of the border states to a meeting at the White House, during which he urged them to adopt a program of gradual, compensated emancipation. Fearful of any kind of emancipation, they demurred.

Shortly thereafter, another Union general precipitated a crisis over slavery. David Hunter, who was nominally in command of Georgia, South Carolina, and Florida, issued a proclamation freeing the slaves in his Department. Radicals hailed Hunter's action, but Lincoln swiftly quashed it by revoking the general's order. For the first time, however, Lincoln publicly suggested that emancipation might be a legitimate war power if it was "a necessity indispensable to the maintainance of the government," but that was a decision, he said, that "I reserve to myself."

Lincoln battled Congress on emancipation and war policy because he believed these concerns were his responsibility as commander-in-chief. Yet on other matters, he adhered to the Whig view that Congress should shape legislation. He took little interest in a series of far-reaching laws that Congress passed in this session to develop the West, fund the war, and organize the economy, and which he signed without a murmur.

THE WAR TOOK a dramatic turn in April, as Grant continued his offensive southward and McClellan finally put the Army of the Potomac in motion. While waiting for reinforcements at Shiloh, Tennessee, Grant's army was surprised on April 6 by Confederate forces. In ferocious fighting over a two-day period, Union troops finally managed to reclaim the ground they had lost the first day, and the Confederates finally withdrew. The Union's victory, however, came at a horrendous cost, with nearly 25,000 combined casualties. Public opinion was unpre-pared for such severe losses, and Grant came under heavy criticism. Lin-coln, however, stood by the shabbily dressed, cigar-champing general. "I can't spare this man," he told one critic. "He fights."

The Union advance in the West continued. Northern forces even-tually captured Corinth, Mississippi, a vital rail juncture, and New Orleans, the Confederacy's largest city and port, fell as well. Union gunboats now controlled the upper and lower Mississippi River.

The navy meanwhile transported McClellan's enormous army to the Virginia coast. Northern papers proclaimed that McClellan's long-awaited campaign would end the war, and the War Department op-timistically closed recruiting offices. All of McClellan's shortcomings as a general, however, became immediately apparent. Wildly over-estimating the size of the opposing forces, he moved with extreme caution and soon lost the initiative. As he inched his way up the peninsula, the Union commander sent a flurry of telegrams to the War Department protesting that he was greatly outnumbered (he ac-tually had a decisive advantage in manpower) and advancing a litany of excuses.

Stanton, who had previously championed McClellan, was increas-ingly hostile and now urged that he be removed, but Lincoln, em-ploying his considerable skills in human management, attempted to make the general useful. In a forthright manner, Lincoln tried to im-press upon McClellan that public opinion, which demanded aggressive action, could not be ignored. "And, once more let me tell you, it is indispensable to *you* that you strike a blow. *I* am powerless to help this." Promising to support the army as fully as possible, the president closed with the blunt warning, *"But you must act."*

Lincoln soon demonstrated that compared with McClellan he was a superior commander as well as strategist. Coming down to Fortress Monroe, in Virginia, to inquire into the army's failure to advance, Lincoln learned that McClellan had done nothing to neutralize the powerful Confederate ironclad, the *Virginia* (*Merrimack*), docked at Norfolk across the bay. Visibly angry, Lincoln personally took charge of planning an expedition that captured the city two days later. Re-treating Confederates blew up the *Virginia*, ending the threat it posed to the Union navy.

On May 31, with McClellan's forces within five miles of Richmond, the Confederate army under the command of Joseph Johnston suddenly attacked at Fair Oaks. The battle was inconclusive, but Johnston was wounded in the fighting and was replaced by Robert E. Lee, a far more daring and dangerous adversary. As soon as he had organized and refitted the Army of Northern Virginia, Lee attacked McClellan at Mechanicsville (June 25). For the next seven days Lee hammered McClellan's lines. McClellan skillfully parried Lee's blows and inflicted fearful losses on the attackers, but he was badly shaken by the fighting and steadily retreated to the James River. In his usual whiney fashion, the frazzled McClellan blamed others for his failure. In an insolent telegram, he lashed out at Stanton and Lincoln, accusing them of failing to sustain the army. "If I save this Army now I tell you plainly that I owe no thanks to you or to any other persons in Washington— you have done your best to sacrifice this Army." The shocked military telegraph supervisor deleted these lines before delivering the message.

Measured against the high expectations when the peninsula campaign began, McClellan's retreat stunned Northerners, who considered the outcome a major defeat. When he called on the president at the White House, his old friend Orville Browning was alarmed at how "weary, care-worn and troubled" he appeared. But Lincoln was as resolute as ever. He assured Seward that "I expect to maintain this contest until successful, or till I die, or am conquered, or my term expires, or Congress or the country forsakes me." Though he feared "a general panic" might ensue, he called for 300,000 more volunteers.

After visiting McClellan at Harrison's Landing in early July, Lincoln was uncertain what to do about the Army of the Potomac. Feeling he needed an experienced military advisor, he summoned Henry Halleck, a paunchy man with a large head and bulging eyes, from the West and named him commanding general. Halleck was known as "Old Brains," but he was in reality an unimaginative plodder who was at home only behind a desk. His surly manner and harsh comments offended virtually every one, and Lincoln once said he was Halleck's friend because no one else was. After conferring with Halleck, Lincoln ordered the peninsula campaign abandoned. The failure of the Union's offensive, which meant the war would continue indefinitely, left Lincoln "as nearly inconsolable as I could be and live."

AT HARRISON'S LANDING, McClellan handed Lincoln a letter discussing war policy. Urging that the war be conducted on "the highest
principles" of civilization, McClellan opposed a war of "subjugation."
He argued that the Union should respect the rights of southern civilians, protect their property, and disavow any interference with slavery.
"A declaration of radical views, especially upon slavery, will rapidly
disintegrate our present Armies," he warned. McClellan continued to
cling to the idea that the war was a struggle between armies rather
than peoples.

Lincoln, however, had about decided that this strategy would never
defeat the Confederacy. Observing that the war could not be fought
"with elder-stalk squirts, charged with rose water," he informed a
Democratic critic, "this government cannot much longer play a game
in which it stakes all, and its enemies stake nothing." By now Lincoln
had run out of patience with southern Unionists, who "will do nothing
for the government" while "demanding that the government shall not
strike its open enemies, lest they be struck by accident!" He also realized that McClellan's idea of fighting a war of maneuver to capture
territory was fatally flawed. The Union had to wage an offensive war
to win, and he increasingly thought the South would have to be conquered to destroy popular resistance.

Believing that a change in leadership as well as strategy was needed,
Lincoln brought John Pope from the western theater to take command of a new army being assembled near Washington and gave him
a free hand to wage war. The vain but pugnacious Pope was an antislavery Republican who now implemented a more stringent form of
warfare. Pope ordered his troops to live off the countryside by widely
foraging, authorized the seizure of private property without compensation, threatened to expel from his lines civilians who refused to take
a loyalty oath, and sanctioned the execution of captured guerrillas.
Southerners charged that this type of war was uncivilized, but Lincoln
for the most part endorsed Pope's orders, as did northern public opinion, which had lost faith in the policy of conciliation and applauded
the idea of a more vigorous war.

Lincoln advocated a harder war in the West as well. Halleck instructed Grant to "take up all active [rebel] sympathizers, and either hold them as prisoners or put them beyond our lines. Handle that class without gloves, and take their property for public use. As soon as the corn gets fit for forage get all the supplies you can from the rebels in Mississippi. It is time that they should begin to feel the presence of war. . . ."

In the wake of the Union's military setbacks in the summer of 1862, attitudes in Congress began to shift. Declaring that the war had to be fought on "different principles," William Pitt Fessenden, a leading Republican moderate, called for an end to "white kid-glove warfare." On July 17, Congress approved the Second Confiscation Act, which provided that any slave owned by a disloyal master who came into Union custody would be emancipated. Unlike the First Confiscation Act, this act did not specify whether a slave had been used for military purposes—the critical test was the owner's political loyalty—which meant that women and children would also now come under congressionally sponsored emancipation. Lincoln objected to the idea that Congress could interfere with slavery in any state and considered vetoing the bill, but in the end he reluctantly signed it and then proceeded to ignore it.

Instead, Lincoln preferred inducing the border states to adopt gradual emancipation as the first step to ending slavery. On July 12 he summoned border-state leaders to a second conference at the White House. He urged them to take advantage of Congress's offer of financial aid, pointing out that the pressure on him to attack slavery was increasing. "The incidents of war can not be avoided," he emphasized, and if they did not act now "the institution in your states will be extinguished by mere friction and abrasion . . . and you will have nothing valuable in lieu of it." Failing to heed Lincoln's blunt warning, the representatives once again turned a deaf ear and voted 20 to 8 to reject his plan.

Following the failure of this meeting, Lincoln believed that it was time to change his policy on slavery. He "had about come to the conclusion that we must free the slaves or be ourselves subdued" and was thinking of issuing a proclamation freeing at least some of the slaves. He explicitly linked emancipation to the idea of a hard war: "We wanted the army to strike more vigorous blows," he told his advisers. "The Administration must set the army an example, and strike at the heart of the rebellion."

Several considerations were involved in this decision. For one thing, he was increasingly convinced that emancipation was both a legitimate war power and, as he phrased it, "a military necessity, absolutely essential to the preservation of the Union." He also believed that if emancipation became a Union war aim, it would be more difficult for England or other European nations to recognize the Confederacy. And finally, he was convinced that the border slave states would remain in the Union even if he took this step. "Things had gone on from bad to worse," he later explained, "until I felt that we had reached the end of our rope on the plan of operations we had been pursuing; that we had about played our last card, and must change our tactics, or lose the game."

Lincoln informed two of his cabinet members, William Seward and Gideon Welles, of his decision on July 13, the day after his second appeal to the border state representatives. A week later, he circulated a draft of his proclamation at a cabinet meeting. He prefaced this action with the statement that he "had not called them together to ask their advice," since he had already "resolved upon this step," but that he welcomed any suggestions they might have. In the ensuing discussion, Seward urged the president to withhold the document until the military situation improved so that it did not seem like "our last shriek, on the retreat." Persuaded by Seward's argument, he put the document back in his desk.

But Lincoln said nothing publicly about his decision. As was his custom, he often argued against his positions in order to see all sides of a question and confirm that his thinking was right. When a group of clergymen that summer presented to him a petition urging emancipation be made a Union war aim, Lincoln asked what authority a proclamation of his would have in areas in rebellion. Implying that he had reached no conclusion, he added, "I can assure you that the subject is on my mind, by day and night, more than any other."

In a carefully timed move, he also resurrected the idea of colonization to undercut popular opposition to emancipation among Northerners. At a meeting with free black leaders in mid-August, he argued that white prejudice was an insuperable barrier to blacks ever being

Francis Carpenter stayed at the White House for six months in 1864 work-
ing on a large painting showing Lincoln presenting his draft of the Eman-
cipation Proclamation to the cabinet. From left, those present are Edwin
Stanton, Salmon P. Chase, Lincoln, Gideon Welles, Caleb B. Smith, Wil-
liam Henry Seward (seated, front), Montgomery Blair, and Edward Bates.
(Illinois State Historical Library)

treated as equals. Whether this feeling was right or wrong, "I cannot
alter it if I would. . . . It is better for us both, therefore, to be separated." Noting that "there is an unwillingness on the part of our people, harsh as it may be, for you free colored people to remain with
us," he urged those present to take the lead in recruiting volunteers
for a pilot colonization project in Central America. Black leaders had
no sympathy for Lincoln's ideas or his proposal. Lincoln was not being
cynical in this appeal—he genuinely believed colonization would benefit blacks—but his primary motive was to facilitate popular acceptance of emancipation.

In the gloom that followed the Union's summer defeats, Horace
Greeley, the mercurial editor of the *New York Tribune*, published an
editorial entitled "The Prayer of Twenty Millions," urging the presi-

dent to attack slavery as part of the war effort. Knowing that emancipation was the most difficult problem he faced because of the strong
feelings it engendered on both sides, Lincoln used this opportunity to
skillfully prepare the public mind for a future change in policy. "I
would save the Union," Lincoln replied on August 22, underscoring
what had been his guiding principle since the beginning of the war.
"I would save it the shortest way under the Constitution. . . . My paramount object in this struggle *is* to save the Union, and is *not* either
to save or destroy slavery. If I could save the Union without freeing
any slave I would do it, and if I could save it by freeing *all* the slaves
I would do it; and if I could save it by freeing some and leaving others
alone I would also do that." Nowhere did he mention that he was
waiting for a military victory to issue his proclamation.

THAT VICTORY did not come quickly or easily. Realizing that the
inactive McClellan posed no threat, Lee lost no time in confronting
Pope. Like McClellan, Pope constantly boasted about what he would
accomplish, but unlike his predecessor, Pope was an aggressive fighter.
On taking command, he announced that henceforth the army would
only advance and that headquarters would be in the saddle, prompting
one wag to comment that his headquarters were where his hindquar-
ters should be. Pope's tactless statements alienated alike officers and
men under him.

Lee clashed with Pope at Manassas, the site of the war's first major
battle, on August 28 and 29. Acidly commenting that his rival should
be left "to get out of his scrape," McClellan ignored orders to rush
reinforcements to Pope, whose army was badly mauled in two days
of fighting. Pope bitterly complained of the treachery of officers loyal
to McClellan, but his public reputation had been destroyed and the
army was overtly hostile to him. A dark depression swept over Lincoln, who, Attorney General Edward Bates reported, "seemed wrung
by the bitterest anguish" and said "he felt almost ready to hang
himself."

Second Manassas also ended Halleck's usefulness as commanding
general. Lincoln had leaned heavily on the ineffective Halleck to direct

Pope and get McClellan to render assistance. Fearful that he would be blamed for future Union military failures, Halleck subsequently sloughed off all decision-making responsibility and limited himself to drafting orders as directed by the president. In a later conversation with John Hay, Lincoln explained that after the second Battle of Bull Run, Halleck "broke down—nerve and pluck all gone—and has ever since evaded all possible responsibility—[he is] little more since that than a first-rate clerk." Halleck's collapse left Lincoln as the Union's chief military strategist, a position he would fill until Grant took command in 1864. Functioning literally as commander-in-chief, Lincoln's role in guiding military affairs now reached its peak.

Lincoln's immediate problem was to find a new commander for the eastern theater. McClellan's politicization of the Army of the Potomac, particularly its officer corps, severely limited his options. McClellan had filled key staff and command positions with Democrats who felt no loyalty to the president, opposed emancipation, and endorsed a limited war strategy. Many of them were nothing more than sycophants of McClellan, whose repeated failures they blamed on Lincoln, Stanton, Halleck, and Washington politicians in general. Unlike in the western armies, openly disloyal talk pervaded the officer corps in Virginia. Fitz John Porter, one of McClellan's top lieutenants, wrote to a New York Democrat in August, "Would that this army was in Washington to rid us of incumbents ruining our country." The hostility and lack of cooperation Pope had encountered ruled out appointing another western general to command, and there was no time to reform the army. Lincoln now paid the price for giving McClellan, whom Hay aptly termed "the grand marplot of the Army," too free a hand in organizing the army and for failing to root out the attitude that the army should dictate public policy.

Believing he had no other choice, Lincoln merged Pope's army with the Army of the Potomac and on September 1 reappointed McClellan to command. He no longer harbored any illusions about McClellan's ability to conduct an offensive campaign; instead, he intended for McClellan to merely stand on the defensive while reorganizing the army. Lincoln took this step without consulting the cabinet, whose members strongly assailed his decision. Stanton, in particular, was livid. It was a bitter pill for Lincoln, too, for he thought McClellan's refusal to help Pope was "unpardonable." Nevertheless, he realized that "McClellan has the army with him," and "if he can't fight himself, he excells in making others ready to fight." Moreover, McClellan's selection offered potential political dividends, since as a Democrat his appointment might bolster that party's wavering support for Lincoln's war policies.

In reappointing McClellan, Lincoln had expected the eastern theater to remain quiet for the moment. The Confederacy, however, now launched a coordinated invasion in both theaters. In the West, the Confederate invasion of Kentucky was finally checked at the Battle of Perryville on October 8, when Buell battled Confederate general Braxton Bragg to a standstill, after which Bragg withdrew. In the East, hoping that a decisive victory would secure diplomatic recognition of the Confederacy, Lee invaded Maryland with the intention of pushing on into Pennsylvania. The war had strengthened Lincoln's sense of fatalism, and he made a vow to God that if the Union army won a victory, he would issue the proclamation on slavery that he had drafted.

Aided by a copy of Lee's orders that fell into his hands, McClellan moved with unaccustomed swiftness and intercepted the Army of Northern Virginia at Sharpsburg, on the Potomac River near Antietam Creek. Possessing a great numerical advantage, McClellan launched a series of uncoordinated attacks on September 17 that Lee barely managed to beat back in desperate fighting. With 5,000 Union and Confederate dead, Antietam was the bloodiest single day of the war. The battle was essentially a draw, but because Lee retreated to Virginia, popular opinion perceived it as a Union victory. McClellan had checked Lee's invasion, but he had fumbled the best opportunity of the war to annihilate Lee's army.

For Lincoln, Antietam was as close to a victory as he expected to come with McClellan as his general. Fulfilling his earlier pledge, he decided to announce his new policy on emancipation. On September 22, he issued the preliminary Emancipation Proclamation. Under its terms, Lincoln gave the rebel states one hundred days to return to their loyalty to the United States. If they did not do so, he announced he would issue a proclamation on January 1, freeing the slaves in areas that were still in rebellion.

The reaction to Lincoln's decision was mixed. Abolitionists and free African Americans hailed the news, though they wished for a more sweeping edict, while southern Unionists felt betrayed. Republicans in Congress in general were pleased, but most Democrats denounced Lincoln for perverting a war to save the Union into a war of emancipation and angrily accused him of promoting a wild social revolution in the South. Like Congress, the northern press divided along partisan lines, with Democratic organs opposed to the war especially vehement in their denunciation of Lincoln's policy. But even the prowar *New York World* assailed Lincoln's "radical fanaticism." Attitudes in the army were mixed as well, and some officers in the Army of the Potomac spoke of marching on Washington. In eventually discountenancing such talk, McClellan noted that the polls were the proper remedy for political errors, a clear thrust at the president.

Public reaction in Britain was initially scornful. The *London Spectator*, for example, sneered that the proclamation's principle "is not that a human being cannot justly own another, but that he cannot own him unless he is loyal to the United States." Nevertheless, the policy of emancipation dealt a serious blow to the Confederacy's hopes for diplomatic recognition. The British cabinet, which had been debating the possibility of recognition, postponed any action. From London Henry Adams was soon reporting that "the Emancipation Proclamation has done more for us here than all our former victories and all our diplomacy." Within a year, with all hope of recognition at an end, the Confederacy recalled its minister.

Unaccustomed to much praise since the war had begun, Lincoln appreciated the endorsements of Republican editors and leaders. "Commendation in newspapers and by distinguished individuals is all that a vain man could wish," he conceded. But both sales of war bonds and volunteering had fallen off since he had issued the proclamation, prompting him to observe, "The North responds to the proclamation sufficiently in breath; but breath alone kills no rebels."

Earlier Lincoln had indicated that he would "not surrender this game leaving any available card unplayed." He now adopted new, more stringent policies for the prosecution of the war. Shortly after issuing his preliminary proclamation, Lincoln suspended the writ of habeas corpus throughout the North for the duration of the war for "any disloyal practice," and for the first time authorized military trials of civilians accused of antiwar activities. Calling for 600,000 more volunteers, he resorted to a questionable interpretation of a law reorganizing the militia to impose a draft on states that failed to fill their enlistment quotas. And he quietly authorized the War Department to begin recruiting black soldiers in the South.

LINCOLN WORRIED about the effect the proclamation would have on the upcoming state and congressional elections in the North. Indeed, in cabinet discussions Montgomery Blair had opposed issuing the proclamation out of fear that it would give the Democrats "a club to be used against us" in the elections. Following the initial burst of bipartisan enthusiasm when the war began, the Democratic party had become increasingly divided over the war and Lincoln's policies. Hoping to cement Democratic support for the war effort, Lincoln appointed a number of prominent Democrats to important military commands, but the hard fighting and heavy losses of 1862, coupled with Lincoln's policies on slavery and civil liberties, ended the possibility of a bipartisan war effort.

Three major Democratic factions emerged. War Democrats were willing to heed Lincoln's call for suspension of partisanship during the war. They generally backed the Lincoln administration and its policies, and in many states joined Republicans in forming Union coalition tickets. A number of war Democrats ended up becoming Republicans. Regular Democrats constituted the largest wing of the party. They supported a war to save the Union, but opposed emancipation and condemned Lincoln's interference with civil liberties. The final group was the peace Democrats. Republicans labeled them Copperheads, after the poisonous snake, and charged they were aiding the Confederacy by trying to kill the Union from within. Peace Democrats called for negotiations with the Confederacy, and many were ready to accept disunion rather than continue the war. They were never a majority of Democrats, but they made a lot of noise and commanded a great deal of attention. In the process, they tarred the Democratic party with the popular image of disloyalty.

The target of various disaffected groups, Lincoln took a hands-off approach in the 1862 fall elections. One reason was that he was unwilling to get involved in the bitter factional quarrels that divided Republicans in many states. But he also knew his unpopularity limited any impact he might have. He conceded to his cabinet, "I believe that I have not so much of the confidence of the people as I had some time since." Observers noted the toll that the war was taking on him. "His introverted look and his half-staggering gait were like those of a man walking in sleep," one visitor to Washington reported. His face "revealed the ravages which care, anxiety, and overwork had wrought." Noah Brooks, who had first met Lincoln in Illinois in 1856, was shocked at the change in his appearance. He seemed "prematurely aged," and in place of the previous sparkle there was "a sunken, deathly look about the large, cavernous eyes."

Focusing on the issues of emancipation, civil liberties, and the conduct of the war, Democrats made a political comeback in the fall elections. In New York, Horatio Seymour was elected governor, and Democrats won control of the legislatures in Indiana and Illinois, which had holdover Republican governors. Moreover, the party picked up thirty-two seats in the next House of Representatives. The Republican *New York Times* pronounced the results a "vote of want of confidence" in the president.

While the 1862 election results were a setback for Lincoln and the Republicans, they were not a clear defeat. Although the Democrats had done well in the lower North, in the upper North—New England and the upper Great Lakes states—the Republican party had triumphed. The Republicans had also been victorious on the Pacific Coast, and while the party's margin had been reduced, it still controlled both houses of Congress. Neither party could view the results as a clear endorsement. The civil liberties issue, and to an even greater extent emancipation, had put the Republicans on the defensive, but they correctly identified the military situation as the major cause for the party's losses. "After a year and a half of trial and a pouring out of blood and treasure, and the maiming and death of thousands, we have made no sensible progress in putting down the rebellion," acknowledged one Republican. "The people are desirous of some change, they scarcely know what."

The elections also marked the end of McClellan's tenure as commander. Following the Battle of Antietam, Lincoln visited McClellan at the battlefield and urged him to vigorously pursue Lee. Instead, McClellan offered one excuse after another. When he claimed that he could not move because his horses needed rest, Lincoln's patience snapped, and he fired back a telegram that read, "Will you pardon me for asking what the horses of your army have done since the battle of Antietam that fatigue anything?" Lincoln's uncharacteristic display of temper in this message revealed the strain and pressure he was under as he saw the chance to cripple Lee's army slipping away. A month elapsed before McClellan put his army across the Potomac, and his movements were so slow, Lee easily eluded him. For Lincoln, this outcome was the last straw.

By now Lincoln realized that a new approach to the war, one that stressed "hard, tough fighting," was required. Both McClellan and the

After the Battle of Antietam, Lincoln visited the Army of the Potomac in a vain effort to get General George McClellan to vigorously pursue the re-treating enemy army. This picture, taken at army headquarters, shows Lincoln in the center towering over McClellan (center foreground), who strikes a characteristic pose. (Library of Congress)

army, he sarcastically commented, expected "to whip the rebels by strategy. . . ." Unable to infuse any vigor into either McClellan or Buell, he concluded that new leadership was needed.

The day after the northern elections were held, Lincoln permanently removed George McClellan from command. Convinced that McClellan would never display the aggressiveness needed to win, he decided that he had "tried long enough to bore with an auger too dull to take hold." He also had no faith in a general whose political convictions (and growing ambition) shaped his military strategy. He named Ambrose Burnside as McClellan's successor.

Earlier, Lincoln had removed Buell, who had come under heavy criticism from western Republican governors and congressmen. Following the Battle of Perryville, Lincoln wanted Buell to liberate the Unionists in eastern Tennessee, which had long been one of his goals. When Buell raised a series of objections, Halleck wrote that the president could not understand "why we cannot march as the enemy marches, live as he lives, and fight as he fights. . . ." Finally in exasperation Lincoln placed William S. Rosecrans in command of Buell's army. Unlike McClellan and Buell, neither Burnside nor Rosecrans was an opponent of the president's policies.

Together with the policy of emancipation, the fall of McClellan marked the end of the limited war. Buell had been McClellan's closest associate, and as Democrats opposed to emancipation they had been the foremost advocates of the concept of a limited war. They were good organizers and administrators, but that was not enough in what had become a new kind of war. Overly cautious and hesitant, they were inflexible in their military philosophy and conceived of war in terms of maneuvering for territory rather than attacking and destroying the enemy's armies, and they were insensitive to the political aspects of the contest and the role of public opinion in the war. Both commanders had scrupulously protected the property of southern civilians and refused to allow their men to forage for supplies. Their failure had demonstrated that the war could not be won by such a strategy. In addition, Lincoln had lost faith in southern Unionists, complaining that they were too few and too timid to rely on. He finally realized that his earlier view—that the bulk of southern whites were essentially loyal—was erroneous. Southern soldiers had displayed a tenacious fighting spirit in the 1862 campaigns, while southern civilians had openly flaunted their Confederate loyalty in the presence of invading Union soldiers.

In removing McClellan and Buell, Lincoln served notice that the rosewater war was over. Henceforth, he intended to pursue a hard war against both Confederate armies and southern civilians, and he was determined to find generals who would successfully carry out this strategy.

WHEN HE ACCEPTED appointment as head of the Army of the Potomac, Burnside protested that he was unfit for the position. It took him little more than a month to prove the accuracy of his assessment. On December 13, after occupying Fredericksburg, Burnside launched piecemeal assaults against an impregnable Confederate position. The result was one of the worst Union defeats of the war, with over 13,000 casualties, compared with less than 5,000 for the enemy. Officers and men openly denounced Burnside, desertions soared, talk of a dictatorship intensified, and some observers feared the army might mutiny.

Lincoln was overcome with despair when he learned the true magnitude of the Union's reverse, and the northern press raised a chorus of denunciation against Lincoln, Burnside, and the administration. *Harper's Weekly*, normally a loyal Republican sheet, admonished that the people "have borne, silently and grimly, imbecility, treachery, failure, privation, loss of friends and means, . . . but they can not be expected to suffer that such massacres as this at Fredericksburg shall be repeated." Morale on the home front sank to its lowest point. "If there is a worse place than Hell," Lincoln observed, "I am in it."

The harried president's problems only got worse. For months Chase had been telling Republican members of Congress that Seward dominated the president and opposed a vigorous prosecution of the war. Following the Fredericksburg debacle, a caucus of Republican senators agreed to send a committee to see Lincoln and demand a shake-up of the cabinet. Informed of these deliberations, and realizing that he was the target of their hostility, Seward submitted his resignation. When he learned of the caucus's action, Lincoln moaned to

Browning that "we are now on the brink of destruction. It appears to me that the Almighty is against us, and I can hardly see a ray of hope." He recognized that he had to head off this congressional challenge to his leadership without destroying his party. If he had let the radicals force Seward out, he later explained to Hay, the cabinet "would all have slumped over one way and we should have been left with a scanty handful of supporters."

Lincoln had entered office determined to be his own man, and as his self-confidence had grown, he had relied less and less on his advisors. Throughout his political career Lincoln had always made crucial decisions by himself, and this approach continued when he became president. Gathering advice from various quarters, he thought long and hard about problems and then made up his mind in solitude.

He conferred with cabinet members on matters relevant to their own department, but on other matters he consulted them sporadically if at all. Welles grumbled that cabinet meetings were "infrequent, irregular and without system"; Seward was frequently absent, preferring to deal with Lincoln privately; and Stanton, fearing leaks, refused to discuss military matters in front of other cabinet members. Lincoln rarely took votes, which he he did not feel bound by in any case. No one was more irritated at this state of affairs than the pompous Chase, who complained that "we . . . are in reality only separate heads of departments, meeting now and then for talk on whatever happens to come uppermost, not for grave consultation on matters concerning the salvation of the country." Members made "no regular and systematic reports of what is done" to the president or the cabinet. Indeed, Chase fumed that if he wanted to know what was going on in other departments, he had to send a clerk to buy a copy of the New York Herald.

The senatorial committee came to the White House on the evening of December 18 and had a long discussion with the president, who requested that they return the following night. Lincoln asked the entire cabinet except for Seward to attend the second meeting with the senators. He acknowledged that he had not regularly consulted the cabinet, but insisted (not entirely accurately) that "most questions of importance had received a reasonable consideration," and added that he "was not aware of any divisions or want of unity." With his fellow cabinet members present, Chase, who was clearly uncomfortable, had no choice but to agree with Lincoln's statement, thereby directly contradicting what he had been telling members of Congress privately. In the meeting, which lasted five hours, Lincoln declined an offer to confer with the Senate about the makeup of the cabinet, thus making it clear that he considered the cabinet his concern and not that of Congress.

The next morning, when a greatly embarrassed Chase hesitantly offered his resignation, Lincoln snatched it from his hands. With both Seward's and Chase's resignations now in his pocket, he wryly commented, "I can ride on now, I've got a pumpkin in each end of my bag." Declaring that he needed both men's services, Lincoln proceeded to reject their resignations. The December cabinet crisis ended with Lincoln in firm control of his administration and free from congressional dictation. Lincoln had once again displayed great skill in maneuvering his way around his critics. As Leonard Swett, a longtime associate in Illinois politics, observed, "He handled and moved man *remotely* as we do pieces upon a chessboard."

In the end, the only cabinet change that occurred was that John Usher replaced the ineffectual Caleb Smith, who resigned as head of the Interior Department. Steering a middle course between the radicals and conservatives, Lincoln conceded to Swett that he had not pleased either group, "but I believe I have kept these discordant elements together as well as anyone could."

EVEN AFTER he issued the preliminary Emancipation Proclamation, Lincoln still preferred a program of compensated emancipation under state control. Thus in his annual message in December 1862, he asked Congress to pass three constitutional amendments to provide federal bonds to any state that abolished slavery before 1900; to secure the freedom of all slaves freed by "the chances of the war," with compensation to loyal owners; and to authorize federal funding for colonizing free blacks outside the United States. He still adhered to the unrealistic view that if the border states enacted a program of emancipation, this action would shorten the war. "The dogmas of the quiet past, are inadequate to the stormy present," he declared. "As our case is new, so we must think anew, and act anew." Lincoln's plan was vague and confusing—perhaps deliberately so—and appealed to many different groups. This scheme of compensated emancipation, which Browning dismissed as an "hallucination," revealed how fundamentally conservative Lincoln was, and how much he hoped to control the revolutionary forces the war had unleashed.

In the message's most famous passage, he affirmed: "Fellow-citizens, *we* cannot escape history. We of this Congress and this administration, will be remembered in spite of ourselves. . . . The fiery trial through which we pass, will light us down, in honor or dishonor, to the latest generation. . . . In *giving* freedom to the *slave*, we *assure* freedom to the *free*—honorable alike in what we give, and what we preserve. We shall nobly save, or meanly lose, the last best, hope of earth."

Lincoln's endorsement of compensated state emancipation alarmed antislavery advocates, who feared that it meant he did not intend to issue the Emancipation Proclamation as promised, but radical senator Charles Sumner reassured one concerned correspondent that on this issue the president "will stand firm." In November, Lincoln told a group of Kentucky Unionists that he would rather die than retract his proclamation. He ignored Chase's advice that there was no possibility Congress would pass any of the amendments he had recommended, and remained hopeful that compensated, gradual emancipation would be acceptable to the border states and even southern Unionists in the occupied Confederacy. "Mr. Lincoln's whole soul is absorbed in his plan of remunerative emancipation and he thinks if Congress dont fail him, that the problem is solved," reported David Davis.

On New Year's Day, the president held the traditional reception at the White House. For three hours, he greeted and shook hands with a parade of well-wishers. The Proclamation had already been copied, but when he arrived at his office to sign it, his hand was badly swollen from the reception. As a small group of officials watched, his hand trembled as he wrote his full name, but he assured those present, "I never, in my life, felt more certain that I was doing right, than I do in signing this paper."

The Emancipation Proclamation applied only to areas the president declared in rebellion. Excluded from its terms were all of Tennessee, which was largely under Union occupation; certain counties in Virginia and Louisiana; and all the border states, including the new state of West Virginia (which Congress had required to adopt a program of gradual emancipation as part of the process of admission). In a decision of great future moment, the proclamation announced for the first time that emancipated slaves would be accepted into the army and navy. Promulgated strictly as a war measure by his authority as commander-in-chief, the proclamation contained none of Lincoln's usual appeals to higher principles. Only in the last sentence, added at Chase's suggestion, did he sound such a note when he asked for "the considerate judgment of mankind, and the gracious favor of Almighty God."

The legal impact of the proclamation was limited. It applied only to areas where the government had no power, whereas the loyal and occupied areas of the South were not touched by its terms. In the Second Confiscation Act, passed in August, Congress had already freed slaves of disloyal masters (in one sense, the proclamation went beyond this law because it applied to all slaves in rebellious areas, regardless of their owner's allegiance). Critics charged that Lincoln had no power to interfere with slavery, and even if the courts upheld his action, its true impact would depend on the outcome of the war. Only a Union victory could make emancipation—even within the scope of the proclamation—lasting. Believing that the proclamation could be constitutionally justified only as a war measure, Lincoln refused subsequently to apply its provisions to the areas excluded from its original terms. To do so, he argued, would be an act of despotism.

Whatever its legal limitations, the Emancipation Proclamation had immense symbolic significance, a point the black abolitionist Frederick Douglass emphasized when he declared that its spirit had "a life and power far beyond its letter." With a stroke of the pen, Lincoln had changed the nature of the war. Both sides understood that the war had been fundamentally transformed, that the Union was no longer fighting to restore the old Union but to create a new one. The *Springfield Republican*, accurately enough, pronounced the Emancipation Proclamation "the greatest social and political revolution of the age." Having wrestled with this decision over the past months, Lincoln fully comprehended that the war had reached a decisive turning point and that there was no going back. The proclamation, he privately acknowledged, would change "the character of the war" into "one of subjugation." The gloves were off. The war had become remorseless revolution.   •

Chapter 6

MIDSTREAM

LINCOLN'S DECISION to adopt emancipation as a Union war aim did not solve either his political or his military problems. To the contrary, his action alienated many northern Democrats from the war effort, failed to mollify his Republican critics, and created deep divisions both at home and within the army's ranks. At the same time, Northerners became increasingly despondent over the Union's military failures and the war's mounting death toll; desertions from the army peaked; and Union generals openly carped at one another and denounced the government.

The only bright news from the front as the new year began was General William Rosecrans's victory at Stones River in Tennessee after a ferocious two-day battle. "I can never forget," Lincoln later told the general, that ". . . you gave us a hard earned victory which, had there been a defeat instead, the nation could scarcely have lived over." But Rosecrans, resenting the president's suggestions for new movements, made no effort to follow up his victory, and gloom again gripped the northern home front, making the winter of 1862–63 the North's Valley Forge. As he approached the midpoint of his term, Lincoln confronted growing criticism over his domestic and military policies.

BY NOW LINCOLN'S daily activities followed a general routine. He was an early riser and began work before breakfast. Never much interested in food, he ate a light breakfast then returned to work in the east wing of the White House. Around one he had lunch, which he sometimes skipped. On Tuesday and Friday the cabinet met at noon. He spent the rest of the afternoon at work, going over various matters and reading the correspondence his secretaries had selected from the pile of mail. If an answer was required, he usually wrote it himself. Likewise, Lincoln wrote his public papers and speeches.

Fearful for her husband's health, Mary Lincoln insisted that he get some exercise and fresh air, so in the late afternoon they usually took a drive in a carriage. When his wife did not join him, Lincoln often went on horseback instead. Dinner was at six, followed by more work unless a formal function was scheduled. Except in summer, Lincoln held a public reception one evening each week, when people high and low could shake his hand and exchange greetings. Mary Lincoln's prolonged mourning after their son Willie's death made these affairs an ordeal for her husband and increased the weight of loneliness that pressed down on him.

Mary Lincoln, who had never been entirely stable emotionally, became more flighty and hysterical in the White House and was increasingly a burden on her weary husband. The loss of Willie, the fault finding of the press regarding her public behavior, the sneers of Washington society, the aspersions against her loyalty because of her Confederate relatives, and the fear for her husband's personal safety all took their toll on her mental balance. Lincoln admitted that his wife's "nerves have gone to pieces; she cannot hide from me that the strain she has been under has been too much for her mental as well as her physical health." She frequently directed volcanic temper tantrums at anyone on the staff who crossed her, and John Nicolay and John Hay, who tried to give her a wide berth, privately designated her "the Hellcat."

When there was no official function, Lincoln spent the evening at work or, more frequently, talking with friends and political cronies. Secretary of State William Henry Seward, whose humor Lincoln enjoyed and whose counsel he valued, was an especially frequent participant in the evening gatherings. Navy secretary Gideon Welles, who was jealous of his cabinet colleague, muttered that Seward spent "a considerable portion of every day with the President, patronizing and instructing him, hearing and telling anecdotes, relating interesting details of occurrences in the Senate, and inculcating his political party notions." Yet as Senator Zachariah Chandler perceptively recognized, Lincoln maintained a personal distance in these sessions and, even when relaxed and at ease, did not reveal his feelings and thoughts on public affairs.

Usually his last act before calling it a day was to go over to the telegraph office in the War Department and check the latest news from the front. Once the operators became accustomed to his nightly visits, they began assembling the daily dispatches in order to make it easier for him to go through them. It was often past midnight when he returned to the White House.

During the humid summer months, Lincoln slept at the Soldier's Home, on the outskirts of Washington, in an effort to escape the heat. The rest of the year, after he returned from his nightly visit to the War Department, he would try to unwind by reading or talking with his wife. "I consider myself fortunate," Mary Lincoln divulged, "if at eleven o'clock, I once more find myself, in my pleasant room and very especially, if my tired and weary Husband, is *there*, resting in the lounge to receive me—to chat over the occurrences of the day." Few presidents have put in longer days, worked harder, or endured greater strain. A government official who called on him early in 1863 observed that he looked "worn and haggard" and that "his hand trembled" when he wrote. Urged to get some rest, Lincoln conceded that "it was a pretty hard life for him."

WHEN HE ISSUED the Emancipation Proclamation, Lincoln announced that black men would be accepted into the army and navy for military service. Although the policy promised to help solve the Union's need for more troops, it was a more radical step than emancipation, and Lincoln adopted it with even greater hesitation. He expected these troops to be used in noncombat roles, but their labor would nevertheless free additional white troops for combat. When northern free black leaders and their white allies protested against this policy, the War Department finally endorsed organizing several elite black combat units.

These units saw their first action in the summer of 1863. Black troops from Louisiana fought at Port Hudson in May, and shortly thereafter regiments of former slaves helped repel a Confederate attack at Milliken's Bend in Louisiana. In both engagements, white observers were impressed by the fighting ability of black troops. Even greater publicity was given to the Fifty-fourth Massachusetts, which was made up largely of free blacks from the North and which was led by socially prominent white officers. Their assault on Fort Wagner, in South Carolina, in July helped sway northern public opinion in favor of black troops, although opposition, both on the home front and in the ranks, did not disappear.

Prior to issuing the final Emancipation Proclamation, Lincoln had continued to advocate the impractical idea of colonization as a means to defuse opposition to emancipation, even going so far as to inaugurate a pilot project on a small island in the Caribbean. The settlement failed ignominiously, and in 1864 Lincoln had the navy bring the survivors back to the United States. Long before this project collapsed, Lincoln had abandoned the idea of colonization, and indeed he made no public appeals for colonization after issuing the Emancipation Proclamation. Lincoln had come to the realization that for the foreseeable future, at least, whites and blacks would have to live together in freedom in the United States.

Lincoln's decision to enlist black soldiers was intended to strengthen the Union war effort and, by lessening the need for white volunteers and conscripts, weaken opposition to emancipation among Northerners. Eventually, more than 180,000 blacks, mostly ex-slaves, served in the army, with another approximately 10,000 in the navy.

THE CONTRIBUTION of black soldiers to the war effort, however, still lay in the future at the beginning of 1863. Matters quickly came to a head in the eastern theater, where grumbling about Burnside's leadership among the senior officers in the Army of the Potomac soon reached the president. Lincoln began to worry that Burnside, for all his fighting spirit, was too reckless, and before long named Joseph Hooker to replace him. Hooker was boastful and indiscreet (he had openly declared that the country needed a dictator), but he had a reputation as a hard fighter, stood high in popular opinion, and was backed by the radicals in Congress.

In what had become his usual practice when dealing with his eastern commanders, Lincoln summoned Hooker to Washington for a meeting. In a letter he handed to the general at this meeting, he offered some sage counsel to his supremely ambitious new commander. Praising the army commander's bravery, his avoidance of politics, and his self-confidence, Lincoln added, "I have heard, in such way as to believe it, of your recently saying that both the Army and the Government needed a Dictator. Of course it was not *for* this, but in spite of it, that I have given you the command. Only those generals who gain successes, can set up dictators. What I now ask of you is military success, and I will risk the dictatorship."

A good organizer, Hooker set about restoring morale in the Army of the Potomac, which had reached its lowest ebb under Burnside. He reorganized the commissary service so that adequate rations were again provided, and desertions, which had been running at more than a hundred a day, dropped dramatically. Boasting that he commanded "the finest army on the planet," Hooker proclaimed, "May God have mercy on General Lee, for I will have none."

Disturbed by Hooker's pronouncements—he had heard this gasconade before from McClellan—Lincoln, who visited the army shortly before campaigning resumed, enjoined Hooker to throw all of his troops into the next battle. Hooker's and his generals' incessant talk about capturing Richmond disturbed him as well. "Our prime object is the enemies' army in front of us, and is not with, or about, Richmond—at all, unless it be incidental to the main object," he emphasized to Hooker in reiterating his ideas on strategy, which by now had fully crystallized.

Lincoln's involvement with military strategy peaked during Hooker's tenure. In what may have been an effort to strengthen Hooker's self-confidence, he encouraged the general to communicate directly with him rather than through Edwin Stanton or Henry Halleck. Lincoln sent advice and suggestions to Hooker directly, often without informing Halleck, and when Hooker came to Washington, he consulted with the president and ignored the commanding general and secretary of war. Lincoln's decision to bypass the traditional chain of command, which often left Halleck in the dark about the Army of the Potomac's movements, was a mistake that demonstrated he still had not fully mastered his role as commander-in-chief. Nor was Lincoln's effort to lead Hooker by suggestion successful, as the general became increasingly resistant to advice.

Hooker devised a strategically sound plan that initially fooled Lee, and he crossed the Rappahannock River without opposition. But Hooker's nerve then failed, and he assumed a defensive position near Chancellorsville. Quickly regaining the initiative, Lee boldly attacked, and after two days of fighting, the psychologically whipped Hooker withdrew across the river on the night of May 3. Ignoring Lincoln's earlier admonition, he had withheld half of his army from the fighting. Yet another of Lincoln's generals had failed.

For several days, Lincoln anxiously awaited word of the battle's outcome. Noah Brooks, a Washington reporter, was at the White House when a telegram confirming the extent of the Union's defeat arrived. As he read it, Lincoln's face turned "ashen," and Brooks had never seen him "so dispirited." Pacing back and forth in his office, the anguished president exclaimed, "My God! my God! What will the country say!"

Following his stunning victory, Lee decided to again invade the North. One of his purposes, he explained to Jefferson Davis, was "to give all the encouragement we can . . . to the rising peace party of the North" in the upcoming elections and thereby undermine northern will. In June, the Army of Northern Virginia crossed the Potomac River.

THE IDEA of the "home front" as part of the war effort dates from World War I. Lacking this concept, Lincoln and other Union leaders did not think of northern society as a separate front in the war, and as a result the government did not produce official propaganda to sustain morale; mobilization of civilians was at best haphazard; and the organization of the northern economy was hit and miss. Lincoln focused on those aspects of the home front that affected raising manpower or materiel.

The initial bipartisan support for the war failed to survive the second year of the fighting. Lincoln had recognized that he needed Democratic support, and he had been especially careful to give Democrats military commands. But the policy of emancipation undercut Democratic support for the war and strengthened the peace elements within the opposition's ranks. Indeed, at the beginning of the year, Lincoln indicated to Senator Charles Sumner of Massachusetts that he feared "the fire in the rear" from peace Democrats more than he did the fighting.

When in September 1862 Lincoln suspended the writ of habeas corpus throughout the Union for cases of disloyalty, he had authorized military trials of civilians who interfered with the war effort. Lincoln necessarily gave his military commanders wide latitude in enforcing his proclamation. On the day the battle of Chancellorsville began, former congressman Clement Vallandigham, a leading peace Democrat, delivered a campaign speech in Ohio that condemned emancipation, termed the draft and suspension of the writ of habeas corpus unconstitutional, and called for an armistice and peace negotiations with the Confederacy. Three days later Union soldiers arrested Vallandigham for violating General Ambrose Burnside's order against expressing sympathy for the enemy. A military court quickly found Vallandigham guilty and sentenced him to imprisonment for the duration of the war.

A storm of protest erupted over Vallandigham's arrest and trial, and even some Republican papers were critical. Privately, Lincoln wished that the army had left Vallandigham alone, but he felt he could not constantly second-guess his generals' decisions. It was testimony to his political skill that he found a way to get out of the dilemma Vallandigham's arrest posed without undercutting his subordinates. As commander-in-chief, the president had to review military convictions, so Lincoln modified Vallandigham's sentence to banishment to the Confederacy. The Ohio Democrat soon left the South on a blockade runner and made his way to Canada, where he cooperated with Confederate agents in seeking to overthrow the Lincoln administration.

Up to this point, Lincoln had made no concerted effort to shape northern public opinion beyond his annual messages and the official documents he issued as president, although Lyman Trumbull's claim that instead of "attempting to form or create public sentiment, he waited till he saw whither it tended" and then simply took advantage

In this anti-Lincoln cartoon, shadowy Union soldiers arrest Clement Val-landigham in his bedroom in the middle of the night as the result of a speech the Ohio Democrat delivered against the war. Democrats portrayed Vallandigham, here shown in white, as a martyr following his arrest. (The Lincoln Museum, Fort Wayne, IN #2579)

of it, was incorrect. In reality, Lincoln had been ahead of public opin-ion on the most controversial domestic issues of the war: emancipa-tion, conscription, and civil liberties. Sensitive to the potential danger the civil liberties issue posed to the war effort, he now took steps to more directly influence public opinion. With Lee's army currently moving toward Maryland and Pennsylvania, states with large disaf-fected populations, Lincoln was justly concerned about disloyalty at home. Earlier he had ignored the resolutions of a meeting of Albany Democrats that condemned Vallandigham's arrest, but now he replied with a carefully crafted, vigorously argued letter directed to Erastus Corning defending his record on civil liberties.

"Under cover of 'Liberty of speech' 'Liberty of the press' and 'Ha-beas corpus,'" Lincoln declared, the rebellion "hoped to keep on foot amongst us a most efficient corps of spies, informers, supplyers, and aiders and abbettors of their cause. . . ." The courts, he argued, were "utterly incompetent" to deal with such an enormous threat. Vallandigham was arrested, not because he opposed the administration politically, but because "he was damaging the army." Lincoln avoided actually examining Vallandigham's words and instead shrewdly invoked one of his most effective images to clinch his point. "Must I shoot a simple-minded soldier boy who deserts," he trenchantly asked, "while I must not touch a hair of a wiley agitator who induces him to desert?"

Republicans were ecstatic in their praise of Lincoln's letter, which was circulated throughout the North as a pamphlet by the Loyal Publication Society. Bolstered by this response, Lincoln issued an even more forceful letter to a group of Ohio Democrats, bluntly accusing Vallandigham of having done more than "any other one man" to encourage desertions and resistance to the draft.

Indeed, one of Lincoln's main motivations for suspending the writ was to enforce conscription. He dismissed the idea that the draft was unconstitutional. The Constitution, he noted, gave Congress the power to raise armies "fully, completely, unconditionally," which, he insisted, included the power to coerce military service if volunteering proved insufficient. When Democratic state judges in Pennsylvania, ignoring his suspension of the writ of habeas corpus, began freeing draftees in 1863, Attorney General Edward Bates reported that Lincoln was "more angry than I ever saw him." Vowing to enforce the law and threatening to arrest any judge who interfered with the draft, Lincoln considered these judicial acts "a formed plan of the democratic copperheads, deliberately acted out to defeat the Government, and aid the enemy." Unwilling to brook any interference with the raising of manpower, Lincoln instructed army officers to ignore these court orders, a tactic that proved effective.

Lincoln had skillfully minimized the damage from the Vallandigham case, but interfering with traditional civil liberties carried great political risks. When Burnside subsequently suppressed the *Chicago Times*, the most important Democratic paper in the West, Lincoln quickly rescinded the order. The civil liberties issue further alienated regular Democrats, already angry over emancipation, from the administration.

FOLLOWING the Battle of Chancellorsville, Lincoln visited the Army of the Potomac and found morale high. Hooker, however, was reluctant to resume the offensive, and the president was not entirely frank when he said to a reporter that his confidence in the Union commander was "unshaken." With Halleck unwilling to offer strategic advice and his faith in Hooker waning, Lincoln felt compelled to exercise more forceful control over the Union's main eastern army by keeping its commander on a short leash. By this point the Union's military setbacks had induced Lincoln to discard his previous deference to professional military men, and he began to exhibit a growing self-confidence in military matters.

Possessing a sounder strategic grasp than his generals, Lincoln found himself stymied by personalities and the Union's inefficient command system. Most of his generals resented civilian meddling in military matters and almost automatically rejected any suggestions the president offered. At the same time, Halleck often dragged his feet when he disagreed with Lincoln's strategic decisions and invented a host of excuses to delay issuing the requisite orders. Halleck's declining reputation in Washington made him an effective shield to deflect congressional criticism, but in other ways he was a severe disappointment to the president. Lincoln in particular complained about what he called Halleck's perpetual "habitual attitude of demur."

In invading Pennsylvania, Lee hoped to score a knockout blow against the Army of the Potomac, then follow up this victory with the capture of a major northern city such as Philadelphia. Uncertain of Lee's intentions, Hooker was slow to react and proposed to advance on Richmond rather than pursue the Confederate army. "I think *Lee's* Army, and not *Richmond*, is your true objective point," the president patiently explained in vetoing this idea, after which Hooker tardily turned north and warily shadowed Lee's movements. With Lee's army strung out along several roads, Lincoln urged Hooker to find a weak point and attack, but the Union commander seemingly had no desire to confront Lee again.

It was by now obvious that Lincoln's attempt to bolster Hooker's confidence by giving him direct personal access had not worked, and he had also come to appreciate that this arrangement hurt the Union military effort by establishing competing channels of authority. Taking decisive action to remedy the situation, Lincoln peremptorily instructed Hooker that he was under Halleck's authority and was to obey the general-in-chief's orders. Lincoln's problems with Hooker gave him a better understanding of the importance of maintaining a clear chain of command, and he therefore corresponded with his generals less frequently in the second half of the war. Moreover, as the war continued he increasingly confined his attention to strategy rather than trying to direct the movement of armies from Washington. Through trial and error, he was developing a sound conception of his role as commander-in-chief.

Nevertheless, the Union still had not developed an effective command structure. Several factors contributed to this situation. Lincoln's lack of military training meant he could not write unambiguous military orders to his generals. He relied on Halleck to do this, but the chief general had had no more luck than Lincoln in getting generals to act quickly in accordance with these orders. Furthermore, the timid, stolid commanding general was unwilling to exert any overall direction on the war. As a result, Lincoln had to be present to deal with problems as they arose and make the crucial strategic decisions, so he rarely left Washington except to visit the army.

In late June, Hooker submitted his resignation in a gambit to regain his previous access to the president. Lincoln responded forcefully to this new crisis. He promptly accepted Hooker's resignation and, without consulting his cabinet, placed George Gordon Meade in command of the Army of the Potomac. Changing commanders in such a fluid military situation was dangerous, but Lincoln believed he had no choice. The army's new commander, its fifth in a year, was a cautious, industrious man who held aloof from politics and was respected by the troops. His quick temper, however, caused one observer to call him a "damned old goggle-eyed snapping turtle."

Only a few days after Meade assumed command, the two armies

accidentally collided outside the small town of Gettysburg, in south-eastern Pennsylvania, and the largest, most costly battle of the war ensued. For three days, from July 1 to 3, the two armies battered one another. In the first day of fighting, Confederate forces pushed the Union troops south of the town, where they formed a new line, but Lee's efforts on the second day to dislodge Meade's left and right flanks failed. On the final day the Confederate commander launched a massive assault, led by General George Pickett, against the Union center. The attacking troops were mowed down by Union artillery and rifle fire. Following this failure, Lee ordered a retreat, but much to Lincoln's chagrin, Meade failed to vigorously pursue, and the Army of Northern Virginia escaped back to Virginia. Lincoln was convinced that Meade had squandered an opportunity to destroy Lee's army and end the war. "Our army held the war in the hollow of their hand," he cried, "and they would not close it." On this occasion, Lincoln's desire to eliminate the threat posed by Lee's army clouded his judgment, and he uncharacteristically exaggerated the ease with which it could have been destroyed.

Still, Lincoln recognized how important this Union victory was. Jefferson Davis had dispatched the Confederate Vice-President, Alexander H. Stephens, on a peace mission, but when it was clear that Lee had been defeated, Lincoln refused to allow Stephens to come to Washington.

THE UNION PURSUED a more aggressive military strategy in the Mississippi Valley, where Ulysses S. Grant was in command. Grant's goal was to capture Vicksburg, a heavily fortified stronghold situated on a high bluff overlooking the Mississippi River. The Union controlled the upper and lower reaches of the Mississippi River, but the 250-mile stretch from Vicksburg to Port Hudson remained in enemy hands. Vicksburg blocked Union shipping and prevented the movement of troops and supplies. It also provided the only link between the trans-Mississippi Confederacy and the rest of the Confederacy and, as such, was an important entry point for food and supplies. Early in the war, Lincoln had correctly observed that Vicksburg was the vital point on the Mississippi line, and "the war can never be brought to a close until that key is in our pocket."

In September 1862 former Illinois Democratic congressman John McClernand presented Lincoln with a plan to gather recruits among his midwestern supporters for a new army that would operate against Vicksburg under his command. Perceiving military and political benefits in this proposal, Lincoln gave his approval the following month, and in accord with Lincoln's instructions Stanton drew up McClernand's orders. In purposely vague language, these orders stated that McClernand would have control of the troops he raised, subject to Halleck's direction, and if they were not needed by Grant. Events would demonstrate that Lincoln and Stanton had left themselves considerable leeway to abandon McClernand's plan, but Lincoln's action badly muddied the situation. He compounded the problem by not informing Grant of McClernand's appointment. As Halleck later grumbled, Lincoln's "fingers itch to be into everything going on."

As was often the case, Lincoln carefully cloaked his true intentions in this matter. On the one hand, the opening of the Mississippi was a critical western demand, and he intended to use the ambitious McClernand to cement western Democrats' support for the war. On the other hand, Vicksburg was in Grant's department, and as Grant later succinctly observed concerning McClernand's appointment, "two commanders on the same field are always one too many." At this point, Lincoln was not yet sold on Grant's abilities, and in a serious misjudgment he greatly overrated McClernand's military talent, but it seems likely that he never intended for the boastful McClernand to exercise independent command unless Grant either refused to attack Vicksburg or completely failed in his operations.

But McClernand proved too obtuse and too blinded by dreams of military glory to fill the role Lincoln had devised for him. Bringing his new bride with him to Memphis, he discovered that Grant had taken control of the troops he had raised and sent them down the river, and that instead of having an independent command, he was in charge of a corps in Grant's army. The indignant McClernand peppered the president with complaints about his treatment and demands for an independent command. "I have too many *family* controversies, (so to speak) already on my hands, to voluntarily . . . take up another," an exasperated Lincoln replied in January. "You are now doing well—well for the country, and well for yourself. . . . Allow me to beg, that for your sake, for my sake, and for the country's sake, you give your whole attention to the better work."

Once again, Lincoln put too much faith in his powers of persuasion to make a general useful. Unmollified, McClernand continued to nurse his grievances until Grant finally sacked him, bringing to an end Lincoln's ill-considered scheme. Still adjusting to his role as commander-in-chief, Lincoln was slowly learning how to assess generals' abilities, as well as the necessity of maintaining clear lines of military authority.

Grant's major problem in operating against Vicksburg was terrain. The only dry land suitable for military operations was south and east of the city, and Grant spent the entire winter unsuccessfully searching for a water route that would take his army south of Vicksburg. Frustration mounted with each new failure. Critics charged that Grant was both incompetent and a drunkard and demanded his removal. Lincoln dispatched several observers to check on Grant, and they sent back a ringing endorsement of the general. Lincoln had never met Grant, but he was impressed with the general's energy and determination and resisted demands he be removed from command. "I think Grant has hardly a friend left, except myself," the president remarked to one of his secretaries.

Grant, however, was amazingly resourceful and not easily discouraged. In a new plan, he marched his army along the western bank of the river to a point below Vicksburg, where Union gunboats that had run past the Confederate guns at night transported his army across the river. After fighting a series of battles, he drove the Confederate army back into Vicksburg's defenses and trapped it inside the town, which surrendered on July 4, 1863. The fall of Port Hudson a few days later brought the entire Mississippi under Union control. In saluting this accomplishment, Lincoln observed that "the Father of Waters again goes unvexed to the sea."

As a westerner and a former flatboat operator, Lincoln understood how critical Grant's victory was. Unlike northern public opinion, which was fixated on the Virginia theater, Lincoln recognized that the western theater was every bit as important to the war's eventual outcome, and that the loss of the Mississippi Valley, with its concentration of slaves and vital food– and cotton–producing areas, was a serious blow to the Confederacy. Grant's operation also had great significance for Union military strategy. Lacking a base of supplies, Grant's troops foraged for food from nearby farms and plantations, increasing the hardship on southern civilians. With Grant's Vicksburg campaign, the Union strategy moved relentlessly closer to that of total war.

Equally important, the Vicksburg campaign highlighted Grant's dogged determination and leadership ability. Lincoln, who had earlier voiced doubts about Grant's strategy, wrote a generous letter to the victorious general in which he declared, "I now wish to make the personal acknowledgement that you were right, and I was wrong." Having developed a new appreciation of Grant's abilities, Lincoln affirmed, "Grant is my man and I am his the rest of the war."

Together, the Union victories at Gettysburg and Vicksburg were a major turning point in the war. "We are now in the darkest hour of our political existence," conceded Jefferson Davis.

THE IMPROVED MILITARY situation, however, did not eradicate the deep divisions over the war on the northern home front. Especially controversial was conscription, which in theory, at least, directly affected large numbers of ordinary Northerners.

When volunteering fell off in 1862, Lincoln had instituted a limited draft, and in March 1863, Congress finally established a full-fledged system of conscription. The conscription law, however, contained two major loopholes. Men who were otherwise eligible could avoid service by either hiring a substitute (which would free one from all subsequent drafts) or paying a $300 commutation fee (which applied only to the current draft call). Democrats raised the cry that it was "a rich man's war and a poor man's fight."

In reality, the draft produced very few men for the army—only 46,000 conscripts and 118,000 substitutes, or less than 10 percent of the total Union strength. The real purpose of the draft was to stimulate volunteering. Nevertheless, coerced military service was bound to be controversial in a society that prided itself on the liberty it granted its citizens, and where conscription had previously been unknown under the Constitution. Festering resentment soon boiled over into violent resistance in a number of states, and antidraft riots occurred in several northern cities.

None of these popular disturbances approached in scope or destruction the draft riots in New York City in July 1863. Violence exploded following the initial drawing of names and continued for four days. Members of the mob cheered for Jefferson Davis and attacked the police, soldiers, well-known Republicans, and the city's black population. "Jefferson Davis rules New York today," George Templeton Strong, a socially prominent Republican, seethed as the riot raged. Eventually the government had to rush troops from Gettysburg in order to restore order. More than a million dollars in property was destroyed and at least 105 people lost their lives, making this riot the most deadly civil disturbance in American history.

Led by New York governor Horatio Seymour, Democrats demanded that Lincoln suspend the draft, alleging that it was unconstitutional and should be tested in court first. Adopting a middle course, Lincoln, who had earlier refused to employ massive force to suppress the rioters, also rejected calls to stop the draft. The Union's need for more men was pressing, and he recognized that suspension of the draft would encourage the Confederacy. Nor was he willing to wait until the Supreme Court ruled on the issue (in fact, the court never dealt with this question during the war). Instead, he postponed resumption of the draft to allow emotions to subside. Then in August, without fanfare, the draft quietly resumed in the metropolis.

As president, Lincoln tended to focus on policy goals rather than constitutional issues. From his perspective, winning the war took priority, and he adopted policies that he believed promoted that objective without anguishing over their constitutionality. His policies were normally responses to specific events and developments rather than based on any constitutional blueprint. Nor was he excessively concerned about the longterm effect of such policies, as he was certain they would cease once peace was restored. In his letter to Erastus Corning, he denied that there was any danger that "the American people will, by means of military arrests during the rebellion, lose the right of public discussion, the liberty of speech and the press, the law of evidence, trial by jury, and Habeas corpus, throughout the indefinite peaceful future . . . any more than I am able to believe that a man could contract so strong an appetite for emetics during temporary illness, as to persist in feeding upon them through the remainder of his healthful life."

To him the government's power to institute a draft was clear, but even so he too easily dismissed northern complaints about this interference with personal liberty. Late in 1863, Lincoln wrote a paper discussing the legal issues raised by conscription. Insisting that the power to raise armies was "expressly" and "unconditionally" granted by the Constitution, he argued that it was "not a power to raise armies *if* State authorities consent; nor *if* the men to compose the armies are entirely willing; but it is a power to raise and support armies given to congress by the constitution, without an if." Lincoln was on shakier ground when he tried to defend the equity of substitution and commutation. In the end, perhaps believing his letter was inadequate, he decided not to send it.

The Union's recent military victories made Lincoln more confident and raised his spirits, which the New York City riots only temporarily deflated. Hay reported in August that Lincoln was "in fine whack. I have rarely seen him more serene and busy. He is managing this war, the draft, foreign relations, and planning a reconstruction of the Union, all at once." Lincoln's show of consulting the cabinet following the crisis in December 1862 soon ended. "I never knew with what tyrannous authority he rules the Cabinet, till now," Hay wrote. "The most important things he decides and there is no cavil."

The summer of 1863 represented the peak of antiwar Democrats' power and influence. In the Midwest, the elections of 1862 had momentarily made radical Copperhead elements dominant in the legislatures in Indiana and Illinois. After repeated clashes, the Republican governors of these states, Richard Yates in Illinois and Oliver P. Morton in Indiana, had, in effect, dispensed with the legislature. In contrast to more excitable Republican leaders, Lincoln was normally levelheaded in his judgments, but the harsh criticism and extreme rhetoric of the opposition over the past year had convinced him that there existed an organized conspiracy to undermine the war effort. Hence he believed that this was no time to stand on constitutional niceties or democratic scruples. When Morton ran out of money to run the

Indiana government, the War Department secretly provided him with an illegal $250,000 subsidy.

In this situation, Democrats in several key states selected prominent peace Democrats to head the party's ticket. The most notorious example was former congressman Clement Vallandigham, currently in exile in Canada, who was nominated for governor in Ohio. In accepting the Democratic nomination Vallandigham declared that the Confederacy could not be defeated and called for peace negotiations. In Pennsylvania, Democrats named controversial state supreme court justice George Woodward, who upheld the right of secession, as their gubernatorial candidate. In both states, Democrats intended to challenge the Republicans not just on the issue of emancipation, but also on the issue of continuing the war.

Although Lincoln's own state did not have a statewide election in 1863, Republicans organized a rally, to be held on September 3, to counteract Democratic calls for peace. When organizers asked Lincoln to speak at the meeting, he was tempted to accept (it would have been his first visit home since the war began), but with a Union offensive in East Tennessee finally under way, he concluded that matters were too pressing to leave Washington. Therefore, he decided to write a public letter, which he promised would be "rather good."

In appealing to Northerners to drop partisan motivations, Lincoln asserted that compromise was impossible and that the only choices were military victory or surrender of the Union. In the letter's most important section, he took up the issue of emancipation and reiterated that "the promise being made, must be kept." To his critics, Lincoln responded, "You say you will not fight to free negroes. . . . Fight you, then, exclusively to save the Union. I issued the proclamation on purpose to aid you in saving the Union." He emphasized that African Americans' assistance in the war was essential if the Union was to be preserved, and noted that some military commanders believed that emancipation and the recruitment of black troops "constituted the heaviest blow yet dealt to the rebellion." Contrasting the patriotic zeal of black soldiers with the sulking disloyalty of Copperheads, Lincoln emphasized that when victory was finally won, "there will be some black men who can remember that, with silent tongue, and clenched teeth, and steady eye, and well-poised bayonet, they have helped mankind on to this great consummation; while, I fear, there will be some white ones, unable to forget that, with malignant heart, and deceitful speech, they have strove to hinder it."

Near the end of his letter, which was addressed to his old friend James Conkling, he observed that "the signs look better" and saluted the contribution of both Union soldiers and sailors: "Thanks to all. For the great republic—for the principle it lives by, and keeps alive—for man's vast future,—thanks to all." Cautioning against over-optimism, he closed, "Let us diligently apply the means, never doubting that a just God, in his own good time, will give us the rightful result."

Once again Lincoln had employed great eloquence in defending his policies. Yet the reaction to the letter divided along predictable partisan lines. Democrats were generally critical, offering no more than a grudging nod to its sentiments, while Republicans applauded it, though the *New York Times* certainly erred when it claimed, "Abraham Lincoln is to-day the most popular man in the Republic." A veteran of many party campaigns, Lincoln knew that eloquence alone did not sway many voters.

LINCOLN HAD LITTLE time to bask in the praise Republicans heaped on this letter before he confronted a new military crisis in Tennessee. Like so many Union generals, William Rosecrans often seemed nearly immobilized. He cited one pretext after another to delay action, and it took constant—and increasingly forceful—prodding from Washington to get him to move. Once finally under way, however, he advanced with unusual speed and deftly maneuvered Braxton Bragg's Confederate army out of Tennessee and occupied Chattanooga, in the southeast corner of the state. Chattanooga, which guarded critical rail and river lines, was almost as vital a strategic site as Vicksburg.

Rosecrans's zeal to push into northern Georgia soon outran prudence, however, and he suffered a major defeat at Chickamauga when Bragg attacked his dispersed forces on September 19–20, sending them fleeing back to Chattanooga, where Bragg's pursuing troops bottled them up. Oscillating between confidence and despair, the Union commander sent contradictory messages about his situation, prompting Lincoln to remark that Rosecrans seemed "confused and stunned like a duck hit on the head." The Union's only supply line to the besieged town was a vulnerable, tortuous road over the mountains, and federal soldiers were soon put on quarter rations.

As was his usual practice, Lincoln acted decisively to deal with this potentially disastrous situation. After an emergency night meeting at the War Department, the government detached 20,000 troops from the Army of the Potomac and sent them west by rail to reinforce Rosecrans's army. In addition, in mid-October Lincoln placed Grant in command of all Union forces between the Appalachians and the Mississippi and gave him sweeping powers to deal with the crisis in Tennessee. Grant immediately removed Rosecrans, who seemed almost paralyzed, and went to Chattanooga to personally take command.

The army's situation at Chattanooga was still precarious when the Ohio and Pennsylvania elections occurred on October 14. Lincoln confessed to Welles that he was exceedingly anxious about the outcome, since Copperhead victories in those two key northern states would be a major, perhaps fatal, blow to the Union cause. Lincoln's concern proved exaggerated, for the results demonstrated that the Democrats had seriously blundered by nominating extreme peace candidates. The Republicans won a narrow victory in Pennsylvania, while in Ohio, Vallandigham was crushed by a margin of over 100,000 votes. Particularly striking was the overwhelming opposition to him among Ohio soldiers, many of whom had been Democrats before the war. Unlike Pennsylvania, Ohio allowed its soldiers to vote in their camps, and about 95 percent cast Republican ballots. The soldier vote revealed how deeply the troops hated the Copperheads, whom they considered traitors.

Elections elsewhere in the North the following month brought more cheering news. Republicans regained control of the New York legislature by a commanding margin, and were generally victorious outside New Jersey and the border states. Republicans believed that Lincoln's public letters had played an important role in the party's improved showing, and the northern elections demonstrated that opinion was beginning to swing in favor of emancipation.

Additional good news soon arrived from Chattanooga. After opening a more reliable supply line to the city and receiving additional reinforcements, Grant assumed the offensive and, following a series of preliminary victories, in late November drove the Confederates from a seemingly impregnable stronghold on Missionary Ridge. The Confederate army retreated to northern Georgia. Both armies went into winter quarters, but the Union army was now poised to invade Georgia when campaigning resumed next year. In addition, the military defeats of 1863 were a death blow to Confederate hopes for European recognition. From London, Henry Adams reported that "the disasters of the rebels are unredeemed by even any hope of success. . . . It is now conceded . . . that all idea of intervention is at an end." Moreover, the capture of Vicksburg and rescue of the army at Chattanooga established Grant as the Union's most impressive commander. Lincoln had finally found the general he was looking for.

A major diplomatic crisis with Britain was resolved as well. Unable to construct a navy, the Confederacy sought to build ships by subterfuge in Great Britain, in violation of international law. Several cruisers, including the *Alabama*, had been built in British shipyards and had inflicted damage totalling millions of dollars on Union shipping. In 1863 a Liverpool firm began constructing two rams powerful enough to destroy the Union blockade. Armed with evidence provided by Charles Francis Adams, the American minister, that these vessels were secretly owned by the Confederacy, the British government finally seized them. This episode marked the last serious diplomatic crisis of the war. The Confederacy was left to stand or fall on its own resources.

LINCOLN'S MANAGEMENT of the war changed after mid-1863. He turned much of the day-to-day direction over to Halleck and Stanton, and he also abandoned his effort to transform generals. His attempts to invigorate McClellan, Hooker, and even Meade had been unsuccessful. The war had winnowed out some of the Union's less competent generals, and Lincoln finally recognized that he could not direct military movements from afar. Concentrating on larger strategic questions, he increasingly relied on his generals to evaluate their own situations in the field.

The military events of the year had confirmed in Lincoln's mind how hard it was to find generals who could administer large armies and also make sound strategic decisions. He was especially frustrated by most of his generals' unwillingness to exploit the enemy's mistakes. "How much depends in military matters on one master mind," he observed during the Gettysburg campaign. He had found such a leader in Grant. But the war was fundamentally a two-theater war, and Grant could not be in both the East and the West. Hoping to instill some energy in the Army of the Potomac, Lincoln considered the possibility in 1863 of bringing Grant east. He rejected this idea for the moment, but the seed had been planted in his mind.

The fighting in 1863 marked a transition phase in the evolution of the Union's military strategy. Lincoln's policy of emancipation made compromise with the rebels impossible. Early in 1863 Halleck wrote to Grant, "The character of the war has very much changed within the last year. There is now no possible hope of reconciliation. . . . We must conquer the rebels or be conquered by them." This attitude resulted in much harsher treatment of civilians.

The Union's new policy toward southern whites was most force-fully directed against committed supporters of the Confederacy, especially slaveholders, but in practice all southern civilians, including slaves, suffered at the hands of the invading armies. By 1863 Union troops considered all southern whites to be essentially disloyal and made no careful discrimination when destroying civilian property.

This new conception of war was most apparent in Grant's operations in the West. Again, Lincoln's policy of emancipation heralded the change in policy. In the fall of 1862 Grant abandoned his earlier approach of trying to protect civilian property and instructed his troops to forage widely for supplies. "Our armies are devastating the land," Union general William Tecumseh Sherman noted early in 1863, "and it is sad to See the destruction that attends our progress—we cannot help it. Farms disappear, houses are burned and plundered and every living animal killed and eaten." The purpose of such action was not to break civilians' will to resist; rather, it was to deny these resources to the Confederate army and to destroy the region's economic value to the Confederacy.

Beginning in 1863, Grant also sought to liberate as many slaves as

possible to weaken the Confederacy even further. It was the policy of
the government, Halleck tersely wrote Grant, "to withdraw from the
use of the enemy all the slaves you can, and to employ those so
withdrawn to the best possible advantage against the enemy." These
policies, which provoked no opposition or criticism from Lincoln, laid
the basis for adoption of the strategy of total war in the final year of
the war.

SHORTLY AFTER the 1863 elections, Lincoln traveled to Gettysburg to
participate in ceremonies dedicating a national cemetery on the battlefield. The famous orator Edward Everett, a former president of
Harvard, was the featured speaker, but the organizers asked Lincoln
to make "a few appropriate remarks." Throughout his presidency, Lincoln routinely declined speaking invitations, and thus observers were
surprised when he agreed to go to Pennsylvania. Several correspon-
dents had previously urged him to address the northern people concerning the basic issues of the war, and he chose this forum to do so.

The national government had no wartime propaganda agency, and
much of the propaganda issued in the North during the war was the
work of civilian organizations such as the Loyal Publication Society
in New York. Nor did Lincoln try to systematically shape popular
opinion. His efforts in this regard, while often effective, were sporadic,
usually precipitated by a crisis, such as Vallandigham's arrest, or by an
official duty, such as his annual messages to Congress.

Lincoln gave considerable thought to what he would say on this
occasion. He intended to describe the larger purpose of the war, and
he carefully prepared a draft before he boarded a special train that
took him and other Washington dignitaries to Gettysburg. He revised
his speech that evening, and the next morning made a clean copy
from which to read.

A larger crowd than expected, perhaps 15,000, was present for the
ceremony. Everett spoke for more than two hours, describing in detail
the battle that had occurred there. Then the president rose and, after adjusting his glasses, delivered the most famous presidential speech in
American history. When he reached the conclusion, he spontaneously

added the phrase "under God," but otherwise stuck to the draft he had prepared. The entire speech lasted only about two minutes. Indeed, the audience, which had expected a longer speech, had hardly begun to pay attention to the president's words when he sat down. In his brief remarks, the former backwoodsman and onetime country lawyer distilled the essence of America and the meaning of the war. Lincoln placed the promise of equality at the heart of the American experience and, anticipating the end of slavery in the Republic, called for a new birth of freedom in the country to redeem the war's terrible cost.

The enduring fame of the Gettysburg Address derives from several qualities: its musical cadences, reminiscent of the Bible Lincoln knew so well; its simple language; its use of repetition; its succinct expression of overarching ideas; and its generous spirit and soaring vision. The structure allowed him to link the country's past, present, and future in one sustained, abstract view. Its effectiveness also rests on Lincoln's shrewd decision not to focus on the recent battle, the events of the war, or the cemetery that was being dedicated. Indeed, the speech could have been delivered on any "great battle-field" of the war. It has been frequently commented on that he used the word "nation" no less than five times in the speech. But equally important was his dating of the nation's birth in 1776, with the Declaration of Independence, and not with the adoption of the Constitution. His ultimate purpose was to justify the transformation of Union war aims during the last year to include not just preservation of the Union, but the destruction of slavery, in order to fulfill the ideals of the Revolution.

Democratic papers generally dismissed Lincoln's effort, while Republican papers were favorable, although some gave it only limited attention. The importance and appreciation of the Gettysburg Address would grow with time, but fair-minded observers discerned its qualities immediately. To Lincoln, Everett frankly confessed, "I should be glad, if I could flatter myself that I came as near to the central idea of the occasion, in two hours, as you did in two minutes."

Yet the harsh political reality was that whatever the power of his address, Lincoln remained a vulnerable president. True, after the grim winter of 1862–63, the Union had made significant military strides. In the East, while Lee's army was still a genuine threat, it no longer had the striking power it had possessed at the beginning of the year. In the West, the Union's achievements were more impressive—and more decisive. The Mississippi River was under Union control, the Confederate army had finally been pushed out of Tennessee, and the heart of the Confederacy was now open to Union invasion.

Northern public opinion, however, failed to grasp the significance of these developments. Fixated on Virginia and correctly recognizing that Lee, if weakened, was hardly defeated, many Northerners continued to doubt Lincoln's leadership ability. Once again, popular hopes at the beginning of spring that the latest Union offensive would end the war had been dashed. As head of the government, Lincoln naturally was the target of this growing impatience and frustration.

The 1863 elections in the North revealed that emancipation enjoyed much broader support than a year earlier, less because of any moral concern for the welfare of black Americans than from a conviction that freeing the slaves would weaken the Confederacy and hasten the end of the war. The *Illinois State Journal*, the Republican state organ in Lincoln's home town of Springfield, claimed that had a referendum been held in the fall of 1862, northern voters would have soundly rejected emancipation, but that it would now win by "an overwhelming majority." While this assertion was an exaggeration, Lincoln acknowledged in his annual message in December that the Emancipation Proclamation had been "followed by dark and doubtful days," but with hostility to emancipation dissipating, he optimistically claimed that, "the crisis which threatened to divide the friends of the Union is past."

Nevertheless, the major lesson of the 1863 elections for Democrats was the necessity of keeping the extreme peace advocates in the background to avoid a popular image of disloyalty. Experienced commentators attributed the recent Republican victories primarily to the Democrats' blunder in nominating men such as Vallandigham, rather than to any groundswell of popular support for Lincoln.

With victory still unattained and murmurings about his leadership growing, Lincoln seemed destined to be a one-term president. Ever a political realist, Lincoln recognized that without a dramatic change in the military situation, he was unlikely to be reelected. Feeling desperately alone, he was determined to persevere in the struggle, but he was increasingly uncertain whether the northern people would sustain him.

Chapter 7

TO FINISH THE TASK

IT IS DIFFICULT today to appreciate Abraham Lincoln's political situation at the beginning of 1864. Blessed with hindsight, the modern observer marvels at his growth in office, at his ability to deal with a discordant group of advisers, at his skillful handling of a wide variety of difficult problems, and at his resolute determination to see the war through to victory. Yet Lincoln's contemporaries, who were denied the advantage of knowing the future, were increasingly critical of the president and his policies. The war had lasted much longer and proven far more costly, in terms of both lives and money, than anyone had anticipated in 1861, and yet after almost three years of fighting the Confederacy remained strong and defiant. The growing frustration over the war welled up in 1864 on the northern home front and seriously threatened Lincoln's chances of reelection.

THROUGHOUT HIS LIFE, Lincoln's ambition to be somebody had driven him ahead. Believing that his leadership was necessary for the Union to be preserved, he was anxious to win a second term in office, but he felt compelled to observe the nineteenth-century propriety of not seeming to seek the nomination. Having endured a torrent of criticism since assuming office, he could not fail but be personally satisfied by the popular endorsement that a victory in November would represent.

While Lincoln had enjoyed a certain measure of support among common citizens, he had never exercised the same hold over party leaders in Washington, who were not in awe of him either personally or politically. Even many Republicans in the capital believed that he was too vacillating to be an effective leader. Illinois Senator Lyman Trumbull told an associate in February, 1864, "You would be surprised, in talking with public men we meet here, to find how few, when you come to get at their real sentiments, are for Mr. Lincoln's reëlection. There is a distrust and fear that he is too undecided and inefficient to put down the rebellion."

The most important group that wanted to put Lincoln aside in 1864 was the radical Republicans. Strongly antislavery, the radical wing of Lincoln's party had clamored for a vigorous war against the Confederacy that would destroy slavery and remodel southern society along lines of that of the North. When Lincoln took the first steps toward instituting a program of Reconstruction in the occupied areas of the South, the radicals privately voiced their unhappiness.

Unlike many Northerners during the war, Lincoln never demonized Southerners or appealed to sectional hatreds to gain personal support. He wanted a lasting peace that would avoid the need for any long-term military occupation of the defeated southern states. In his first message to Congress, on July 4, 1861, he glanced ahead to the problem of Reconstruction. "Lest there be some uneasiness . . . as to what is to be the course of the government, towards the Southern States, *after* the rebellion shall have been suppressed," he said with an obvious eye toward reassuring southern whites, "the Executive deems it proper to say, it will be his purpose then, as ever, to be guided by the Constitution, and the laws." Yet by the time he formulated a program of Reconstruction, the war had already forced him to stretch the Constitution in ways he had never imagined when it began.

In devising a program of Reconstruction, he carefully balanced his instinctive desire for a generous peace with the necessity of fashioning a political consensus. The majority of Democrats, who wanted simply to restore the Union as it existed in 1861 and opposed any penalties on southern whites, were out of step with northern sentiment and could be ignored. The division within the Republican party, however, was more significant and troubling. Moderate and conservative Republicans opposed any sweeping revolution in southern society, but at the minimum they insisted on maintaining emancipation, and some favored penalties against at least the leaders of the Confederacy. The radicals, on the other hand, favored instituting fundamental change in southern values and society. In addition to emancipation, they wanted blacks to be given greater rights and for the government to protect those rights. Most wanted to extend legal equality to the former slaves, and some went so far as to advocate black suffrage in the South after the war.

For a substantial period after the war began, Lincoln had clung to the belief that secession was the act of a minority, and the majority of whites in the seceded states wished to return to the Union. As long as he held this view, Reconstruction seemed a rather straightforward and simple problem. But the unexpected resiliency of the Confederate military effort in 1862 undercut these assumptions and forced him to formulate a more comprehensive program.

He devoted his greatest attention to Louisiana, which he intended to serve as a model for other states. After the Union captured New Orleans in 1862, Lincoln urged General Benjamin F. Butler, the Union commander in the city, to waste no time in organizing a loyal state government. Venturing into uncharted constitutional waters, Lincoln instructed Butler to "follow the forms of law as far as convenient." Unlike the president, neither Butler nor his successor, Nathaniel P. Banks, gave priority to this task and little had been accomplished by the summer of 1863. Finally, in November, Lincoln alerted the dilatory Banks that "time is important" and pressed him to directly intervene to start the process of organizing a loyal state government. "Without waiting for more territory, . . . go to work and give me a tangible nucleus which the remainder of the State may rally around as fast as it can, and which I can at once recognize and sustain as the true State government." With matters moving more slowly in Louisiana than he had hoped—Banks did not hold an election until February 1864, and it was even longer before a new state constitution was approved—Lincoln decided to officially frame a program of Reconstruction.

In issuing the preliminary Emancipation Proclamation, Lincoln had been sensitive to the question of timing, not wishing his action to be perceived as stemming from military weakness. The same consideration influenced his announcement of a program of Reconstruction. The Union's military victories in 1863, capped by Grant's success at Chattanooga, prompted the president to outline his policy in his message to Congress in December of that year. Other considerations were pertinent as well. Unwilling to wait until the war was over, he was anxious to get the process started, in part because he believed creating loyal governments would weaken the Confederacy, but also because the war powers of the presidency (which would cease in peacetime) strengthened his hand against congressional interference.

Reflective of his ingrained conservative nature, he placed first emphasis on the need to establish loyal governments in the South, rather than on changing racial or social arrangements. For Lincoln, future loyalty, not past actions, was what counted, and he proposed a liberal oath that "accepts as sound whoever will make a sworn recantation of his former unsoundness." The task, as he saw it, was to induce southern whites to return to their previous loyalty while preventing die-hard rebels from exercising power. "The practical matter for decision," he commented to John Hay shortly before he outlined his program in 1863, "is how to keep the rebellious populations from overwhelming and outvoting the loyal minority."

In conjunction with his annual message, he also issued a proclamation concerning pardon and amnesty, which outlined the oath of allegiance southern whites had to take to regain their political rights. He excluded certain high-ranking Confederate political, judicial, and military officials from being eligible to take this oath; they would have to apply for individual pardons, but he indicated he would be generous in granting these.

The president specified that once 10 percent of the number of voters in 1860 had taken the stipulated oath, they could establish a new state government. Those taking the oath had to support the Emancipation Proclamation and the laws passed by Congress concerning slavery, but Lincoln did not insist upon immediate and universal emancipation. Conceding to Banks earlier that restrictions on black freedom might initially be necessary, he suggested that "a reasonable temporary arrangement, in relation to the landless and homeless freed people" would be acceptable, but that he was publicly committed to "their permanent freedom." He thought it especially important that blacks be given access to education, a manifestation of his longstanding belief in self-improvement.

A political realist, Lincoln did not underestimate the tenacious power of antiblack racism in American society, nor the difficulty of eradicating such deep-seated feelings. Yet his views on race, and on black Americans' place in postwar society, were evolving, and he now privately endorsed limited black suffrage in the South. In discussing voting rights in Louisiana, he suggested that some blacks be included, particularly "the very intelligent, and especially those who have fought gallantly in our ranks."

Lincoln's program skillfully blended points that would satisfy radicals and conservatives. His pledge to maintain the existing southern states with their boundaries and laws appealed to conservatives, who rejected the radical argument that these states had ceased to exist. Radicals, on the other hand, endorsed the president's insistence that slaves freed during the war could not be reenslaved, and that all Southerners had to take a loyalty oath that included acceptance of emancipation.

Republicans publicly praised the president's message, but privately a number of party leaders believed that his program was too lenient and rested on too small a kernel of loyalty, and many were uncertain exactly what the condition of former slaves would be under these new governments. The famous abolitionist Wendell Phillips, a persistent critic, harshly accused Lincoln of seeking nothing beyond freedom for southern blacks and being willing to leave the old landowning aristocracy in power in the South. He dismissed Lincoln's policy as designed to "make as little change as possible!"

More concerned with pragmatic political objectives than ideological rigor, Lincoln conceded that a larger base of popular support was desirable, but he argued that the governments he had launched in 1864 in Louisiana and Arkansas would with time grow stronger. Such a government "is only to what it should be as the egg is to the fowl," he subsequently declared, but "we shall sooner have the fowl by hatching the egg than by smashing it."

The applause that greeted Lincoln's Reconstruction program caused radicals to rein in their criticism for the time being, but there was considerable grumbling in Congress over Lincoln's leadership on this and other matters. David Davis, Lincoln's 1860 campaign manager, who was now a member of the Supreme Court, reported, "The politicians in and out of Congress . . . would put Mr. Lincoln aside if they dared."

ENCOURAGED BY THIS intraparty sniping, Secretary of the Treasury Salmon P. Chase decided to challenge Lincoln for the Republican nomination. Supremely ambitious, the egotistical Chase had unsuccessfully sought the Republican nomination in 1860, and though he subsequently accepted a place in the cabinet, he never could get it out of his head that he was more qualified to be president than Lincoln—or indeed, anyone else in the country. Chase's "theology is unsound," Ohio Senator Benjamin F. Wade acidly observed during the war. "He thinks there is a fourth Person in the Trinity. . . . "

The relationship between the informal, genial Lincoln and the stiff-backed, humorless Chase had steadily deteriorated, particularly since the cabinet crisis in December 1862. While Lincoln did not personalize opposition, Chase was one individual he genuinely disliked, and over the course of the war their personal relations had become increasingly icy. In response, Chase began to regularly absent himself from cabinet meetings. Never realizing the degree to which he was dependent on Lincoln's support to remain in office, Chase had on several occasions resorted to the strategy of threatening to resign in order to get his way on some matter. This strategy would work, however, only as long as Chase was politically essential to the president.

Chase was also unhappy with Lincoln's management style, which left each cabinet member to run his own department without any general consultation on policy. Convinced that Lincoln was too cautious and hesitant, particularly on the slavery issue, Chase advocated universal emancipation as part of any postwar settlement and believed that Reconstruction required granting greater rights to former slaves, including suffrage.

As Secretary of the Treasury, Chase controlled a vast number of jobs, and he systematically used this patronage to advance his presidential ambitions. Insisting that Chase was doing a good job in his post, Lincoln looked the other way as the secretary built up a personal machine through his department's patronage. Time would show that this approach was a mistake. In much the same way that the rot McClellan had fostered in the Army of the Potomac continued to fester after he was no longer its commander, the Treasury Department politically hurt Lincoln in 1864. Only in the final weeks of the campaign, when Lincoln finally reorganized the New York Custom House, did its employees fall in line behind the president's re-election campaign.

Chase's actions were too transparent to fool veteran political leaders. Fully informed of the secretary's schemes, Lincoln outwardly adopted a bemused attitude toward "Chase's mad hunt after the Presidency," telling Hay with a laugh, "I suppose he will, like the bluebottle fly, lay his eggs in every rotten spot he can find." This pose masked cool political calculation. Lincoln could not force Chase out of the cabinet without offending the radicals and deepening the internal divisions in the Republican party. Believing a rupture was inevitable, Lincoln decided to wait until Chase put himself in a disadvantageous position before taking action.

Chase always wore political blinders when it came to judging men's character or assessing his own political situation. It was extremely awkward for a cabinet member to oppose the president under whom he served, yet Chase moved serenely ahead, confident that his moral superiority and great intellect would prevail over the ineffective, self-educated frontier bumpkin in the White House.

In late February 1864 a group of Chase's supporters, led by Senator Samuel Pomeroy of Kansas, issued a circular openly calling for his nomination. The move recoiled upon its promoters. The circular galvanized Lincoln's supporters to more active efforts at the same time that it sparked considerable criticism of Chase's seeming disloyalty, and the Chase boom quickly fizzled. Disingenuously denying any knowledge of these movements on his behalf, an embarrassed Chase offered to resign, but Lincoln declined to accept his resignation. Shortly thereafter, when the Republican convention in his own state of Ohio endorsed Lincoln, Chase withdrew as a candidate, but Lincoln's supporters were certain if the opportunity subsequently presented itself, he would resume his candidacy.

Lincoln's unpretentious manner, his folksy ways, and his obvious sincerity and good-heartedness all carried weight with the common people. Even the *Chicago Tribune*, long critical of the president, conceded that Lincoln "has the confidence of the people, and even the respect and affections of the masses." Such support was important in the election, but party regulars and officeholders played a much more crucial role in selecting the nominee.

One of Lincoln's great strengths as president was the skill with which he ran the party machinery. He adeptly used the patronage to shore up his support among party workers and made sure that his friends carefully managed the election of delegates to the national convention. Indeed, with so many federal officeholders who were beholden to the president for their places selected as delegates, Lincoln's renomination was a forgone conclusion. Republican leaders who hoped to derail the presidential express suffered another setback when the National Committee rejected proposals to postpone the convention. Desirous of dumping Lincoln from the ticket, Horace Greeley, the erratic editor of the *New York Tribune*, glumly concluded that unless the war went badly, Republicans were saddled with Lincoln as their candidate.

The pressure of office was beginning to show on Lincoln. He had noticeably aged under the strain of trying to hold his cabinet and party together while energizing the army. Albert G. Riddle, an Ohio Republican who called on Lincoln in late April, was struck by how much he had changed in the half-year since he last saw him. He "looked like a man worn and harassed with petty faultfinding and criticisms," Riddle wrote, "until he had turned at bay, like an old stag pursued and hunted by a cowardly rabble of men and dogs."

CONFIDENT OF RENOMINATION, Lincoln nevertheless expected a difficult electoral contest and recognized that his political prospects in 1864 very much depended on the progress of the Union's arms. In response, he manifested a grimmer determination to continue the war, and he called for more troops for the Union war machine: 500,000 men in February and 200,000 more a month later.

But the Union war effort needed more than additional troops; what it needed most was an effective commanding general. By now neither Lincoln nor Congress had any faith in Henry Halleck, who was nominally the general-in-chief. In February 1864, Congressman Elihu B. Washburne of Illinois, long Ulysses S. Grant's personal champion, introduced a bill to revive the rank of lieutenant general, last held by

George Washington, and to designate the recipient the commanding general of all the Union armies. Once Congress approved the bill, Lincoln, as expected, bestowed the honor on Grant and summoned him to Washington. Lincoln was eager to meet Grant and also wanted to sound him out about strategy. On March 9, he formally presented Grant with his commission.

By now, Lincoln had developed a firm understanding of his position as commander-in-chief and a greater self-confidence in his own strategic abilities. His dealings with generals such as George McClellan, Joseph Hooker, and Halleck had served to lessen his deference to professional military men. Lincoln was particularly frustrated by his inability to get his eastern generals to adopt a more aggressive strategy and abandon their fixation on Richmond. He reminded Halleck that since the first year of the war, "I have constantly desired the Army of the Potomac, to make Lee's army, and not Richmond, it's objective point. If our army can not fall upon the enemy and hurt him where he is, it is plain to me it can gain nothing by attempting to follow him over a succession of intrenched lines into a fortified city." He had greater faith in Grant, having pronounced Grant's Vicksburg campaign "one of the most brilliant in the world," and expected the new commander to infuse more energy into the Union's main army.

Grant did not initially fully comprehend the demands of his new position. Wishing to isolate himself from the intrigues of Washington, he indicated that he wanted to remain in the western theater, where because of the distance from Washington, Union generals were subject to less interference. Northern public opinion, however, expected the Union's leading general to take charge of the war in the eastern theater, where Union arms had experienced only limited success. Lincoln made it clear to Grant that for political reasons he had to come east. Grant bowed to this necessity and placed his chief subordinate, William Tecumseh Sherman, in command of his old army, but he was determined to avoid becoming a desk general in Washington, so he decided to accompany the Army of the Potomac in the field. George Meade would remain nominally in command of that army, while Grant would communicate with the other Union armies via telegraph through the War Department. Lincoln accepted this arrangement but insisted that Halleck become something like a modern chief of staff.

Relieved of decision-making responsibilities, Halleck functioned well in this new position, relaying Grant's orders to Union generals in the field and keeping Lincoln and Secretary of War Edwin Stanton informed of military developments.

Grant's appointment ended Lincoln's attempt to manage the details of the war in Virginia. In an interview, he told Grant that only the slowness of his generals and the pressure of public opinion had caused him to interfere with military movements in the past. He wrote the Union commander that "the particulars of your plans I neither know, or seek to know," adding, "I wish not to obtrude any constraints or restraints upon you."

Despite such assurances, Lincoln continued to take an active role in military matters. He refused to allow Grant to remove several political generals whose support he needed, particularly Benjamin F. Butler, a favorite of the radicals, and Franz Sigel, the German American leader. The impression Grant gave in his *Memoirs* that Lincoln knew little about strategy and left the conduct of the war to him is demonstrably false. After his frustration in dealing with McClellan, Lincoln never completely entrusted the war to any of his generals.

A case in point was his reaction to Grant's proposal to invade North Carolina by sea and operate against Lee's communications. Grant was certain that Lee would have no choice but to leave the defenses of Richmond and come south to confront him. Lincoln failed to grasp the logic of Grant's plan, which would produce fewer casualties than a head-on thrust against Lee's veteran army. Always placing first priority on the security of Washington, Lincoln had no faith in the ability of other Union generals to protect the capital (a belief subsequently justified by the army's ineffectual response to Jubal Early's raid in July 1864), and he wanted Grant nearby. Lincoln also knew that northern public opinion, which was obsessed with Lee and the Virginia theater, expected Grant to make the constricted region between the two national capitals his area of operation. He vetoed Grant's plan.

Grant eventually devised a strategy to have five Union armies coordinate movements along a front extending more than a thousand miles from Virginia to New Orleans. The Confederacy was too weak to defend every threatened point, he explained, and somewhere the Union would be able to break through. This was the strategy of a simultaneous advance, which Lincoln had been trying unsuccessfully to get his commanders to employ since 1862. When Grant outlined his plan, Lincoln observed, "Those not skinning can hold a leg."

A Union strategy of total war now began to come together under Grant. To the idea of relentless pressure along a broad front, Grant added the notion of destroying the southern economy in order to weaken the Confederate armies in the field. These tactics would inevitably inflict hardship and suffering on southern civilians, white and black. Unlike northern Virginia, which had been ravaged by three years of fighting, Georgia, which lay open to Sherman's army, was relatively untouched, its farms bursting with food and supplies. Grant's orders to Sherman were to "get into the interior of the enemy's country as far as you can, inflicting all the damage you can against their war resources."

When the Army of the Potomac broke camp on May 4, Northerners anticipated a decisive campaign that would bring the war to a close by fall. For the next month, from the Wilderness to Spotsylvania to Cold Harbor, Grant vainly tried to break Lee's lines. Too weak to confront Grant in the open field, Lee adopted a strategy of attrition, hoping to inflict such heavy losses on his opponent that northern public opinion would abandon Lincoln and the war effort. And in fact, Grant's losses were staggering: 60,000 men in one month of heavy fighting.

In the capital the president, haggard and weary from lack of sleep, seemed overburdened with sorrow and anxiety. As he paced back and forth in his office impatiently awaiting news from the front, he exclaimed to one congressman, "Is it ever to end!" The painter Francis Carpenter, who saw Lincoln close-up at this time, reported that "he scarcely slept at all." Encountering him early one morning in the executive mansion, Carpenter found the president alone with his thoughts, with "great black rings under his eyes, his head bent forward upon his breast,—altogether such a picture of the effects of sorrow, care, and anxiety. . . ." Day after day the wounded continued to arrive in Washington, until Lincoln admitted to his old friend Isaac Arnold, "I cannot bear it. This suffering, this loss of life is dreadful."

Grant's strategy, however, failed to produce the victory Lincoln so desperately needed. The Union armies commanded by Benjamin F. Butler at Fortress Monroe, Franz Sigel in the Shenandoah Valley, and Nathaniel Banks in New Orleans, all political generals, abysmally failed to achieve their assigned objectives. Union hopes for victory, and Lincoln's political prospects, therefore rested on the shoulders of Grant and Sherman. Unable to flank Lee, Grant finally changed tactics and mounted a siege of Petersburg, a key transportation center south of Richmond. Meanwhile, the lanky, red-headed Sherman, who overflowed with nervous energy, relentlessly worked his way toward Atlanta but won no decisive victory in battle that would uplift northern morale. Surveying the military situation, a Democratic paper declared, "Patriotism is played out. . . . Each hour is but sinking us deeper into bankruptcy and desolation."

WHILE GRANT FUTILELY assaulted Lee's lines, dissident antislavery supporters assembled in Cleveland at the end of May to nominate an independent ticket. With most prominent radical leaders conspicuously absent, the convention nominated John C. Frémont, whose 1861 emancipation edict in Missouri made him a favorite of advanced antislavery elements, as the presidential candidate of the Radical Democracy. Some considered Frémont merely a stalking horse for Chase, but the real motive for his nomination was to defeat Lincoln by splitting the Republican vote.

As Republican delegates passed through Washington on their way to the national convention, Lincoln made it clear that he wanted the party platform to endorse a constitutional amendment abolishing slavery. Such an amendment would remove all legal doubt about the Emancipation Proclamation. It would also end slavery in the border states and other areas of the South that were exempted from the proclamation's provisions. Otherwise, Lincoln left the convention to its own will.

The Republican convention, which was rechristened the Union convention, assembled in Baltimore on June 7. With his supporters in complete control, Lincoln was easily renominated, with only the anti-Blair Missouri delegation opposed. The platform urged a vigorous prosecution of the war, demanded the "unconditional surrender" of the Confederacy (without defining that term's meaning), endorsed a constitutional amendment against slavery, and vaguely called for harmony in the cabinet, a swipe at Postmaster General Montgomery Blair, who was a vitriolic critic of the radicals. Because of the deep divisions in the Republican ranks, the platform said nothing about Reconstruction. For vice-president, the delegates named Andrew Johnson, a staunch Tennessee Unionist, to balance the ticket with a Southerner and a Democrat. As the events of Reconstruction would prove, Lincoln's hands-off approach which led to Johnson's nomination was a serious mistake.

After the convention adjourned, Blair submitted his resignation, which Lincoln rejected. Nevertheless, Blair gave Lincoln an undated letter of resignation, knowing that political pressures would probably force the president to accept it.

It was not the conservative Blair, however, but the radical Chase who now left the cabinet. Still smarting over the humiliating fiasco of his recent presidential bid, the Secretary of the Treasury continued to resist Lincoln's wishes on patronage appointments in his department. Twice already Chase had prevailed in these disputes by threatening to resign. When he found himself at loggerheads with the president over another appointment, he played the game once again and on June 30 submitted his resignation. Now that Lincoln had been renominated, Chase posed less of a political threat, and to the secretary's shock and dismay, Lincoln accepted his resignation. Acknowledging Chase's ability and service, the president nevertheless added, "You and I have reached a point of mutual embarrassment in our official relation which it seems can not be overcome, or longer sustained, consistently with the public service." After his first nominee declined, Lincoln named William Pitt Fessenden of Maine, chairman of the Senate Finance Committee, as Chase's successor.

At the beginning of July, Robert E. Lee sent Jubal Early on a raid toward Washington, hoping to relieve the pressure on his army by drawing Union troops out of Virginia. As Early approached the capital's outer defenses, Lincoln pressed Grant to take charge of the situation. The Union commander finally dispatched veteran troops to the scene, and Early soon retreated, but not before he had given Washington the worst scare of the war. Northern despondency and war weariness intensified. The New York Republican George Templeton Strong, who outwardly kept up a hopeful demeanor, noted that even truly loyal people "seem discouraged, weary, and faint-hearted." Maintaining that he saw "no bright spot anywhere," he concluded that "the blood and treasure spent on this summer's campaign have done little for the country."

The war news continued to be discouraging. At Petersburg, Grant was confident that his siege would force the eventual evacuation of Richmond, but he knew it would take time and that he would not achieve the military victory Lincoln so desperately needed before the November election. All through the summer, Sherman moved relentlessly toward Atlanta as Joseph Johnston, the Confederate commander, steadily retreated. Jefferson Davis became increasingly impatient with this defensive strategy, however, and finally in mid-July replaced Johnston with John Bell Hood, a much more aggressive fighter. Hood quickly seized the offensive, but after unsuccessfully assaulting Sherman's lines he retired to the city's defenses. Nevertheless, Confederate leaders were confident that the southern army could hold Atlanta, which was one of the most heavily fortified cities in the Confederacy. Grant was bogged down in Virginia, Atlanta stubbornly defied Sherman, and no end to the war was in sight.

The heavy losses in the summer of 1864 deepened Lincoln's fatalism. Perhaps the only way he could confront the immense suffering was by believing that events were beyond his control. Visitors now often found him seeking solace by reading the Bible. In a letter to a Kentucky editor discussing the evolution of his policy on slavery, Lincoln invoked his deeply rooted fatalism. "I claim not to have controlled events, but confess plainly that events have controlled me," he wrote, adding, "Now, at the end of three years struggle the nation's condition is not what either party, or any man devised, or expected. God alone can claim it." Earlier Lincoln had talked sternly about the necessity of hard fighting, but he was unnerved by Grant's heavy losses. Visiting the army in June outside Petersburg, he expressed the hope that "all may be accomplished with as little bloodshed as possible."

Yet his determination to persevere, his courage when confronted with disappointment, did not waver. Indeed, Lincoln's resiliency in defeat was one of the defining characteristics of his presidential leadership. "I have seen your despatch expressing your unwillingness to break your hold where you are," he telegraphed Grant in August, when his political fortunes were bleakest. "Neither am I willing. Hold on with a bull-dog gripe [*sic*], and chew and choke, as much as possible."

Grant's heavy losses necessitated obtaining more men to replenish the Union ranks, but Republican leaders paled at the thought of a new draft call. When they urged Lincoln to postpone such a step until after the election in order to enhance his chances of reelection, he pointedly observed, "What is the Presidency worth to me if I have no country?" On July 19, he called for a half million more men and scheduled a new draft for early September if the quotas were not met. Rarely was Lincoln's moral courage more evident. When the draft was announced, a Democratic editor gleefully predicted, "Lincoln is *deader* than dead."

IN THE SUMMER of 1864 Lincoln found himself under attack from all sides. Radicals were unhappy with his policies on slavery and Reconstruction, conservatives doubted his leadership abilities, and everyone blamed him for failing to end the war. In this dark and discouraging period, he manifested his steadfastness in the face of criticism, his determination to do what he believed right, and his refusal to seek mere partisan advantage.

When the new government in Louisiana, established under Lincoln's guidelines, failed to grant additional rights to African Americans, opposition in Congress to Lincoln's program increased. Two leading radicals, Benjamin F. Wade in the Senate and Henry Winter Davis in the House, introduced a bill that established a more stringent program of Reconstruction. The Wade–Davis bill placed the Confederate states temporarily under a military governor. Rather than Lincoln's nucleus of 10 percent, it required a majority of a state's 1860 voters to take the loyalty oath before forming a new state government. Large categories of southern whites were disqualified from participating in the restoration process by mandating they take a so-called iron-clad oath that they had never voluntarily supported the Confederacy. In addition, slavery was abolished in the state, and Confederate officials barred from holding office. With strong radical support, the bill passed Congress on July 2, shortly before adjournment.

Radical leaders rushed to the White House to press Lincoln to sign the bill, but he laid it aside. When Senator Zachariah Chandler stressed the importance of its provision abolishing slavery in the reconstructed states, Lincoln replied, "That is the point on which I doubt the authority of Congress to act." Reminded that he had issued the Emancipation Proclamation, Lincoln answered, "I conceive that I may in an emergency do things on military grounds which cannot be done constitutionally by Congress." While Lincoln had issued the Emancipation Proclamation as a military act based on the executive's war powers, he never believed Congress had the constitutional power to abolish slavery in a state. In the end, he pocket-vetoed the bill (if a president does not sign a bill after Congress has adjourned, it has the effect of a veto).

Lincoln then issued a proclamation explaining his action. Declaring that he was unwilling "to be inflexibly committed to any single plan of restoration," he objected to abandoning the new governments already in place in Louisiana and Arkansas. He further roused the radicals' ire by noting that the Wade–Davis bill provided one plan, which the people of the South were free to accept if they wished (an unlikely occurrence, as he well knew).

Wade and Davis responded by publishing a manifesto that harshly assailed Lincoln as a political usurper, bent on creating "shadows of Governments" in the South to aid his reelection. Insisting that "the authority of Congress is paramount" on the matter of reconstruction, they characterized Lincoln's proclamation as a "studied outrage on the legislative authority of the people." Wade and Davis's vehemence sorely tried Lincoln's well-known patience. "To be wounded in the house of one's friends," he lamented, "is perhaps the most grievous affliction that can befall a man."

The division between Lincoln and the radicals over Reconstruction involved more than whether Congress or the president would play the major role in formulating a program of Reconstruction. Also involved were different perceptions of how best to restore loyal governments in the South. Radicals had little faith in white southern Unionists and believed that blacks were the only loyal group of any size in the South. Therefore, they demanded immediate emancipation and saw black suffrage as the best way to establish loyal governments. Lincoln, in contrast, shrank from inaugurating a fundamental upheaval in southern society and mores, and by stressing future over past loyalty, he was willing to allow recanting Rebels to dominate the new southern governments. Moreover, Lincoln believed that the best strategy was to introduce black suffrage in the South by degrees in order to accustom southern whites to blacks voting. How far he was willing to go in extending rights to former slaves remained unclear, but his gradualist approach to social change remained intact, just as when he had tried to get the border states in 1862 to adopt gradual emancipation. Finally, the radicals and Lincoln held quite different views of the relationship of Reconstruction to the war effort. By erecting impossibly high standards that no southern state could meet, the Wade–Davis bill sought to postpone Reconstruction until the war was over. For Lincoln, in contrast, a lenient program of Reconstruction would encourage southern whites to abandon the Confederacy and thus was integral to his strategy for winning the war.

At the same time, Lincoln was harshly denounced by antiwar Democrats. Northern war weariness, which peaked in the summer of 1864, fostered a powerful peace movement on the home front. The extreme Copperheads claimed that a negotiated settlement was possible if Lincoln would only drop his insistence on emancipation. Lincoln correctly understood that Jefferson Davis would never agree to a restoration of the Union, but many Northerners, sickened by the bloodshed, clutched almost in desperation at any hope for peace.

Already under attack from the peace wing of the Democratic party, Lincoln came under heavy pressure from Horace Greeley to open peace negotiations with the Confederacy. "Our bleeding, bankrupt, almost dying country also longs for peace—shudders at the prospect of fresh conscriptions, of further wholesale devastations, and of new rivers of human blood," Greeley plaintively wrote in early July. Informed that Confederate diplomats with authority to negotiate a peace settlement were in Niagara Falls, Greeley urged the president to confer with them. The belief that the administration did not favor peace, he added, was doing great political damage and was certain to do even more as the election approached.

Tired of Greeley's censorious attitude and his flip-flops on public pol-icy, Lincoln hit upon the brilliant strategy of sending the New York edi-tor to Niagara Falls to meet these purported commissioners. He drafted a letter, addressed "To Whom It May Concern," laying out his peace terms, which he gave to his secretary, John Hay, to take to Niagara Falls. "Any proposition" from the Confederate government, the letter read, "which embraces the restoration of peace, the integrity of the whole Union, and the abandonment of slavery . . . will be received and consid-ered by the Executive government of the United States, and will be met by liberal terms on other substantial and collateral points."

Lincoln no doubt smiled as he sent Greeley on what he knew was a wild goose chase. When Greeley reported (as Lincoln suspected all along) that the Confederates had no power to conduct peace negoti-ations, the editor of the *Tribune* found himself the target of northern ridicule. His eyes twinkling, Lincoln chuckled to Charles A. Dana, one of Greeley's former associates who was now working in the War Department, "I sent Brother Greeley a commission. I guess I am about even with him now."

Realizing that a negotiated peace was impossible, Lincoln adopted the strategy of appearing to be willing to open peace talks, while setting the preconditions high enough that Davis would reject them out of hand. His demand for the abandonment of slavery in his letter outlining his peace terms was more sweeping than the terms of his Emancipation Proclamation and the ambiguous language of his Re-construction program.

Lincoln's strategy backfired. All through the summer, Democrats made effective use of his "To Whom It May Concern" letter to argue that Lincoln was prolonging the war because of a fanatical desire to end slavery. That demand out of the way, Democrats insisted, a set-tlement with the Confederacy could quickly be reached. The un-friendly *New York Herald* proclaimed that the letter "sealed Lincoln's fate in the coming Presidential campaign."

In this battle for northern public opinion, Lincoln was ironically aided by Jefferson Davis, who blundered by not proposing an armistice and peace talks without conditions. He also benefited when two unofficial emissaries, following an interview with Davis in Richmond, quoted the Confederate president as having delivered an ultimatum that "the war . . . must go on . . . *unless you acknowledge our right to self-government. We are not fighting for slavery. We are fighting for Independence,*—and that, or extermination, we *will* have."

Even so, Lincoln remained on the defensive. His peace terms failed to mollify the radicals, still smarting over his veto of the Wade–Davis bill, while they constituted a sharp blow to the prowar Democrats, who were opposed to emancipation as a Union war aim. Conservative and moderate Republicans were also discontented, believing that Lincoln's letter would strengthen Confederate resistance; they also feared that it would usher in wild scenes of revolutionary upheaval in the postwar South. With the president under attack whichever way he turned, his old friend Orville Browning flatly pronounced him a "failure" as president.

Nevertheless, Lincoln decided to stick to his position. He could not give up the nearly 130,000 black men now serving in the Union ranks, he explained, nor would he consent that slaves once freed be reenslaved. "I should be damned in time and in eternity for so doing." In an interview with several Wisconsin Republicans, Lincoln insisted that the war was being waged solely to save the Union, but that "no human power can subdue this rebellion without using the Emancipation lever as I have done."

By the beginning of August, despair was evident among Republicans, who believed that they were staring defeat in the face. Military victory appeared as far away as ever, party divisions were deepening, and Lincoln seemed unable to rally public opinion to his side. There had been griping all summer among disaffected Republicans about Lincoln's candidacy, but the movement to convene a new convention and dump Lincoln now came to a head. At a meeting in New York City, a number of prominent Republicans canvassed the possibility and a call soon appeared, urging that a convention be held in Cincinnati on September 28. "Mr. Lincoln is already beaten," Greeley contended in endorsing the call. "He cannot be elected. And we must have another ticket to save us from utter overthrow."

Disheartened reports from party leaders in a number of key states poured in to Henry J. Raymond, chairman of the Republican National Committee and editor of the *New York Times*. Raymond attributed Lincoln's problems to the military situation and the prevailing opinion that the administration was prolonging the war solely to end slavery. "The suspicion is widely diffused that we *can* have peace with Union if we would," he wrote the president on August 22. "It is idle to reason with this belief—still more idle to denounce it. It can only be expelled by some authoritative act, at once bold enough to fix attention and distinct enough to defy incredulity and challenge respect." He urged that a commissioner be appointed to negotiate with Davis, specifying only reunion as a condition for peace. Davis would certainly reject such terms, Raymond added, but the offer would dampen the cry in the North for peace negotiations. At a subsequent meeting at the White House with the leaders of the National Committee, Lincoln rejected this proposal, insisting that it "would be worse than losing the Presidential contest—it would be ignominiously surrendering it in advance."

Gloom pervaded the White House. "Everything is darkness and doubt and discouragement," Nicolay reported in late August. Lincoln remained outwardly determined, but in reality he was deeply dis-couraged. On August 23, after reading Raymond's bleak letter, he took out a sheet of paper and wrote the following: "This morning, as for some days past, it seems exceedingly probable that this Administration will not be re-elected. Then it will be my duty to so co-operate with the President elect, as to save the Union between the election and the inauguration; as he will have secured his election on such ground that he can not possibly save it afterwards." Lincoln was certain that party pressure would force any Democratic president, no matter how com-mitted to the war, to agree to an armistice, which he knew would be fatal to the Union cause. After sealing this statement in an envelope, he had each of his cabinet members sign the back without revealing the contents to them. Only after the election was over did he open the envelope and read to his advisers the statement they had blindly endorsed.

The Democrats had postponed their convention until the end of August in order to see what the military situation was before selecting a ticket. Among the delegates who assembled in Chicago was Clement Vallandigham, the Copperhead leader who had been banished the year before, and who now returned from Canada breathing fire and daring the administration to arrest him. Lincoln instructed his generals to leave Vallandigham alone, convinced that he was doing more harm to the Democrats than the Republicans.

The Democrats nominated former general George McClellan for president. McClellan was the choice of the regular Democrats, who favored a war to save the Union but balked at emancipation. The platform, however, reflected the views of the peace wing of the party. Largely written by Vallandigham, the 1864 Democratic platform pronounced the war a failure and called for an armistice and peace negotiations with the Confederacy. "After four years of failure to restore the Union by the experiment of war," the controversial plank read, ". . . justice, humanity, liberty, and the public welfare demand that immediate efforts be made for a cessation of hostilities, with a view of an ultimate convention of the States, or other peaceable means, to the end that, at the earliest practicable moment, peace may be restored on the basis of the Federal Union. . . ." In his acceptance letter, McClellan repudiated the assertion that the war was a failure and, after much indecision, rejected the idea of an armistice.

Privately, Confederate leaders considered McClellan their last hope of victory. His triumph would signal the North's unwillingness to continue the war; certainly it would revive southern morale and determination. McClellan's election would lead to southern independence, the *Charleston Mercury* assured its readers following the Democratic convention, and thus it was "essential" that "for the next two months *we hold our own and prevent military success by our foes.*"

DEMOCRATS'—AND CONFEDERATES'—optimism was short lived. Word soon arrived from Sherman that "Atlanta is ours, and fairly won," which completely transformed the existing political situation. Sherman's capture of the city on September 2 came on the heels of Admiral David Farragut's stirring success at Mobile Bay. Shortly thereafter, Philip Sheridan smashed Jubal Early's army and began to devastate the Shenandoah Valley so that Lee could no longer draw supplies from that fertile agricultural region. It was apparent that the Union was much closer to victory than Northerners had previously realized. Republican spirits revived, and Democratic ones correspond-

This Republican cartoon contrasts the two presidential candidates' approaches to peace. McClellan holds out an olive branch to a defiant Jefferson Davis while allowing him to re-enslave a black Union soldier, whereas Lincoln resolutely demands unconditional submission and the end of slavery. (The Library of Congress)

ingly declined. Almost overnight, Abraham Lincoln became the favorite to win the 1864 presidential election.

The prospect of a Republican victory in November did wonders to close the party's internal breach. The movement to hold a new national convention promptly collapsed, and even "sorehead republicans," in the words of the *New York Herald*, scrambled aboard the Lincoln bandwagon. At this point Zachariah Chandler, who considered McClellan a traitor, apparently worked out an arrangement whereby Frémont would withdraw from the race and Montgomery Blair, the radicals' chief nemesis, would leave the cabinet. Lincoln disliked giving up Blair, who had been a loyal supporter, but he realized that Blair's endless personal quarrels and slashing attacks on his critics negated his political usefulness. In late September Frémont withdrew as a candidate, and Lincoln accepted Blair's long-standing offer to resign and named William Dennison of Ohio the new Postmaster General. Radicals took to the campaign trail, though sometimes stumping with less than good grace for the national ticket.

Three key northern states—Pennsylvania, Ohio, and Indiana—held their state elections in October. Unlike the other two states, Indiana failed to adopt a procedure that would allow Union soldiers to vote in the field. With an eye on the contest, Lincoln asked Sherman to furlough as many Indiana troops as possible to go home and vote in the state election. Sherman complied, and two of his generals, John Logan and Frank Blair, Jr., both notable politicians and former Democrats, campaigned for Lincoln in the state and elsewhere. When the Republicans, aided by the soldier vote, carried all three states, Lincoln's success in November seemed likely, but the result in Pennsylvania was uncomfortably close. Two days later, Lincoln estimated that he would narrowly squeak through in the November balloting.

As was the custom for presidential candidates in the nineteenth century, Lincoln refrained from actively campaigning, but he kept a close eye on developments in various states. Indeed, Fessenden reported that "the President is too busy looking after the elections to think of anything else." He especially used his enormous tact and great powers of persuasion to paper over personal feuds and party divisions in several states, including Pennsylvania. "I confess that I desire to be re-elected," Lincoln remarked. "God knows I do not want the labor and responsibility of the office for another four years. But I have the common pride of humanity to wish my past four years Administration endorsed."

Following such a heated campaign, the balloting on November 8 was surprisingly peaceful. Election day was "dull, gloomy and rainy" in Washington. Calling around noon, Noah Brooks found the White House virtually deserted. In talking to Hay during the day, Lincoln reflected, "It is a little singular that I who am not a vindictive man, should have always been before the people for election in canvasses marked for their bitterness." Except for the 1846 congressional race, "the contests in which I have been prominent have been marked with great rancor." That evening Hay accompanied the president as he went over to the War Department to receive the returns by telegraph, just as Lincoln had done four years earlier at the office of the *Illinois*

State Journal in Springfield. The early returns were generally favorable, and the Republican trend grew more pronounced as the evening wore on. Lincoln was in a genial mood, and it was not until around three that he at last went home.

The final returns gave Lincoln a popular majority of more than 400,000 votes. Lincoln carried all but three states (New Jersey, Delaware, and Kentucky) and won an overwhelming victory in the electoral college, 212 to 21. The election was closer than these numbers suggest, however, for Lincoln's margin was very small in several key states, including New York. His vote in 1864 followed the same lines as in 1860, except in the border states, where the Republican party now was much stronger.

One of the most striking features of the balloting was Lincoln's support among Union soldiers. Nineteen states made provisions for troops to vote in their camps. Lincoln won almost 80 percent of the their votes, evidence of the great affection ordinary soldiers had for him, as well as the deep resentment they bore toward the Copper-

Most loyal states made provisions for Union soldiers to vote in their camps in the 1864 presidential election. This sketch shows the voting in one camp. Union soldiers overwhelmingly voted for Lincoln. (The Library of Congress)

heads and the Democratic platform. One Democratic soldier who voted for Lincoln explained, "I had rather stay out here a lifetime (much as I dislike it), than consent to a division of our country. . . . We all want peace, but none *any* but an *honorable* one." The vote of soldiers provided Lincoln's margin of victory in New York and Connecticut, and probably Indiana and Maryland as well.

During the course of the war, Lincoln had developed a very special relationship with Union troops, who affectionately called him "Uncle Abe" and "Father Abraham." His unpretentious manner, common looks, and homespun ways appealed to ordinary soldiers, who felt a kinship with him. When he reviewed the troops, he did not cut a dashing figure on horseback (one of Grant's aides said he reminded him of "a country farmer riding into town wearing his Sunday clothes"), but the men spontaneously broke into cheers as he rode by. A New York soldier wrote home after Lincoln visited the army in 1862, "The boys liked him. In fact, his popularity with the army is and has been universal." On another occasion, when Lincoln reviewed the Army of the Potomac, Noah Brooks observed, "It was noticeable that the President merely touched his hat in return salute to the officers, but uncovered to the men in the ranks." The troops appreciated the interest he took in their condition and treatment, and when he told them to bring their personal problems to his attention, many did. This relationship grew stronger as the war continued, and the 1864 election confirmed that Union soldiers were the strongest supporters Abraham Lincoln had.

Two nights later Lincoln made a brief speech to a crowd of well-wishers who came to the White House. "The election was a necessity," he affirmed. "We can not have free government without elections; and if the rebellion could force us to forego, or postpone a national election, it might fairly claim to have already conquered and ruined us." The election caused strife, but it also did good. "It has demonstrated that a people's government can sustain a national election, in the midst of a great civil war."

The election of 1864 marked the final turning point of the Civil War. Its outcome constituted a great personal triumph for Lincoln after four years of vicious and unrelenting criticism. It also evinced the renewed commitment of the northern people, after the Union's recent military victories, to continue the struggle until the war was won. Finally, it represented an endorsement of the policy of emancipation, against which Democrats had directed their fire in the recent campaign, and ended any doubt that slavery would be abolished as a result of the war. "The crisis has been past," George Templeton Strong wrote in his diary, "and the most momentous popular election ever held since ballots were invented has decided against treason and disunion."

To be sure, Jefferson Davis remained defiant and announced that the Confederacy would fight on until independence was achieved, but in the wake of Lincoln's victory southern morale rapidly deteriorated. With the defeat of the Confederacy now only a matter of time, Lincoln turned his thoughts to peace.

Chapter 8

WITH MALICE TOWARD NONE

AMONG THOSE who gathered in the War Department on election night was Gustavus V. Fox, the Assistant Secretary of the Navy. As the returns came clattering in over the telegraph, he expressed particular pleasure that Henry Winter Davis, one of the president's harshest Republican critics, had been defeated for reelection to Congress. "You have more of that feeling of personal resentment than I," Lincoln commented. "Perhaps I may have too little of it; but I never thought it paid. A man has no time to spend half his life in quarrels. If any man ceases to attack me I never remember the past against him." This outlook would continue to guide his policies in the last months of his presidency.

IN THE AFTERMATH of Lincoln's reelection, the final component was added to the Union's military strategy. In a series of escalating steps, the Union army had confiscated private property in the South, expelled disloyal civilians from Union lines, emancipated slaves, utilized black soldiers, and waged a grinding, all-out form of warfare. To this mix was now added the dimension of psychological warfare designed to break the will of southern civilians. This was the nineteenth-century equivalent of the strategy of total war.

After the fall of Atlanta, John Bell Hood had led the Confederacy's western army back into Tennessee in order to draw William Tecumseh Sherman out of Georgia. Unwilling to chase Hood all over the state, Sherman instead proposed to lead 60,000 men on a destructive march across Georgia. With no Confederate army to oppose him, Sherman's purposes were political and psychological rather than military. "If we can march a well appointed Army right through [Jefferson Davis's] territory," he argued, "it is a demonstration to the World, foreign and domestic, that we have a power which Davis cannot resist. This may not be war, but rather Statesmanship. . . ." Sherman's proposed movement was risky, but after Grant gave his approval, Lincoln did too.

On November 16, Sherman's army pulled out of the smoldering ruins of Atlanta. Moving about ten miles a day, the army cut a swath of destruction sixty miles wide to the sea. The troops foraged widely, burned homes and buildings, tore up railroad tracks, and then twisted the rails so they could not be used again. In late December, Sherman captured Savannah. With the Confederacy steadily shrinking, evidence of despair could be seen everywhere on the southern home front, and an officer who accompanied Sherman concluded that southern whites were whipped.

Elsewhere in the West the military news was equally encouraging. Recklessly attacking his stronger, better-equipped foe, Hood suffered a costly defeat at Franklin on November 30. Nevertheless, he pushed on to Nashville, where Union general George Thomas attacked him on December 15 and all but annihilated Hood's army. Jefferson Davis restored Joseph Johnston to command of the shattered Army of Tennessee, but the war was essentially over in the West.

Sherman's successful march reaffirmed Lincoln's confidence in Grant and led him to adopt more of a hands-off approach in the final stages of the war. "What next?" he asked Sherman after he occupied Savannah, adding, "I suppose it will be safer if I leave General Grant and yourself to decide."

WITH THE WAR EFFORT at last in capable hands, Lincoln concentrated his attention on political matters. For one thing, he had to make several key appointments. Edward Bates, who had been a dutiful but unimaginative adviser, resigned as Attorney General, and William Pitt Fessenden now left the Treasury Department to return to the Senate. Lincoln selected James Speed of Kentucky, the brother of his old friend Joshua Speed from his early years in Springfield, to succeed Bates. For Secretary of the Treasury, Lincoln finally tapped the uninspiring Hugh

McCulloch of Indiana. In addition, when John Usher, the undistinguished Secretary of the Interior, resigned in March 1865, Lincoln selected Iowa Senator James Harlan to fill the post.

Lincoln's reconstituted cabinet differed from the original body in that none of the new members was an important party leader or an aspirant for the presidency. The cabinet still contained a variety of political viewpoints, but the radical influence had been strengthened, as William Dennison (who had earlier replaced Montgomery Blair as Postmaster General) and Speed were identified with that faction. Perhaps the most important difference was that all its members, including holdovers William Henry Seward, Gideon Welles, and Edwin Stanton, were personally loyal to the president.

Lincoln also needed to name a successor to Chief Justice Roger Taney, who had died in October. The leading candidate was former Treasury Secretary Salmon P. Chase, whose appointment would please the radicals. Moreover, Chase's elevation would offer assurances that the government's controversial war policies on slavery and the currency would be constitutionally sustained. But Lincoln worried that Chase's "head was so full of Presidential maggots" that he would use the position to futilely pursue that office. As always, Chase's efforts at self-promotion were clumsy and transparent. When he suddenly wrote Lincoln during the 1864 campaign about the political prospects in Ohio, the president handed the letter to John Nicolay with the sarcastic comment, "File it with his other recommendations."

Lincoln, however, never favored political vendettas, and on more than one occasion remarked to John Hay that he was "in favor of short statutes of limitations in politics." On December 6, he nominated Chase to be chief justice. As was normally the case, Lincoln did not consult his cabinet concerning this appointment and was very tight-lipped about his motives. Chase enjoyed wide support for the post in the Republican party, and Lincoln certainly needed to foster better relations with the radicals in his own party. But probably an equally crucial consideration was Lincoln's concern for the legal security of emancipation. Lincoln was confident that under Chase's direction, the Supreme Court would never invalidate the Emancipation Proclamation.

Congress assembled for its lame-duck session in December. Lincoln's reelection and the improved military situation made Republican congressmen reluctant to challenge him, and he encountered far less hostility than in the previous session. Lincoln urged the House to pass the proposed Thirteenth Amendment abolishing slavery (the Senate had already approved it in the previous session by the required two-thirds' majority). The results of the recent election, he argued, demonstrated popular support for this action. "It is the voice of the people now, for the first time, heard upon the question." The next Congress, with its overwhelming Republican majorities, would certainly pass the amendment, but better to do it now, he advised, and start the process of ratification.

As president, Lincoln rarely intervened in the legislative process, either to shape legislation or to lobby for votes, relying instead on members of his cabinet in these matters. He felt very strongly about this issue, however, and therefore used all the resources at his command, including the patronage, to secure the votes of wavering Democrats. While the fastidious might balk at such tactics, Charles Dana pronounced Lincoln "a supreme politician. He understood politics because he understood human nature." There was no "shabby philanthropy" in him. "He was all solid, hard, keen intelligence combined with goodness."

The vote on January 31 was close but sufficient: 119 to 56. Lincoln was relieved, for the proposed amendment, which he pronounced "a King's cure for all the evils," removed all the legal uncertainty pertaining to wartime emancipation, and it covered areas exempted from the terms of the Emancipation Proclamation. The next day, when a procession of well-wishers came to the White House, Lincoln noted that he was especially proud that his own state of Illinois was the first to ratify the amendment. Illinois's action was testimony to the revolution the war had produced. Only a few years earlier, in his 1858 senatorial campaign, Lincoln had been constantly on the defensive because of his assertion that slavery eventually had to end in the United States.

Lincoln failed, however, to reach an accord with Congress on the question of Reconstruction. Moderate Republicans helped defeat a revised version of the Wade–Davis bill, but Congress refused to recognize the loyal governments established under Lincoln's program in

Louisiana and Arkansas. The inability of Congress to agree on a program was a victory for Lincoln because it kept the problems of Reconstruction in his hands, at least until December 1865 when the new Congress would assemble.

♒

MEANWHILE THE MILITARY noose steadily tightened around the beleaguered Confederacy. On January 15, 1865, Union forces captured Fort Fisher and closed Wilmington's harbor, the last important port in Confederate hands. At Petersburg, Grant continued to extend his lines, stretching Lee's army to the breaking point. And after refitting his army in Savannah, Sherman turned north and entered South Carolina, intending eventually to join Grant in Virginia. His passage through the state, which was the symbol of secession, was even more destructive than his march through Georgia had been. Influenced by despondent letters from home, Confederate soldiers began to desert in droves, further weakening the Confederate cause.

Despite a new flurry of peace overtures, Lincoln continued to doubt that Jefferson Davis would ever agree to reunion. In his message to Congress in December, Lincoln contended that Davis "would accept nothing short of severance of the Union—precisely what we will not and cannot give. His declarations to this effect are explicit and oft-repeated. He does not attempt to deceive us. He affords us no excuse to deceive ourselves." But hoping to detach the southern people from Davis and divide Confederate leaders, Lincoln reaffirmed the generous terms he had outlined a year earlier, accompanied by a warning that "the time may come—probably will come—when . . . more rigorous measures . . . shall be adopted."

To repel the charge that he did not want peace, however, Lincoln gave the elder Francis P. Blair permission in early January to go to Richmond to see Davis. In their meeting, Davis agreed to appoint peace commissioners "with a view to secure peace to the two countries." Recognizing the import of Davis's words, Lincoln replied that he would receive any agent authorized to secure peace "to the people of our one common country." In the end Davis, whose primary aim was to neutralize the peace movement in the Confederacy, appointed three commissioners to negotiate with Union leaders, but he undercut any possibility of success by instructing them to insist on the recognition of southern independence.

When these commissioners arrived at the Union lines, Lincoln sent Major William Eckert to inspect their credentials. Eckert confirmed that, as Lincoln suspected, Davis had not accepted the specified preconditions, but Grant reported that after talking to the commissioners he was convinced that their motives were sincere. Lincoln therefore decided to join Secretary of State William H. Seward in a conference with them at Hampton Roads, Virginia.

Lincoln and Seward received the Confederate delegates on February 3, 1865, on the steamer *River Queen* off Fortress Monroe. The participants agreed to keep no official record of their talks. In the discussion, which lasted four hours, Lincoln reiterated his terms for peace: cessation of hostilities, reunion, and emancipation. To soften the last point, he indicated his belief that slaveowners should be compensated for their loss of property. Lincoln refused to negotiate the terms of reconstruction, however, without a cessation of hostilities and acceptance of reunion. From the Confederate perspective, these terms were "nothing less . . . than unconditional submission," and the meeting ended without any agreement.

In these discussions, Lincoln's desire for a liberal peace that would lessen sectional hatreds overcame his political judgment. Compensation would require Congress's approval, which by this point was a political impossibility. In a cabinet meeting two days later, when Lincoln circulated a bill to appropriate $400 million to compensate slaveholders if the war ended by April 1, his advisers unanimously disapproved of his proposition, arguing it was inappropriate and politically infeasible. Lincoln quietly shelved the proposal.

When Lee subsequently proposed to meet with Grant to resolve "the present unhappy difficulties," Lincoln rejected the idea. He was willing that Grant discuss only purely military matters with Lee. "You are not to decide, discuss, or confer upon any political question," Stanton wrote to Grant in relaying instructions that Lincoln had carefully written out. "Such questions the President holds in his own hands; and will submit them to no military conferences or conventions."

The failure of the Hampton Roads conference demonstrated, as Lincoln had realized all along, that peace depended on military victory. His instructions to Grant in disapproving a conference with Lee were blunt and to the point: "You are to press to the utmost, your military advantages."

THE STRAIN of the war was evident in Lincoln's gaunt, haggard face and in the flecks of white in his black hair. Visiting him at about this time, his old friend Joshua Speed found him "jaded and weary." His friends repeatedly urged him to rest, but Lincoln replied that "the tired part of me is inside and out of reach." The full weight of the war had

These two photographs show how badly Lincoln had aged under the strain of the war. In contrast to the vigorous presidential candidate in the first picture, taken in the summer of 1860, a tired and weary president appears in the last photograph of Lincoln, made on April 10, 1865, just four days before his assassination. (Left: Library of Congress; right: National Portrait Gallery, Washington, DC/Art Resource, NY)

borne down on him, and he confronted daily what Hay termed "that vast sum of human misery involved in civil war." Day after day weeping mothers, bulldozing congressmen, greedy office-seekers, and irate critics gobbled up his time; to the end he remained the most accessible of presidents and saw as many of them as possible. Nicolay thought it "impossible to portray . . . the labor, the thought, the responsibility, the strain of intellect and the anguish of soul" he experienced.

His kindhearted nature was especially apparent in dealing with court-martial verdicts. Part of each Friday, which Lincoln designated as "butcher's day," was set aside to review capital sentences, a task he heartily disliked, and he looked for any reason to pardon soldiers convicted of falling asleep, going home without authorization, running from battle, or deserting. Many were what he termed "leg cases": soldiers whose legs were stronger than their courage. He commuted the bulk of these sentences and ordered the soldier returned to the ranks where, he explained, "we may at least get some work out of him."

When James Madison Cutts, who was related to Lincoln's old adversary Stephen A. Douglas, was sentenced to be dismissed from the army for quarreling, Lincoln penned a fatherly letter filled with wisdom. "You have too much of life yet before you, and have shown too much of promise as an officer, for your future to be lightly surrendered. . . . The advice of a father to his son 'Beware of entrance to a quarrel, but being in, bear it that the opposed may beware of thee,' is good, and yet not the best. Quarrel not at all. No man resolved to make the most of himself, can spare time for personal contention. Still less can he afford to take all the consequences, including the vitiating of his temper, and the loss of self-control."

The burden of death was overwhelming. Among the war's toll were individuals close to him: Elmer Ellsworth, his former law clerk, who was killed in the first month of the war; Senator Edward Baker, for whom he had named his second son, lost at Ball's Bluff; and his favorite child, Willie. Then there were members of his wife's family: her half-brothers Sam, David, and Alec, all of whom died fighting for the Confederacy, and her sister Emilie's husband, Benjamin Helm, the

Confederate general. And finally the thousands of young soldiers in both armies, struck down in the bloom of life by orders he had given. To a Democratic congressman, Lincoln shared the observation, "Doesn't it seem strange that I should be here—I, a man who couldn't cut a chicken's head off—with blood running all around me?"

From the depths of his own personal anguish, he wrote in late 1864 to Lydia Bixby of Boston, who he had been erroneously informed had lost five sons fighting for the Union. "I feel how weak and fruitless must be any words of mine which should attempt to beguile you from the grief of a loss so overwhelming. But I cannot refrain from tendering to you the consolation that may be found in the thanks of the Republic they died to save. I pray that our Heavenly Father may assuage the anguish of your bereavement, and leave you only the cherished memory of the loved and lost, and the solemn pride that must be yours, to have laid so costly a sacrifice upon the altar of Freedom."

One way he coped with the relentless pressure was through his well-known sense of humor. Congressman Isaac Arnold of Illinois once rebuked Lincoln for his levity in time of war. The president broke down, tears streaming down his cheeks. "If I could not get momentary respite from the crushing burden I am constantly carrying" by telling stories, he explained, "I should die."

Reading was a diversion and source of relaxation, particularly comic stories. Late one evening, Lincoln came chuckling into Hay's office to read his secretaries a humorous story by Thomas Hood. "What a man it is!" Hay exclaimed in his diary. "Occupied all day with matters of vast moment, deeply anxious about the fate of the greatest army of the world, with his own fame and future hanging on the events of the passing hour, he yet has such a wealth of simple bonhommie and good fellow ship that he gets out of bed and per-ambulates the house in his shirt to find us that we may share with him the fun of one of poor Hoods queer little conceits."

At the end of the day, Lincoln would often unwind by sitting around with friends, swapping stories. At these sessions "his wit and rich humor had free play," Hay remembered, and "he was once more the Lincoln of the Eighth Circuit, the cheeriest of talkers, the riskiest of story tellers." Besides Seward, others frequently present included old friends Ward Hill Lamon, Orville Browning, and Elihu Washburne from Illinois. Yet Lincoln kept even these associates emotionally at a distance and never fully confided in them.

The theater was another refuge from his daily cares. Here he could escape the hordes of office-seekers and the weight of decision-making while being diverted by the performance. He especially tried to attend when a famous actor was featured and enjoyed both comedies and tragedies. Having never seen Shakespeare performed on the stage until he came to Washington, he eventually concluded that the comedies were more enjoyable when performed, but he preferred reading the tragedies.

Indeed, Shakespeare became a constant companion. Lincoln had liked his plays since he was a youth, but the tribulations of the war heightened his appreciation, particularly of the tragedies. "Some of Shakspeare's plays I have never read," he told James H. Hackett, a well-known Shakespearean actor, "while others I have gone over perhaps as frequently as any unprofessional reader. Among the latter are Lear, Richard Third, Henry Eighth, Hamlet, and especially Macbeth. I think nothing equals Macbeth. It is wonderful."

As this letter indicated, Lincoln's favorite plays focused on power and politics, issues central to his own life. Like Shakespeare's tragic figures, Lincoln was also ambitious, but he derived little personal pleasure from the exercise of power. Instead, he found it only an ordeal, which grew heavier as the war continued, and his deeply ingrained melancholy drew him to the darkness of Shakespeare's tragedies. Increasingly he found in the will of God the means to carry on under the weight of responsibility.

THE WAR NOT ONLY deepened Lincoln's sense of fatalism, it also had a significant impact on his religious outlook. He had always believed in providence—a higher power that ordered human events— and often used the word God to describe this power. But prior to the war he had taken a rather complacent view of God's designs, which he thought were manifested through cause and effect and irresistibly promoted progress through historical processes. This view limited God's motive force in human affairs and conceived of the Deity as more a force or law than a divine personality.

The dark shadows of the war, however, gave a harder edge to Lincoln's religious thought, and he more frequently invoked God during his presidency than he ever had before. Initially he thought of God as a means to assist the Union in the struggle, but as the war continued despite his best efforts to end it, Lincoln increasingly emphasized the power of God's often inscrutable will. In doing so, he embraced the concept of a more judgmental God, and searched for the larger meaning—God's purpose—in the cataclysm of war. "He had sometime[s] thought that perhaps he might be an instrument in God's hands of accomplishing a great work," he divulged to a group of religious leaders in 1862, but added pointedly that perhaps "God's way of accomplishing the end . . . may be different from theirs."

Sometime in the fall of 1862, he penned a meditation on the war: "The will of God prevails. In great contests each party claims to act in accordance with the will of God. Both *may* be, and one *must* be wrong. God can not be *for*, and *against* the same thing at the same time. In the present civil war it is quite possible that God's purpose is something different from the purposes of either party. . . . I am almost ready to say this is probably true—that God wills this contest, and wills that it shall not end yet."

By 1864 Lincoln had combined his religious ideas into a new outlook that emphasized national sin, emancipation as God's will, and the war as part of God's design. He no longer spoke, as he had earlier, of the war as needless. God "intends some great good to follow this mighty convulsion," he wrote in 1864, "which no mortal could make, and no mortal could stay."

He brought these ideas together in his second inaugural address on March 4. The day was "somber and drizzly," but just as Lincoln stepped forward to thunderous applause, "the sun . . . burst forth in its unclouded meridian splendor. . . ." Delivered on the eve of victory after almost four years of bloody conflict, the speech was remarkable for its compassion, its humility, and its profound comprehension of the tragedy the nation had suffered. As Lincoln noted, the speech was much shorter (only 703 words) than the one he had given four years earlier. After the opening paragraph, Lincoln did not refer to himself, and he did not discuss any of his policies during the last four years. Nor did he refer by name to either the North or the South, or the Union or the Confederacy, and he made only the most general reference to the military situation.

He studiously avoided imputing blame for the war. "All dreaded it —all sought to avert it," but one party "would *make* war rather than let the nation survive; and the other would *accept* war rather than let it perish. And the war came." "All knew" that slavery, the issue that most deeply divided the American people, "was, somehow, the cause of the war."

Yet neither side had expected a war of this magnitude and duration. "Both read the same Bible, and pray to the same God; and each invokes His aid against the other. . . . The prayers of both could not be answered; that of neither has been answered fully." The war demonstrated the fundamental truth that "the Almighty has His own purposes."

Declining to offer glib assurances of the North's moral superiority, Lincoln interpreted the war as God's punishment of America for the sin of slavery, which the North shared with the South. To remove the offense of slavery, God gave "to both North and South, this terrible war, as the woe due to those by whom the offence came." All prayed for a speedy conclusion to the conflict. "Yet, if God wills that it continue" until all the wealth created by slaves was destroyed, "and until every drop of blood drawn with the lash, shall be paid by another drawn with the sword, . . . still it must be said 'the judgments of the Lord, are true and righteous altogether.'" This was as harsh a moral pronouncement as any American president has ever rendered.

Having disassociated himself from the moral arrogance which military victory spawns, Lincoln closed with an eloquent plea for a just peace and a better future: "With malice toward none; with charity for all; with firmness in the right, as God gives us to see the right, let us strive on to finish the work we are in; to bind up the nation's wounds; to care for him who shall have borne the battle, and for his widow, and his orphan—to do all which may achieve and cherish a just, and lasting peace, among ourselves, and with all nations."

Sensitive commentators immediately grasped the significance of Lincoln's speech, none more so than the elitist Charles Francis Adams, Jr., the scion of the famous Massachusetts family. "That rail-splitting lawyer is one of the wonders of the day," he wrote in applauding Lincoln's speech. "Once at Gettysburg and now again on a greater occasion he has shown a capacity for rising to the demands of the hour. . . . This inaugural strikes me in its grand simplicity and directness as being for all time the historical keynote of this war." Lincoln himself believed it would "wear as well as—perhaps better than—anything I have produced."

As he began his second term, Lincoln's power and prestige were at a peak. Military victory was imminent, emancipation was secure, the radicals had been thwarted on Reconstruction, and after almost four years of withering criticism, Lincoln was genuinely popular and respected in the North. The *New York Herald* anointed him "the unquestioned master of the situation in reference to American affairs, at home and abroad." How had he come to be such a successful president?

ABRAHAM LINCOLN was not born a great president. Indeed, he was one of the least experienced men to be elected president in American history, and he had to grow into the office by mastering the many responsibilities that fall on a president in wartime. His touch became more sure as the war continued, but he brought to the office certain qualities of leadership forged in his career in Illinois politics that were crucial to his eventual success as president.

His hardscrabble early life and experience stumping the state had given him a knowledge of and faith in ordinary people, with whom he had a genuine rapport. Putting together legislative and political coalitions in Illinois taught him the art of working with men of diverse viewpoints. He understood the ways of the political world and the imperfections of human character and was not easily fooled, displayed a firm grasp of the workings of party machinery, and knew how to manage men. Moreover, his participation in rough-and-tumble state campaigns had toughened him to criticism, strengthened his belief in democracy, and taught him to rely on his own judgment and not to depend on advisers or cronies.

At the same time, he had developed personal qualities that stood him in good stead as president. He exhibited an extraordinary patience, which his numerous political failures and difficult marriage surely reinforced, and had learned to control his temper. Long before he became president, he manifested a generous spirit and an unwillingness to nurse political grudges or seek revenge. His many defeats and disappointments before 1860 fostered a resiliency in the face of adversity that would prove vital during his presidency. The *New York Herald* observed, "Plain common sense, a kindly disposition, a straightforward purpose, and a shrewd perception of the ins and outs of poor weak human nature, have enabled him to master difficulties which would have swamped almost any other man."

These qualities shaped his presidency. Preeminently his own man, he did not rely on his cabinet to determine policy, and he never felt bound by the sentiment of its members. "The relations between him and all the Secretaries were perfectly cordial always and unaffected," Charles Dana observed, ". . . but it was always his will, his order, that determined a decision." In seeking the opinions of others, he rarely revealed his own thoughts until he had made up his mind. "He always told enough only, of his plans and purposes, to induce the belief that he had communicated all," Leonard Swett, an Illinois Republican, commented. "Yet he reserved enough, in fact, to have communicated nothing." At the same time, he did not isolate himself from dissenting viewpoints or inflexibly adhere to policies if they failed. Through a combination of persuasion, tact, and iron determination, he controlled his administration and the war effort. "He could have dispensed with any one of his cabinet and the administration not been impaired," an admiring Gideon Welles concluded, "but it would have been difficult if not impossible to have selected any one who could have filled the office of chief magistrate as successfully as Mr. Lincoln. . . . "

Lincoln understood that patronage was the glue that held parties together in the nineteenth century, and he devoted more time and energy to patronage matters than to any other issue except the military. He recognized all factions in the distribution of offices and never singled out his party critics for political annihilation. Lincoln's careful attention to the party machinery oiled his surprisingly easy renomination in 1864. Yet he realized that he never could satisfy everyone because, as he mused to an Illinois colleague, he "always had more horses than oats."

Furthermore, he could take the political pounding and could not be intimidated, as his resistance to the radicals' pressure on emancipation in 1862 and the popular cry for peace negotiations in 1864 showed. He endured personal slights, social humiliation, unprecedented ridicule, and vicious criticism without descending to pettiness or vindictiveness. He said of the press's relentless carping, "Those comments constitute a fair specimen of what has occurred to me through life. I have endured a great deal of ridicule without much malice; and have received a great deal of kindness, not quite free from ridicule. I am used to it."

Like most strong presidents, Lincoln found Congress a severe trial, and it was not just coincidence that his most decisive assertions of presidential power usually occurred when Congress was not in session. On matters he deemed beyond his responsibility, such as economic legislation, he generally deferred to Congress. His most forceful exertions of executive authority came on questions of war policy, emancipation, and reconstruction, which he considered his responsibility because of his war powers as commander-in-chief. On all of these issues, however, he made concessions to Congress, and his relations with the legislative branch, while often strained, never broke down completely, in part because Lincoln maintained a basic flexibility in his approach, but also because he understood the need to maintain party unity.

Lincoln devoted considerable attention to military affairs, and in the process redefined the nature of the president's role as commander-in-chief. Despite his limited military background, he displayed a keen aptitude for military strategy, and as his self-confidence grew, he became more assertive in promoting his ideas, while displaying enormous skill in dealing with his generals. Military performance, not personal relations or partisan affiliations, counted most with Lincoln. He never shared the widespread hostility in Washington to West Point officers, and he rejected the view that Democratic generals lacked the commitment to win the war. When the German Republican leader Carl Schurz upbraided him for giving military commands to Democrats, Lincoln retorted that the war "should be conducted on military knowledge" and not "on political affinity." Referring to the many Republicans who had received such commands, he trenchantly observed, "I do not see that their superiority of success has been so marked as to throw great suspicion on the good faith of those who are not Republicans."

The powers Lincoln exercised were breathtaking in their extent and significance. He spent money without congressional authorization, suspended the writ of habeas corpus throughout the Union, authorized military trials of civilians, dictated the terms of peace, and abolished slavery by presidential edict. With exceptional deftness, he walked the thin line between failing to respond vigorously and abuse of power. Exercising unprecedented power, he was neither corrupted by it nor viewed it as an end in itself. "Lincoln certainly was the *safest* leader a nation could have" at a time when constitutional rights had to be suspended, Harriet Beecher Stowe argued. "A reckless, bold, theorizing, dashing man," she concluded, ". . . might have wrecked our Constitution and ended us in a splendid military despotism."

In dealing with the greatest crisis in American history, Lincoln became an accomplished and extraordinary president. He had a sure sense of political timing, knew when to stand firm and when to compromise, and displayed an absolute genius for getting individuals of diverse viewpoints to work together. "Slow and careful in coming to resolutions" and basing his decisions on facts rather than "illusions" of what "might be," he possessed the ability to weigh alternatives and to perceive clearly the consequences of his acts, and, as Noah Brooks noted, was "never crushed at defeat or unduly excited by success" but remained calm in the face of both. He never lost sight of his larger objectives, yet he remained flexible in his approach and not afraid to change his mind or admit that he had been wrong. As he began his second term, the *New York Herald* commented, "He has proved himself, in his quiet way, the keenest of politicians, and more than a match for his wiliest antagonists. . . ."

His two secretaries, John Nicolay and John Hay, marveled at his unsurpassed ability "to still the quarrels of factions, to allay the jealousies of statesmen, to compose the rivalries of generals, to soothe the vanity of officials, to prompt the laggard, to curb the ardent, [and] to sustain the faltering." Even in the darkest hours of the war, he never lacked faith in his ability to lead the nation through this crisis. Indeed, probably his most remarkable quality as president was his unwavering belief in himself, what Welles termed his "wonderful self-reliance."

THE WAR HAD EXACTED a heavy physical toll on Lincoln, and he needed to get away from the daily grind of Washington. Indeed, the normally robust president was so exhausted that in mid-March the cabinet met in his bedroom. As a result, he decided to visit Grant at his headquarters in City Point, Virginia. His wife and Tad accompanied him, and they were reunited with Robert, who had graduated from Harvard and was now a member of Grant's staff.

Lincoln disembarked at City Point on March 24. After Sherman arrived by sea from North Carolina, the president met with Grant, Sherman, and Admiral David Porter on March 28 aboard the *River Queen*, which had brought him from Washington. In discussing the military situation, Lincoln expressed the hope that the war could be concluded without another major battle. When the discussion turned to matters once the fighting was over, Lincoln reiterated his desire for a generous peace that would foster sectional reconciliation and avoid anarchy in the South. As for Confederate soldiers, Lincoln advised, "Let them all go, officers and all. I want submission, and no more bloodshed." He advocated the same approach toward Jefferson Davis and the political leaders of the Confederacy. Rejecting any idea of vengeance, Lincoln said with a wink that he would not complain if they somehow managed to elude Union forces and successfully flee the country.

Once again, Mary Lincoln proved an emotional cross for her already overburdened husband. Her public behavior made this trip excruciatingly painful for Lincoln. The First Lady exploded in a jealous rage when the president rode alongside the pert wife of a Union general as he reviewed the troops. At a subsequent dinner party she

This picture, entitled "The Peacemakers," shows Lincoln conferring with (from left) General William Tecumseh Sherman, General Ulysses S. Grant, and Admiral David Porter in a cabin on the steamship River Queen *a few weeks before the end of the war. (Chicago Historical Society)*

accused General Grant's wife, Julia, of trying to upstage her and publicly berated her husband for allegedly flirting with another general's wife; Lincoln's efforts to cajole her were unavailing. He probably breathed a sigh of relief when she decided to return to Washington.

Indeed, a major scandal was brewing over Mary Lincoln's abuse of her position to extort favors from merchants. Shopping gave her a welcome diversion from the pressures of her public position and the constant criticism of the press, yet she failed to see that her extravagant spending on clothing and luxuries, which she schemed to charge to the government, was inappropriate in a wartime nation draped in black. In 1864 Mary had been terrified that Lincoln would be defeated and her expenditures revealed. His reelection postponed the day of

reckoning, but she persisted in her spending habits and had accumu-
lated debts totaling thousands of dollars. Only death spared Lincoln,
who in his wife's words was "almost a monomaniac on the subject
of honesty," from having to deal with her disreputable actions.

Mary's tantrums and imperiousness caused Nicolay and Hay, who
heartily disliked her, to finally seek reassignment. In March, Lincoln
appointed Nicolay to be consul to Paris, and he intended to make Hay
secretary to the American legation in France. Noah Brooks, a reporter
whom Lincoln had known for almost a decade and who enjoyed Mrs.
Lincoln's support, was designated to take Nicolay's place. While loyal
to the president, Nicolay's harsh and curt demeanor made him many
enemies, and the more congenial Brooks promised to handle these
duties more effectively.

On April 3, while Lincoln was still at City Point, Union troops
entered Richmond after Lee was forced to pull out of the lines at
Petersburg. Lincoln decided to visit the former capital of the Confederacy. To Stanton's concern about the danger of such a visit, Lincoln
replied, "I will take care of myself."

The next morning the president traveled on a Union naval vessel
up the James River to Richmond. Accompanied by Admiral Porter
and a small escort of seamen, he walked through the ruins of the
burned-out city to General Godfrey Weitzel's headquarters in the former Confederate White House. Whites, especially those of higher
status, were generally sullen and stayed largely out of sight, but the
city's black residents jubilantly welcomed the United States president
and marched along behind him.

When Lincoln had met Grant in Petersburg after its fall he had
reiterated his desire for a generous peace. He repeated this wish during
his visit to Richmond. He dissented when a Union officer, after view-
ing the city's military prisons, urged that Davis be hanged. And when
Weitzel sought advice about how to handle the people of Richmond,
Lincoln replied, "If I were in your place, I'd let 'em up easy, let 'em
up easy."

Lee and the remnants of his army moved westward, hoping eventually to turn south and join Johnston. But at Sayler's Creek a de-
tachment of Grant's army captured half of Lee's troops. Sheridan

This engraving, based on a drawing by an artist who was present, shows Lincoln riding through the Confederate capital of Richmond in April 1865 to the enthusiastic cheers of the city's black population. (Library of Congress)

wired Grant, "If the thing is pressed I think that Lee will surrender." Reading this message, Lincoln tersely responded, "Let the *thing* be pressed."

While in Virginia, he insisted on visiting the 7000 sick and wounded soldiers in the hospital at City Point and personally greeting most of them, including those who were Confederates. An agent for the United States Sanitary Commission noted that when talking to rebel soldiers, "he was just as kind, his handshakings just as hearty, his interest just as real for the welfare of the men, as when he was among our own soldiers."

News that Seward had been seriously injured in a carriage accident prompted Lincoln to return to Washington. He arrived on April 9 and quickly called on the bedridden secretary of state. "I think we are near the end, at last," he quietly informed his colleague. Indeed, later that evening word arrived from Grant that Lee had surrendered at Appomattox Court House.

When the news was announced the next morning, it set off a day-long celebration in the capital. Mary reported that an immense crowd swarmed around the White House, singing songs and repeatedly shouting for the president. That evening the weary chief executive finally came out on the balcony and said a few brief words. Then noticing that a band was present, he asked its members to play one of his favorite songs: "Dixie."

"ALL SEEMS WELL WITH US"
"From Our Special War Correspondent, City Point, Virginia"

This illustration from Harper's Weekly, *drawn during his visit to Grant's army in 1865, was published the day Lincoln died. Reflecting Lincoln's image as Father Abraham, it conveys the affection countless Northerners felt for the unpretentious president.*

THE NEXT EVENING, April 11, Lincoln delivered a public address, which he had carefully written out, on the problem of Reconstruction. Refusing to indulge in the speculative argument of whether the seceded states had ever been out of the Union, Lincoln, as was his wont, emphasized instead the practical problem of restoring these states to their normal relationship with the federal government. "Let us all join in doing the acts necessary to restoring the proper practical relations between these states and the Union. . . ." In an appeal to the radicals, he granted that Congress had a legitimate role in Reconstruction. Once again, flexibility and political dexterity were the hallmarks of Lincoln's position. Noting that "no exclusive, and inflexible plan can safely be prescribed as to details and colatterals," he indicated that he might soon make a new announcement to the people of the South concerning Reconstruction, and he also suggested that he might favor different programs for different states. This thought was left undeveloped, but Lincoln may have been considering that states that did not yet have a program of Reconstruction under way could be subject to different (and more stringent) terms than those that did. Certainly such an approach would help assuage radicals' fears while preserving his governments in Louisiana and Arkansas. So would his public endorsement for the first time of limited black suffrage in the Reconstructed South. The audience, however, had expected a triumphant speech on the occasion, and many present became inattentive or wandered off.

Despite his defense of his wartime governments in the occupied South, Lincoln was troubled by developments in Louisiana. As radicals had feared, without military intervention conservatives had seized control of the government, and the new governor began appointing former Copperheads and even Confederates to office. In response to protests from Unionists in New Orleans, Lincoln ordered Nathaniel P. Banks, his military commander who had come to Washington to lobby members of congress to recognize the new state government, to return to Louisiana to put the program back on course.

Banks's return and Lincoln's speech indicated that he was reconsidering the whole process of Reconstruction. The need to establish loyal governments as a way to win the war no longer existed, and the conservative reaction in Louisiana, which boded ill for Unionists and blacks alike, was a major cause for concern. In his speech, Lincoln acknowledged that perhaps his 10 percent requirement was too low, and he also apparently had abandoned his earlier willingness to accept a transition period from slavery to freedom for former slaves.

There were other indications as well that Lincoln was reaching out to the radicals on Reconstruction in hopes of establishing common ground with Congress. He asked Stanton, who was known to favor black suffrage, to draw up a plan to establish military governments in the defeated states of the Confederacy. He also signed the Freedmen's Bureau bill, enacted by Congress in February, which established a special agency within the War Department to aid refugees and supervise the situation of former slaves in the South. As was often the case, Lincoln left himself room to maneuver as events dictated. What was clear was that his program of Reconstruction was in the process of evolution, and that he was moving in the direction of greater rights and safeguards for black Americans, although he had not yet thought through the problem of what position former slaves would occupy in the postwar South.

The change in Lincoln's thinking on race over the past four years was striking. He had sloughed off the idea of colonization and embraced universal black freedom as one of the consequences of the Union's triumph. He was the first American president to officially receive African Americans at the White House, and when a group of black residents hesitatingly showed up at the President's annual New Year's reception in 1865, Lincoln, according to one witness, welcomed them "with a heartiness that made them wild with exceeding joy." Two months later, blacks were allowed for the first time to participate in the inaugural parade. Frederick Douglass, the famous black abolitionist, testified, "In all my interviews with Mr. Lincoln I was impressed with his entire freedom from popular prejudice against the colored race." Lincoln was, according to Douglass, "emphatically the black mans President: the first to show any respect for their rights as men."

Among those in the audience listening to Lincoln's speech was John Wilkes Booth, the famous actor and a Confederate sympathizer. When he heard Lincoln endorse black suffrage, he muttered to an associate, "That means nigger citizenship," and promised, "That is the last speech he will ever make."

~~

LINCOLN HAD APPOINTED Ward Hill Lamon, who was an old friend from the Illinois circuit, marshall of the District of Columbia. A large, burly man, Lamon undertook to protect a president who seemed oblivious to security. Heavily armed, he sometimes slept in the hallway outside the Lincoln's room in the White House to guard against intruders, and he repeatedly criticized the president for not taking proper precautions in public.

Lincoln had never forgotten the ridicule he was subjected to when he secretly entered Washington in February 1861, and he was determined henceforth not to show any fear. Ignoring the hatreds the war had created, he adhered to the traditional view that the ruler of a free people should not be surrounded by guards. "It would never do for a President to have guards with drawn sabres at his door," he maintained, "as if he fancied he were, or were trying to be, or were assuming to be, an emperor." Pointing to a batch of threatening letters, he once told newspaper editor John W. Forney, "I know I am in danger," but he was convinced that "no precautions he could take would be availing" against a determined assassin.

Over the course of the war security measures were tightened, but by modern standards they remained amazingly lax. Lincoln often walked on the streets or went to the War Department late at night alone. Not until November 1864 were District police regularly stationed at the White House. In 1862, Stanton, who shared Lamon's fears, ordered an Ohio company to guard the White House, and in the summer he detailed a cavalry unit to escort the president to the Soldiers' Home. Even so, in August 1864 as he was riding to the Home, a shot fired from the bushes caused his horse to bolt, and he lost his hat; when soldiers retrieved the hat, they found a bullet hole in it. The incident was hushed up, but Stanton augmented the heavy guard that accompanied the president.

On April 14, Good Friday, the cabinet assembled at eleven with

General Grant as an invited guest. The president's spirits were high, and Stanton reported that he was "grander, graver, more thoroughly up to the occasion than he had ever seen him." In the ensuing discussion, Lincoln conceded that perhaps he had tried to move too fast on Reconstruction, but he nevertheless expressed the view that it would be easier to work out a suitable program with Congress no longer in session. "We could do better; accomplish more without than with them," he predicted. He hoped to have new governments in operation by the time Congress convened in December.

Lincoln also renewed his call for a generous peace. When his advisers asked what was to be done with Davis and the leaders of the Confederacy, Lincoln replied, "Frighten them out of the country" as he gestured with his hands as if he were shooing chickens. He criticized the vengeful mood of some members of Congress, saying that he wanted "no persecution, no bloody work, after the war was over." Explicitly disavowing any "feelings of hate and vindictiveness," he insisted that he would not "take any part in hanging" any Confederate leaders. "Enough lives had been sacrificed."

Late in the afternoon Lincoln went for a drive with his wife. "We must *both*, be more cheerful in the future," he said to Mary. "Between the war and the loss of our darling Willie—we have both, been very miserable." Lincoln acted as if a great weight had been removed from his shoulders, and observers reported that as in olden times, his face was animated, his outlook cheerful.

It had been announced that President and Mrs. Lincoln would attend Ford's Theater that evening to see the comedy *Our American Cousin*. They arrived at the theater at about 8:30. When the president entered the special box, the audience broke into thunderous cheers as the orchestra performed "Hail to the Chief." Once the play had resumed, the guard assigned to the presidential box soon left to get a better view of the play.

Earlier that evening in a Washington hotel, John Wilkes Booth had met with a group of Confederate sympathizers, who had been part of an earlier abortive plot to kidnap the president. The defeat of the Confederacy had left Booth despondent, and he was drinking heavily. He now unveiled a plan to murder Lincoln and other government officials, and assigned to himself the task of killing the president. Booth was motivated by more than a desire to avenge the South: He was also a strong defender of slavery and was enraged by the prospect of black equality.

Booth entered the theater after the play was under way and, showing his card to the White House footman, was allowed to go to the door of the presidential box. During the third act, while the audience roared at a particularly funny line, Booth quietly opened the door and shot the president behind the ear with a derringer from only a few inches away. With a flair for the dramatic, Booth then leapt down to the stage, only to break his leg when he landed awkwardly. Brandishing a knife, he shouted something that sounded like "*Sic semper tyrannis,*" the motto of the state of Virginia, and hobbled out the side door. Two weeks later, Union troops killed Booth in a Virginia barn.

The unconscious president was taken across the street to a private home and placed diagonally on a bed. Cabinet members and other government officials quickly assembled at the house. The doctors present announced that Lincoln's condition was hopeless, and the end came at 7:22 in the morning. He was fifty-six years old. After a minister offered a short prayer, Stanton, fighting to hold back tears, commented, "Now he belongs to the ages."

A military funeral was held on Wednesday, April 19, in the East Room of the White House. Mary Lincoln was too distraught to attend, and only official dignitaries were invited. Following the funeral, the body was taken to the Capitol, where it lay in state so the residents of Washington could pay their last respects. Unable to reach their assigned position, a regiment of black soldiers symbolically led the procession down Pennsylvania Avenue. Finally, on April 21, a week after the assassination, a special funeral train left Washington to carry Lincoln's casket back to Springfield. It mostly followed the same 1600-mile route that Lincoln had taken in February 1861 when he had come to Washington. The twenty-day trip from Washington to Springfield transported the martyred president to immortality.

Thousands silently stood along the tracks as the train slowly passed, and thousands more viewed the body as it lay in state in principal cities along the way. All told, well over a million Americans viewed the body of their fallen leader on this journey home. "History has no parallel to the outpouring of sorrow which followed the funeral *cortége* on its route from Washington to Springfield," declared General E. D. Townsend, who was on the train. In New York City, when officials tried to prevent African Americans from taking part in the official ceremony, Stanton ordered the train not to stop in the nation's metropolis unless they were included, and the order prohibiting their participation was quickly rescinded. Even in death, Lincoln could not escape the power of antiblack prejudice.

On May 3, after the train reached Springfield, the casket was taken to the state capitol in a special hearse and placed in the hall of the House of Representatives, where Lincoln had delivered his House Divided speech seven years earlier. For hours, thousands of friends, acquaintances, supporters, and neighbors filed slowly past to bid him farewell. The next day, Lincoln's body was interred at Oak Ridge Cemetery, two miles outside of Springfield, as his widow wished. Abraham Lincoln had come home to the Illinois prairie where, more than three decades before, as a penniless young man, he had begun his journey to greatness.

CHRONOLOGY OF ABRAHAM LINCOLN

1809	February 12	Born in Hardin County, Kentucky
1811	Spring	Family moves to Knob Creek farm
1815	Autumn	Attends first school
1816	December	Family moves to Indiana
1818	October 5	Mother, Nancy Hanks Lincoln, dies
1819	December 2	Father marries Sarah Bush Johnson
1824		Formal schooling ends
1827		Operates a passenger ferry on the Ohio River
1828	Spring–Summer	Travels to New Orleans by flatboat
1830	March	Family moves to Illinois
	Summer	Makes first political speech in Illinois
1831	April–July	Second trip to New Orleans
	Late July	Arrives in New Salem
1832	March 9	Writes platform as candidate for legislature
	April–July	Serves in Black Hawk War
	August 6	Defeated for legislature in first political race
1833	January	Lincoln–Berry store established
	May 7	Appointed postmaster (serves until May 1836)
1834	August 4	Elected to state legislature
	Autumn	Begins studying law
	December 1	Takes seat in legislature

1835	March 7	Personal possessions sold for debt
	August 25	Ann Rutledge dies
1836	August 1	Reelected to legislature
	September 9	Receives law license
1837	March 3	Enters legislative protest against slavery
	April 15	Moves to Springfield; joins law partnership with John T. Stuart
1838	August 6	Reelected to legislature
1840	August 3	Reelected to legislature
	Fall–Winter	Engaged to Mary Todd; breaks engagement
1841	March	Forms legal partnership with Stephen T. Logan
1842	September 19	Challenged to duel by James Shields
	November 4	Marries Mary Todd
1843	August 1	Son Robert Todd Lincoln born
1844	December	Forms legal partnership with William Herndon
1846	March 10	Son Edward Baker (Eddie) Lincoln born
	August 3	Elected to Congress
1847–	December 3–	Serves in Congress
1849	March 4	
1850	February 1	Son Eddie dies
	December 21	Son William Wallace (Willie) Lincoln born
1853	April 4	Son Thomas (Tad) Lincoln born
1854	October 16	Peoria speech
	November 7	Elected to the legislature; resigns to seek U.S. Senate seat
1855	February 8	Defeated for senator
	September 20–21	McCormick reaper patent trial
1856	February 22	Joins movement to organize the Republican party in Illinois
	May 29	Attends Republican state convention; nominated for presidential elector

	June 19	Finishes second in balloting for Republican vice-presidential nomination
	Fall	Campaigns for Republican ticket
1857	September 8	Mississippi River bridge case
1858	May 7	Almanac trial
	June 16	Nominated for senator by Republican convention; delivers House Divided speech
	August 21–October 15	Lincoln–Douglas debates
	November 4	State election foreshadows defeat for Senate
1859	January 5	Defeated for senator
1860	February 27	Cooper Union address
	May 10	State convention instructs delegates for Lincoln
	May 18	Nominated for president
	November 6	Elected president
	December 20	South Carolina secedes

CIVIL WAR

1860–	December–March	Opposes compromise
1861	December–April	Fort Sumter crisis
1861	February 11	Leaves Springfield to go to Washington
	March 4	Inaugurated
	April 12	Fort Sumter bombarded
	April 15	Calls for 75,000 volunteers
	April 19	Institutes blockade
	April 27	Suspends writ of habeas corpus in Maryland
	July 4	First message to Congress
	July 21	Battle of Bull Run
	July 22–25	Crittenden resolution approved
	July 26	McClellan takes command of the army at Washington
	August 6	First Confiscation Act
	September 12	Revokes Frémont's proclamation
	November 1	Appoints McClellan commanding general
	November–December	*Trent* affair

1862	February 6–16	Forts Henry and Donelson captured
	February 20	Son Willie dies
	March–July	Peninsula Campaign
	April 6–7	Battle of Shiloh
	April 25	Farragut captures New Orleans
	May 19	Revokes Hunter's emancipation proclamation
	June 26–July 2	Seven Days' Battles
	July 12	Meets with border state representatives
	July 17	Second Confiscation Act approved
	July 22	Circulates draft of Emancipation Proclamation to cabinet
	July 23	Names Halleck general-in-chief (serves until March 9, 1864)
	August 4	Institutes militia draft
	August 30	Second Battle of Bull Run
	September 17	Battle of Antietam
	September 22	Issues preliminary Emancipation Proclamation
	September 24	Suspends writ of habeas corpus throughout the Union
	October 8	Battle of Perryville
	October 24	Removes Buell from command
	October–November	Democrats gain in fall elections
	November 5	Removes McClellan from command, replaced by Burnside
	December 13	Battle of Fredericksburg
	December 16–20	Cabinet crisis
	December 31– January 1	Battle of Stones River
1863	January 1	Issues final Emancipation Proclamation
	January 25	Hooker replaces Burnside
	May 2–4	Battle of Chancellorsville
	May 6	Vallandigham arrested
	May–July	Siege of Vicksburg
	June 7	Black troops fight at Battle of Milliken's Bend
	June 28	Names Meade commander of Army of the Potomac
	July 1–3	Battle of Gettysburg
	July 4	Vicksburg captured
	July 13–16	New York City draft riots
	September 19–20	Battle of Chickamauga
	October–November	Democrats suffer severe defeats in state elections
	November 19	Gettysburg Address

	November 23–25	Battle of Chattanooga
	December 8	Announces Reconstruction program
1864	February 20	Pomeroy Circular published
	March 9	Names Grant commanding general
	April 8	Thirteenth Amendment passes the Senate
	May–June	Grant's offensive in Virginia
	June 8	Renominated
	June 19	Siege of Petersburg begins
	June 30	Chase leaves the cabinet
	July 4	Pocket vetoes Wade–Davis bill
	July 11	Early's invasion reaches outskirts of Washington
	July 18	Greeley's peace mission
	August 5	Battle of Mobile Bay
	August 29	McClellan nominated
	August 30	Call for new Republican convention circulated
	September 2	Sherman captures Atlanta
	September 17	Frémont withdraws as a presidential candidate
	September 23	Blair resigns from the cabinet
	November 8	Reelected
	November– December	Sherman's march
	December 6	Appoints Chase Chief Justice
	December 15–16	Battle of Nashville
	December 22	Sherman captures Savannah
1865	January 31	Thirteenth Amendment passes Congress
	February 3	Hampton Roads Conference
	March 3	Freedmen's Bureau established
	March 4	Second inauguration
	April 3	Richmond falls
	April 9	Lee surrenders
	April 11	Last speech on Reconstruction
	April 14	Shot at Ford's Theater by John Wilkes Booth; dies the next morning
	April–May	Funeral train procession
	April 26	Booth killed
	May 4	Burial in Springfield

LIST OF ABBREVIATIONS

Brooks, *Washington*   Noah Brooks, *Washington in Lincoln's Time* (New York: Century, 1895).

Browning   Theodore C. Pease and James G. Randall, eds., *The Diary of Orville Hickman Browning*, 2 vols. (Springfield: Illinois State Historical Library, 1933).

CW   Roy P. Basler et al., eds., *The Collected Works of Abraham Lincoln*, 8 vols. (New Brunswick, N.J.: Rutgers Univ. Press, 1954).

Carpenter   Francis Carpenter, *Six Months in the White House with Abraham Lincoln* (New York: Hurd and Houghton, 1866).

Donald   David Herbert Donald, *Lincoln* (New York: Simon and Schuster, 1995).

Hay, *Correspondence*   Michael Burlingame, ed., *At Lincoln's Side: John Hay's Civil War Correspondence and Selected Writings* (Carbondale: Southern Illinois Univ. Press, 2000).

Hay, *Inside*   Michael Burlingame and John R. Turner Ettlinger, eds., *Inside Lincoln's White House: The Complete Civil War Diary of John Hay* (Carbondale: Southern Illinois Univ. Press, 1997).

Herndon's Lincoln   William H. Herndon and Jesse W. Weik, *Herndon's Life of Lincoln*, ed. Paul M. Angle (Cleveland: World Publishing, 1942).

HI   Douglas L. Wilson and Rodney O. Davis, eds., *Herndon's Informants* (Urbana: Univ. of Illinois Press, 1998).

Johannsen	Robert W. Johannsen, *The Lincoln–Douglas Debates of 1858* (New York: Oxford Univ. Press, 1965).
McClellen Papers	Stephen W. Sears, ed., *The Civil War Papers of George McClellan* (New York: Ticknor and Fields, 1989).
McPherson	James M. McPherson, *Battle Cry of Freedom* (New York: Oxford Univ. Press, 1988).
Nicolay, *Oral History*	Michael Burlingame, ed., *An Oral History of Abraham Lincoln: John G. Nicolay's Interviews and Essays* (Carbondale: Southern Illinois Univ. Press, 1996).
Nicolay, *With Lincoln*	Michael Burlingame, ed., *With Lincoln in the White House: Letters, Memoranda, and Other Writings of John G. Nicolay, 1860–1865* (Carbondale: Southern Illinois Univ. Press, 2000).
OR	*The War of the Rebellion: A Compilation of the Official Records of the Union and Confederate Armies*, 128 vols. (Washington: Government Printing Office, 1880–1901).
Recollected Words	Don E. Fehrenbacher and Virginia Fehrenbacher, *Recollected Words of Abraham Lincoln* (Stanford, Calif.: Stanford Univ. Press, 1996).
Thomas	Benjamin Thomas, *Abraham Lincoln: A Biography* (New York: Alfred A. Knopf, 1952).
Welles	Howard K. Beale, ed., *Diary of Gideon Welles*, 3 vols. (New York: W. W. Norton, 1960).

NOTES

In the notes that follow, I have indicated the sources only for quotations in the text. In addition to my own research, I have also had many occasions to consult the two best modern biographies of Abraham Lincoln: Benjamin Thomas, *Abraham Lincoln: A Biography* (New York: Alfred A. Knopf, 1952), and David Herbert Donald, *Lincoln* (New York: Simon and Schuster, 1995). Also of particular importance have been Mark E. Neely, Jr., *The Abraham Lincoln Encyclopedia* (New York: McGraw-Hill, 1982), and Earl Schenck Miers, ed., *Lincoln Day by Day*, 3 vols. (Washington: Lincoln Sesquicentennial Commission, 1960).

Preface

ix "shut-mouthed man": *Herndon's Lincoln*, xxxix.
ix "or Expect to see": David Davis *HI, 348.*
ix "inclined to silence": *CW*, v. 4, p. 209.
ix "speak of any relative": Leonard Swett, *HI,* 159.
ix "as I should of had": George Spears, *HI,* 393.
x "ends he had in view": Horace White, *The Life of Lyman Trumbull* (Boston: Houghton Mifflin, 1913), 427.
x "cheat posterity": *Herndon's Lincoln*, 353.
xi "this place": Michael Burlingame, ed., *Lincoln Observed: Civil War Dispatches of Noah Brooks* (Baltimore: Johns Hopkins Univ. Press, 1998), 202.

Chapter 1: A Son of the Frontier

1 "farm work": *CW*, v. 3, pp. 511–12.
1 "simple annals of the poor": John Scripps, *HI,* 57.
1 "open a farm": *CW*, v. 3, p. 511.
1 "wandering laboring boy": *CW*, v. 4, p. 61.
2 "a tinker": Nathaniel Grigsby, *HI,* 113.
2 "bunglingly sign his own name": *CW*, v. 4, p. 61.
2 "short periods": ibid.
3 "naturally anti-slavery": *CW*, v. 7, p. 281.
3 "a wild region": *CW*, v. 3, p. 511.

3   "plowing and harvesting seasons": *CW*, v. 4, p. 62.

3   "taught him to work": John Romine, *HI*, 118.

4   "ragged and dirty": Dennis Hanks, *HI*, 41.

4   "more human": Sarah Bush Lincoln, *HI*, 106.

4   "the best boy I Ever Saw": ibid., 108.

5   "his best Friend in this world": Augustus H. Chapman, *HI*, 136.

5   "looked upon as a wizzard": *CW*, v. 3, p. 511.

6   "went to school no more": Anna Gentry, *HI*, 131

6   "cipher to the Rule of Three": *CW*, v. 3, p. 511.

6   "ambition for education": ibid.

6   "soared above us": Nathaniel Grigsby, *HI*, 114.

6   "not Energetic Except in one thing": Matilda Johnson Moore, *HI*, 109.

7   "understand Every thing": Sarah Bush Lincoln, *HI*, 107.

7   "treated him rather unkind": A. H. Chapman, *HI*, 134.

7   "slash[ed] him" and "Stubborn": Dennis Hanks, *HI*, 41.

7   "pulled a trigger": *CW*, v. 4, p. 62.

8   "naturally assumed the leadership of the boys": Nathaniel Grigsby, *HI*, 114.

8   "making all happy": ibid.

8   "on his Simple word": Joseph C. Richardson, *HI*, 120.

8   "make him quit": Matilda Johnson Moore, *HI*, 110.

8   "argued much from Analogy": Nathaniel Grigsby, *HI*, 114–15.

8   "6 or more inches": ibid., 113.

9   "a kind of news boy": Dennis Hanks, *HI*, 105.

9   "talked Evry thing over": Nathaniel Grigsby, *HI*, 114.

9   "roughest work": *Herndon's Lincoln*, 52.

9   "wider and fairer before me": Carpenter, 97–98.

10   "lived Easy": Nathaniel Grigsby, *HI*, 113.

11   "a piece of floating driftwood": *Herndon's Lincoln*, 66.

11   "penniless" and "friendless": *CW*, v. 1, p. 320.

11   "as ruff a specimen": David C. Mearns, *The Lincoln Papers* (Garden City, N.Y.: Doubleday and Co., 1948), v. 1, 151.

12   "without any hat": Walter B. Stevens, *A Reporter's Lincoln*, ed. Michael Burlingame (Lincoln: Univ. of Nebraska Press, 1998), 9.

12   "intellegence far beyond": Jason Duncan, *HI*, 539.

12   "centre of the circle": Robert L. Wilson, *HI*, 201.

12   "story to tell": N. W. Branson, *HI*, 91.

14   "done with the Bible": *Herndon's Lincoln*, 67–68.

14   "people relied implicitly": Robert B. Rutledge, *HI*, 386.

14   "flabby and undone": Emanuel Hertz, *The Hidden Lincoln: From the Letters and Papers of William H. Herndon* (New York: Blue Ribbon Books, 1940), 165.

14   "men's foibles": Jason Duncan, *HI*, 541.

14   "for miles around": N. W. Branson, *HI*, 91.

14 "studied English grammar": *CW*, v. 4, p. 62.
15 "than any other Man": Abner Y. Ellis, *HI*, 501.
15 "Doctrine of Necessity": *CW*, v. 1, p. 382.
16 "great popularity": *CW*, v. 4, p. 64.
16 "peculiar ambition": *CW*, v. 1, p. 8.
16 "to recommend me": *CW*, v. 1, pp. 8–9.
17 "morality, sobriety": *CW*, v. 1, p. 8.
17 "so much satisfaction": *CW*, v. 4, p. 64.
17 "mixt Jeans Coat": Abner Y. Ellis, *HI*, 171.
17 "short and sweet": *Herndon's Lincoln*, 86.
17 "direct vote of the people": *CW*, v. 4, p. 64.
18 "without a better education": *CW*, v. 4, p. 65.
18 "wait on the Ladies": Abner Y. Ellis, *HI*, 170.
18 "deeper in debt": *CW*, v. 4, p. 65.
18 "national debt": Mearns, *Lincoln Papers*, v. 1, 153.
18 "in his hat": *Herndon's Lincoln*, 101.
18 "a man better pleased": Mearns, *Lincoln Papers*, v. 1, 157.
19 "soul and body together": *CW*, v. 4, p. 65.
19 "by day and by night": N. W. Branson, *HI*, 90.
19 "reading as he walked": Robert B. Rutledge, *HI*, 426.
19 "eyes would Sparkle": Robert L. Wilson, *HI*, 201–2.
19 "clear Shrill monotone": ibid., *HI*, 203.
20 "in good earnest": *CW*, v. 4, p. 65.
20 "said he was crazy": Mearns, *Lincoln Papers*, v. 1, 158.
20 "Great God Almighty": Russell Godbey, *HI*, 450.
22 "your happiness": *CW*, v. 1, pp. 94–95.
22 "chain of womans happiness": Mary Owens Vineyard, *HI*, 256.
22 "in love with her": *CW*, v. 1, pp. 117–19.
23 "one long step removed": *CW*, v. 1, pp. 65–66.
23 "injustice and bad policy": *CW*, v. 1, pp. 74–75.
23 "so much generosity": *CW*, v. 4, pp. 64–65.

Chapter 2: Thwarted Ambition

25 "experiment as a lawyer": Joshua F. Speed, *Reminiscences of Abraham Lincoln* (Louisville: John P. Morton, 1884), 21–22.
25 "I am moved": ibid.
25 "quite as lonesome": *CW*, v. 1, p. 78.
25 "could have avoided it": ibid.
26 "school in the county": Isaac N. Arnold, *The Life of Abraham Lincoln* (Chicago: A. C. McClurg, 1884), 56.
28 "studied very much": Nicolay, *Oral History*, 37.
28 "shoot too high": *Herndon's Lincoln*, 262.
29 "of any consequence": *CW*, v. 2, p. 126.

29   "whig in politics": *CW*, v. 3, p. 512.

29   "from an offended God": Joshua F. Speed, *HI*, 477–78.

29   "10 or 12 feet": James A. Herndon, *HI*, 460.

29   "many friends": J. Rowan Herndon, *HI*, 51.

30   "defend ourselves with it": *CW*, v. 1, pp. 205, 314.

30   "organize the whole State": *CW*, v. 1, p. 201.

30   "sharing the privileges": *CW*, v. 1, p. 48.

30   "one great living principle": *CW*, v. 1, p. 507.

31   "his opponents ridiculous": Douglas L. Wilson, *Honor's Voice: The Transformation of Abraham Lincoln* (New York: Alfred A. Knopf, 1998), 213.

31   "hard to foil": Earl Schenck Miers, ed., *Lincoln Day by Day*, vol. 1 (Washington: Lincoln Sesquicentennial Commission, 1960), 144.

31   "plead guilty to the charge": Ninian Edwards, *HI*, 447.

32   "unimpassioned reason": *CW*, v. 1, p. 115.

32   "deepest chagrin": *Herndon's Lincoln*, 159–60.

33   "object of government": *CW*, v. 2, p. 221.

34   "to improve his manners": Thomas, 86.

35   "Scarcely Said a word": Elizabeth Todd Edwards, *HI*, 443.

35   "of the courting": Nicolay, *Oral History*, 1.

35   "most miserable man living": *CW*, v. 1, p. 229.

35   "the chief gem": *CW*, v. 1, p. 289.

35   "marry that girl": James Matheny, *HI*, 251.

35   "to hell": Albert J. Beveridge, *Abraham Lincoln, 1809–1858*, vol. 1 (Boston: Houghton Mifflin, 1928), 355.

35   "of profound wonder": *CW*, v. 1, p. 305.

36   "look like somebody": Jean H. Baker, *Mary Todd Lincoln* (New York: W. W. Norton, 1987), 133.

37   "women folks out": Harriet Chapman, *HI*, 646.

37   "played merry war": Baker, *Mary Todd Lincoln*, 133.

37   "put on *Style*": Harriet Chapman, *HI*, 512.

37   "scoffer at, religion": *CW*, v. 1, p. 382.

38   "never was much interested": *CW*, v. 1, pp. 347–48.

39   "extending slave territory": *CW*, v. 1, p. 476.

39   "sort of necessity": *CW*, v. 1, p. 454.

39   "distracting question": ibid.

40   "more assiduously than ever before": *CW*, v. 3, p. 512.

41   "lack of discipline": *Herndon's Lincoln*, 247.

41   "nearly mastered": *CW*, v. 4, p. 62.

41   "dripped from him": *Herndon's Lincoln*, 473.

41   "whistle off sadness": David Davis, *HI*, 350.

41   "Strong Emotional feelings": ibid., 348.

41   "more painful than pleasant": *CW*, v. 2, pp. 96–97.

41   "Loved his farther": Dennis Hanks, *HI*, 176.

42   "was hipocritical": ibid., 177.

42   "look in this": *Herndon's Lincoln*, 254.
42   "remember it better": *Herndon's Lincoln*, 268.
43   "place of Enjoyment": David Davis, *HI*, 349.
43   "heartier than his": *Herndon's Lincoln*, 250.
43   "kept for ten years": Henry C. Whitney, *Life with Lincoln on the Circuit* (Boston: Estes and Lauriat, 1892), 32.
43   "had no *nap*": Henry C. Whitney, *HI*, 617.
44   "back in a ditch": Leonard Swett, *HI*, 635–36.
44   "profession in this state": Donald, 151.
45   "long armed Ape": ibid., 186.
45   "roughly handled": *Herndon's Lincoln*, 287.
45   "*not*, a demonstrative man": Justin G. Turner and Linda Levitt Turner, *Mary Todd Lincoln: Her Life and Letters* (New York: Alfred A. Knopf, 1972), 293.
46   "love him better" and "paid no attention": James Gourley, *HI*, 453.
47   "gutted the room": Thomas, 100.
47   "garret or cellar": Nicolay, *Oral History*, 1.
48   "could not tempt him": Donald, 161.
48   "leave one's country no better": Emanuel Hertz, *The Hidden Lincoln* (New York: Blue Ribbon Books, 1940), 75.
48   "become abstracted": Donald, 163.
48   "picture of dejection and gloom": Jonathan Birch, *HI*, 727–28.

Chapter 3: Rise to Power

49   "aroused him": *CW*, v. 4, p. 67.
49   "of a storm": David M. Potter, *The Impending Crisis, 1848–1861*, edited and completed by Don E. Fehrenbacher (New York: Harper and Row, 1976), 160.
51   "a *lullaby*": *CW*, v. 2, p. 262.
51   "utter antagonisms": *CW*, v. 2, p. 275.
51   "our ancient faith": *CW*, v. 2, p. 276.
51   "a slave of another": *CW*, v. 2, p. 266.
51   "but *self-interest*": *CW*, v. 2, p. 255.
51   "robe is soiled": *CW*, v. 2, p. 276.
52   "the existing institution": *CW*, v. 2, p. 255.
52   "be safely disregarded": *CW*, v. 2, p. 256.
52   "a GREATER one": *CW*, v. 2, p. 270.
52   "instantly give it up": *CW*, v. 2, p. 255.
53   "a little engine": *Herndon's Lincoln*, 304.
53   "activity and vigilance": ibid., 302.
54   "moderately": *CW*, v. 2, p. 306.
54   "personal to myself": *CW*, v. 2, p. 307.

54 "crumbs of last year": *CW*, v. 2, p. 317.
55 "no pretense of loving liberty": *CW*, v. 2, pp. 322–23.
55 "personal friends": *CW*, v. 2, p. 316.
56 "its territorial parts": *CW*, v. 2, p. 341. The newspaper report put this passage in italics.
57 "maxim for free society": *CW*, v. 2, p. 406.
58 "could not at all recognize it": *CW*, v. 2, p. 404.
58 "equal *in all respects*": *CW*, v. 2, pp. 405–6.
58 "rapidly combining against him": *CW*, v. 2, p. 404.
59 "first and only choice": *Illinois State Journal*, June 17, 1858.
60 "half *slave* and half *free*": *CW*, v. 2, pp. 461–62.
60 "the latter condition": *CW*, v. 2, p. 462.
60 "welcome or unwelcome": *CW*, v. 2, p. 467.
61 "voted *down* or voted *up*": *CW*, v. 2, p. 465.
61 "made *Illinois* a *slave* State": *CW*, v. 2, p. 467.
61 "assumption of superiority": Joseph Gillespie, *HI*, 181.
61 "splendid success": *CW*, v. 2, p. 383.
61 "have my hands full": John W. Forney, *Anecdotes of Public Men*, vol. 2 (New York: Harper and Brothers, 1881), 179.
61 "against the South": Johannsen, 29.
62 "founded on the white basis": Johannsen, 33.
63 "showed his rough boots": Edwin Earle Sparks, ed., *The Lincoln–Douglas Debates of 1858* (Springfield: Illinois State Library, 1908), 206–7.
63 "battle-ground in the Union": Donald, 214.
63 "clenching his fists": Carl Schurz, *The Reminiscences of Carl Schurz*, vol. 2 (New York: McClure, 1907), 95.
63 "emphasis to his arguments": Henry Villard, *Memoirs of Henry Villard*, vol. 1 (Boston: Houghton Mifflin, 1904), 93.
65 "assigned to the white race": Johannsen, 162.
65 *"equal of every living man"*: ibid., 52–53.
65 "social and political wrong": ibid., 316.
66 "sink out of view": *CW*, v. 3, p. 339.
66 "absolutely without money": *CW*, v. 3, p. 337.
67 "fit for the Presidency": *CW*, v. 3, p. 377.
68 "the precise fact": *CW*, v. 3, p. 550.
68 "our duty as we understand it": ibid. In the pamphlet version published in 1860 that Lincoln corrected, this sentence was entirely in capital letters.
68 "taste *is* in my mouth": *CW*, v. 4, p. 45.
69 "not the *first* choice": *CW*, v. 4, p. 34.
70 "neither [to] write or speak": *CW*, v. 4, p. 80.
70 "bears his honors meekly": Browning, v. 1, 415.
70 "thorough organization": *CW*, v. 4, p. 109.
70 *"bored badly"*: Donald, 254.

70 "bursting by iron hoops": Nicolay, *Oral History*, 155–56.
71 "the ladies like whiskers": *CW*, v. 4, p. 130.
71 "silly affect[at]ion": *CW*, v. 4, p. 129.
71 "joined the Republicans": William E. Gienapp, "Who Voted for Lincoln?,"
   in John L. Thomas, ed., *Abraham Lincoln and the American Political Tradition* (Amherst: Univ. of Massachusetts Press, 1986), 51.

Chapter 4: A People's Contest

72 "bed of roses": *CW*, v. 2, p. 89.
72 "have just commenced": *Recollected Words*, 460.
73 "trick": Nicolay, *With Lincoln*, 7.
74 "accessible to the public": *CW*, v. 4, pp. 139–40.
74 "beg forgiveness": *CW*, v. 4, p. 152.
74 "tug has to come": *CW*, v. 4, pp. 149–50.
75 "consent of the others": *CW*, v. 4, p. 154.
75 "to govern themselves": Hay, *Inside*, 20.
76 "makes no change": *Herndon's Lincoln*, 390.
77 "an affectionate farewell": *CW*, v. 4, p. 190.
77 "put the foot down firmly": *CW*, v. 4, p. 237.
77 "run no risk": Isaac N. Arnold, *The Life of Abraham Lincoln* (Chicago:
   A. C. McClurg, 1885), 186–87.
78 "gentleman": William Howard Russell, *My Diary North and South*, ed. Eugene H. Berwanger (1863; rpt., New York: Random House, 1988), 45.
79 "yourselves the aggressors": *CW*, v. 4, pp. 266, 268, 271.
79 "words of affection": Frederick Seward, *Seward at Washington as Senator and Secretary of State*, vol. 2 (New York: Derby and Miller, 1891), 513.
79 "better angels of our nature": *CW*, v. 4, p. 271.
79 "national destruction consummated": *CW*, v. 4, p. 424.
80 "fair game for everybody": Henry Villard, *Memoirs of Henry Villard*, vol. 1 (Boston: Houghton, Mifflin, 1904), 156.
80 "entirely ignorant": Robert L. Wilson, *HI*, 207.
81 "I must do it": *CW*, v. 4, p. 317.
81 "the best of us": Seward, *Seward at Washington*, v. 2, p. 590.
81 "troubles and anxieties": Browning, v. 1, p. 476.
82 "course of judicial proceedings": *CW*, v. 4, p. 332.
82 "disaffection lurked": Thomas, 263.
82 "must have troops": *CW*, v. 4, pp. 341–42.
83 "be violated": *CW*, v. 4, p. 430.
83 "readily ratify them": *CW*, v. 4, p. 429.
84 "to the scaffold": Welles, v. 1, p. 549.
84 "insurrectionary combinations": *CW*, v. 4, p. 353.
84 "a People's contest": *CW*, v. 4, p. 438.

84   "domestic foes": *CW*, v. 4, p. 426.
85   "who doubted were wrong": Edward Cary, *George William Curtis* (Boston: Houghton Mifflin, 1894), 147.
86   "so much rosewater": *New York Times*, June 30, 1861.
86   "fault of ABRAHAM LINCOLN": *Harper's Weekly*, May 4, 1861.
86   "green alike": William Henry Hurlbert, *General McClellan and the Conduct of the War* (New York: Sheldon and Co., 1864), 103.
87   "so let it be": *Chicago Tribune*, July 23, 1861.
87   "in the fire": Nicolay, *With Lincoln*, 52.
87   "a little fussy": Russell, *My Diary*, 317.
88   "in favor of disunion": *CW*, v. 4, p. 437.
88   "utmost care": *CW*, v. 4, p. 332.
89   "over the mill dam": Thomas, 275.
89   "lose the whole game": *CW*, v. 4, p. 532.
89   "surrender of the government": *CW*, v. 4, pp. 531–32.
90   "at a time": *Recollected Words*, 173.
90   "confused disorder": Hay, *Inside*, 6.
90   "at all hours": Robert L. Wilson, *HI*, 207.
91   "than any of them": John Hay, *HI*, 332.
91   "want the office": Robert L. Wilson, *HI*, 206.
91   "as it was made": Hay, *HI*, 331.
91   "must see them": Henry Wilson, *HI*, 562.
91   "away from him": Hay, *HI*, 331.
91   "public-opinion baths": *Recollected Words*, 194.
92   "eyes almost shut": Helen Nicolay, "Characteristic Anecdotes of Abraham Lincoln," *Century Magazine*, 84 (September 1913): 699.
92   *"damned old house"*: Benjamin B. French, *Witness to the Young Republic*, eds. Donald B. Cole and John J. McDonough (Hanover, N.H.: Univ. Press of New England, 1989), 382.
95   "a good time": Julia Taft Bayne, *Tad Lincoln's Father* (Boston: Little, Brown, 1931), 107.
95   *"air of success"*: Stephen W. Sears, *George B. McClellan: The Young Napoleon* (New York: Ticknor and Fields, 1988), 111.
95   "power of the land": *McClellan Papers*, 70.
95   "in one campaign": ibid., 75.
96   "own way": Hay, *Inside*, 25.
96   "taken into the account": ibid., 29.
96   "for Jeff Davis": Donald, 320.
96   "do it all": Hay, *Inside*, 30.
96   "offensive was demanded": James B. Fry, "McClellan and His 'Mission,' " *Century Magazine* 48 (October 1894): 934.
96   "a well meaning baboon": *McClellan Papers*, 135, 106.
97   "bad faith": Allan Nevins, *The War for the Union*, vol. 1 (New York: Charles Scribner's Sons, 1959), 305.

97   "personal dignity": Hay, *Inside*, 32.
97   "hold McClellan's horse": Ida M. Tarbell, *The Life of Abraham Lincoln*, vol.
     2 (New York: McClure, Phillips, 1900), 70.
98   "out of the tub": "General M. C. Meigs on the Conduct of the Civil
     War," *American Historical Review* 26 (January 1921): 292.
98   "exceedingly discouraging": *CW*, v. 5, p. 95.
98   "ruining us": *CW*, v. 5, p. 92.
98   "our being two nations": Earl Schenck Miers, ed., *Lincoln Day by Day*,
     vol. 3 (Washington: Lincoln Sesquicentennial Commission, 1960), 87.

Chapter 5: From Limited War to Revolution

99   "revolutionary struggle": *CW*, v. 5, pp. 48–49.
100 "Constitutional rights of all": *McClellan Papers*, 125.
100 "concentrating his scattered forces": Stephen D. Engle, "Don Carlos Buell:
     Military Philosophy and Command Problems in the West," *Civil War History* 41 (June 1995): 92.
100 "defer to General McClellan": Donald, 329.
100 *"borrow it"*: William Swinton, *Campaigns of the Army of the Potomac* (New
     York: Charles B. Richardson, 1866), 80.
100 "his own hands": Donald, 331.
101 "advising general plans": Nicolay, *With Lincoln*, 59.
101 "threaten all their positions": Browning, v. 1, 523.
104 "end of the struggle": *New York Tribune*, February 13, 1862.
104 "is gone": Nicolay, *With Lincoln*, 71.
105 "within state limits": *CW*, v. 5, p. 145.
106 "reserve to myself": *CW*, v. 5, p. 222.
107 "he fights": Alexander K. McClure, *Abraham Lincoln and Men of War-Times*
     (Philadelphia: Times Publishing, 1892), 196. McClure put this quotation in
     italics.
107 *"you must act"*: *CW*, v. 5, p. 185.
108 "sacrifice this Army": *McClellan Papers*, 323.
108 "and troubled": Browning, v. 1, 559.
108 "general panic": *CW*, v. 5, p. 292.
108 "nearly inconsolable": *Recollected Words*, 137.
109 "disintegrate our present Armies": *McClellan Papers*, 344–45.
109 "rose water": *CW*, v. 5, p. 346.
109 "enemies stake nothing": *CW*, v. 5, p. 350.
109 "struck by accident": *CW*, v. 5, p. 345.
110 "the presence of war": *OR*, ser. I, v. 17, pt. 2, p. 150.
110 "kid-glove warfare": Allan G. Bogue, *The Earnest Men: Republicans of the
     Civil War Senate* (Ithaca, N.Y.: Cornell Univ. Press, 1981), 162.
110 "valuable in lieu of it": *CW*, v. 5, p. 318.

110   "or be ourselves subdued": Welles, v. 1, p. 70.

111   "heart of the rebellion": Gideon Welles, "The History of Emancipation," *Galaxy* 14 (December 1872): 843.

111   "a military necessity": ibid.

111   "lose the game": Carpenter, 20–21.

111   "on the retreat": ibid., 21–22.

111   "more than any other": *CW*, v. 5, p. 425.

112   "to remain with us": *CW*, v. 5, pp. 371–72.

113   "I would save the Union": *CW*, v. 5, p. 388.

113   "his scrape": *McClellan Papers*, 416.

113   "hang himself": *CW*, v. 5, p. 404n.

114   "a first-rate clerk": Hay, *Inside*, 191–92.

114   "ruining our country": T. Harry Williams, *Lincoln and His Generals* (New York: Alfred A. Knopf, 1952), 146.

114   "the grand marplot": Hay, *Inside*, 37.

115   "unpardonable": ibid., 39.

115   "the army with him": Welles, v. 1, p. 113.

115   "others ready to fight": Hay, *Inside*, 39.

116   "radical fanaticism": Donald, 380.

116   "loyal to the United States": John Hope Franklin, *The Emancipation Proclamation* (Garden City, N.Y.: Doubleday, 1963), 68–69.

116   "all our diplomacy": Worthington Chauncey Ford, ed., *A Cycle of Adams Letters*, vol. 1 (Boston: Houghton Mifflin, 1920), 243.

116   "kills no rebels": *CW*, v. 5, p. 444.

116   "card unplayed": *CW*, v. 5, p. 343.

117   "disloyal practice": *CW*, v. 5, p. 437.

117   "be used against us": Welles, "Emancipation," 847.

118   "confidence of the people": David Donald, ed., *Inside Lincoln's Cabinet: The Civil War Diaries of Salmon P. Chase* (New York: Longmans, Green, 1954), 151.

118   "overwork had wrought": Mary Livermore, *My Story of the War* (Hartford: A. D. Worthington, 1889), 555, 560.

118   "prematurely aged": Michael Burlingame, ed., *Lincoln Observed: Civil War Dispatches of Noah Brooks* (Baltimore: Johns Hopkins Univ. Press, 1998), 13.

118   "want of confidence": *New York Times*, November 7, 1862.

118   "scarcely know what": McPherson, 560–61.

119   "fatigue anything": *CW*, v. 5, p. 474.

120   "by strategy": Livermore, *My Story*, 556.

120   "too dull to take hold": Donald, 389.

120   "fight as he fights": *OR*, ser. I, v. 16, pt. 2, p. 627.

121   "shall be repeated": *Harper's Weekly*, December 27, 1862.

121   "worse place than Hell": McPherson, 574.

122   "a ray of hope": Browning, v. 1, p. 600.

122   "handful of supporters": Hay, *Inside*, 104.

122 "without system": Welles, v. 1, p. 136.
122 "salvation of the country": Robert Warden, *The Private Life and Public Services of Salmon Portland Chase* (Cincinnati: Wilstach, Baldwin, 1874), 484.
122 "want of unity": Francis Fessenden, *Life and Public Services of William Pitt Fessenden*, vol. 1 (Boston: Houghton Mifflin, 1907), 243.
123 "end of my bag": Frederick Seward, *Seward at Washington as Senator and Secretary of State*, vol. 3 (New York: Derby and Miller, 1891), 148.
123 "pieces upon a chessboard": Leonard Swett, *HI*, 168.
123 "as well as anyone could": ibid., 165n.
123 "act anew": *CW*, v. 5, pp. 530, 537.
124 "hallucination": Browning, v. 1, p. 591.
124 "best, hope of earth": *CW*, v. 5, p. 537.
124 "will stand firm": Thomas, 358.
124 "whole soul is absorbed": Harry E. Pratt, ed., *Concerning Mr. Lincoln* (Springfield: Abraham Lincoln Association, 1944), 95.
124 "signing this paper": Seward, *Seward at Washington*, 151.
125 "favor of Almighty God": *CW*, v. 6, p. 30.
125 "far beyond its letter": Franklin, *Emancipation Proclamation*, 135.
125 "revolution of the age": *Springfield Republican*, September 24, 1862.
125 "subjugation": McPherson, 558.

Chapter 6: Midstream

126 "scarcely have lived over": *CW*, v. 6, p. 424.
127 "gone to pieces": Katherine Helm, *The True Story of Mary, Wife of Lincoln* (New York: Harper and Brothers, 1928), 225.
127 "Hellcat": Hay, *Correspondence*, 20.
127 "political party notions": Welles, v. 1, p. 136.
128 "occurrences of the day": Justin G. Turner and Linda Levitt Turner, *Mary Todd Lincoln: Her Life and Letters* (New York: Knopf, 1972), 187.
128 "hard life for him": Benjamin B. French, *Witness to the Young Republic*, eds. Donald B. Cole and John J. McDonough (Hanover, N.H.: Univ. Press of New England, 1989), 417.
130 "risk the dictatorship": *CW*, v. 6, pp. 78–79.
130 "I will have none": T. Harry Williams, *Lincoln and His Generals* (New York: Alfred A. Knopf, 1952), 229–30.
130 "incidental to the main object": *CW*, v. 6, pp. 164–65.
131 "the country say": Brooks, *Washington*, 57–58.
131 "peace party of the North": Clifford Dowdey, ed., *The Wartime Papers of Robert E. Lee* (Boston: Little, Brown, 1961), 508.
132 "fire in the rear": Edward L. Pierce, *Memoir and Letters of Charles Sumner*, vol. 4 (Boston: Roberts Brothers, 1893), 114.

132   "saw whither it tended": Horace White, *The Life of Lyman Trumbull* (Boston: Houghton Mifflin, 1913), 428.

134   "wiley agitator": *CW*, v. 6, pp. 263–64, 266.

134   "one man": *CW*, v. 6, p. 304.

134   "unconditionally": *CW*, v. 6, p. 446.

134   "aid the enemy": Howard K. Beale, ed., *The Diary of Edward Bates, 1859–1866* (Washington: Government Printing Office, 1933), 306.

135   "unshaken": Donald, 438.

135   "attitude of demur": Brooks, *Washington*, 37.

135   "true objective point": *CW*, v. 6, p. 257.

136   "snapping turtle": Thomas, 383.

137   "would not close it": Hay, *Inside*, 64–65.

138   "in our pocket": David D. Porter, *Incidents and Anecdotes of the Civil War* (New York: D. Appleton, 1885), 95–96.

138   "everything going on": Stephen E. Ambrose, *Halleck: Lincoln's Chief of Staff* (Baton Rouge: Louisiana State Univ. Press, 1962), 110.

138   "one too many": Ulysses S. Grant, *Personal Memoirs of U. S. Grant*, vol. 1 (New York: Charles L. Webster, 1885), 426.

139   "attention to the better work": *CW*, v. 6, p. 70.

139   "except myself": Thomas, 373.

139   "unvexed to the sea": *CW*, v. 6, p. 409.

140   "I was wrong": *CW*, v. 6, p. 326.

140   "Grant is my man": T. Harry Williams, *Lincoln and His Generals* (New York: Alfred A. Knopf, 1952), 271.

140   "our political existence": Dunbar Rowland, ed., *Jefferson Davis, Constitutionalist, His Letters, Papers, and Speeches*, vol. 5 (Jackson: Mississippi Department of Archives and History, 1923), 554.

141   "rules New York today": Allan Nevins and Milton Halsey Thomas, eds., *The Diary of George Templeton Strong*, vol. 3 (New York: Columbia University Press, 1952), 336.

142   "his healthful life": *CW*, v. 6, p. 267.

142   "without an if": *CW*, v. 6, p. 446.

142   "there is no cavil": Hay, *Correspondence*, 49

143   "rather good": John Nicolay and John Hay, *Abraham Lincoln: A History*, vol. 7 (New York: Century, 1890), 385.

143   "in saving the Union": *CW*, v. 6, p. 409.

144   "strove to hinder it": *CW*, v. 6, pp. 409–10.

144   "signs look better": ibid

144   "most popular man": *New York Times*, September 7, 1863.

145   "hit on the head": Hay, *Inside*, 99.

146   "is at an end": Worthington Chauncey Ford, ed., *A Cycle of Adams Letters*, vol. 2 (Boston: Houghton Mifflin, 1920), 59–60.

147   "one master mind": Welles, v. 1, p. 344.

147   "or be conquered by them": *OR*, ser. I, v. 24, pt. 3, p. 157.

147   "are devastating the land": Brooks D. Simpson and Jean D. Berlin, eds., *Sherman's Civil War* (Chapel Hill: Univ. of North Carolina Press, 1999), 373.

148   "all the slaves you can": OR, ser. I, v. 24, pt. 3, p. 157.

148   "appropriate remarks": Donald, 460.

149   "under God" and "great battle-field": CW, v. 7, pp. 22–23.

149   "in two minutes": CW, v. 7, p. 25.

150   "overwhelming majority": V. Jacque Voegli, *Free but Not Equal: The Midwest and the Negro during the Civil War* (Chicago: Univ. of Chicago Press, 1967), 131.

150   "dark and doubtful days": CW, v. 7, pp. 49–50.

Chapter 7: To Finish the Task

152   "to put down the rebellion": Horace White, *The Life of Lyman Trumbull* (Boston: Houghton Mifflin, 1913), 218.

152   "there be some uneasiness": CW, v. 4, p. 439.

153   "as far as convenient": CW, v. 5, p. 462.

153   "a tangible nucleus": CW, v. 7, p. 1.

154   "his former unsoundness": CW, v. 7, p. 51.

154   "outvoting the loyal minority": Hay, *Inside*, 106.

154   "permanent freedom": CW, v. 7, pp. 1–2.

155   "gallantly in our ranks": CW, v. 7, p. 243.

155   "little change as possible": McPherson, 701.

155   "than by smashing it": CW, v. 8, p. 404.

155   "if they dared": Thomas, 410–11.

156   "in the Trinity": Hay, *Inside*, 77.

157   "rotten spot he can find": ibid., 103.

157   "affections of the masses": Donald, 478.

158   "rabble of men and dogs": ibid., 497.

159   "into a fortified city": CW, v. 6, p. 467.

159   "most brilliant": CW, v. 6, p. 230.

160   "restraints upon you": CW, v. 7, p. 324.

161   "hold a leg": Hay, *Inside*, 194.

161   "all the damage you can": OR, ser. 1, v. 32, pt. 3, p. 246.

161   "ever to end": Allen Thorndike Rice, *Reminiscences of Abraham Lincoln* (New York: North American Review, 1888), 337.

161   "sorrow, care, and anxiety": Carpenter, 30–31.

161   "is dreadful": Isaac N. Arnold, *The Life of Abraham Lincoln* (Chicago: A. C. McClurg, 1884), 375.

162   "bankruptcy and desolation": Frank L. Klement, *The Copperheads in the Middle West* (Chicago: Univ. of Chicago Press, 1960), 233.

163   "unconditional surrender": Kirk H. Porter and Donald Bruce Johnson,

comp., *National Party Platforms, 1840–1968* (Urbana: Univ. of Illinois Press, 1970), 35.

163   "point of mutual embarrassment": *CW*, v. 7, p. 419.

164   "little for the country": Allan Nevins and Milton Halsey Thomas, eds., *The Diary of George Templeton Strong*, vol. 3 (New York: Columbia University Press, 1952), 467, 474.

164   "events have controlled me": *CW*, v. 7, pp. 281–82.

164   "bloodshed as possible": Horace Porter, *Campaigning with Grant* (New York: Century, 1897), 223.

165   "a bull-dog gripe": *CW*, v. 7, p. 499.

165   "have no country": John Nicolay and John Hay, *Abraham Lincoln: A History*, vol. 9 (New York: Century, 1890), 364.

165   "*deader* than dead": Klement, *Copperheads*, 233.

166   "constitutionally by Congress": Hay, *Inside*, 218.

166   "single plan of restoration": *CW*, v. 7, p. 433.

166   "authority of the people": *New York Tribune*, August 5, 1864.

166   "can befall a man": Brooks, *Washington*, 170.

167   "rivers of human blood": *CW*, v. 7, p. 435.

168   "collateral points": *CW*, v. 7, p. 451.

168   "even with him now": Charles A. Dana, *Recollections of the Civil War* (New York: D. Appleton, 1898), 180.

168   "sealed Lincoln's fate": Donald, 523.

169   "we *will* have": *Atlantic Monthly* 14 (September 1864): 379.

169   "failure": James G. Randall, *Lincoln the Liberal Statesman* (New York: Dodd, Mead, 1947), 81.

169   "lever as I have done": *CW*, v. 7, p. 507.

169   "from utter overthrow": Burton J. Hendrick, *Lincoln's War Cabinet* (Boston: Little, Brown, 1946), 454.

170   "suspicion is widely diffused": *CW*, v. 7, pp. 517–18.

170   "surrendering it in advance": Nicolay and Hay, *Lincoln*, v. 9, p. 221.

170   "doubt and discouragement": Nicolay, *With Lincoln*, 152.

170   "possibly save it afterwards": *CW*, v. 7, p. 514.

171   "four years of failure": Porter and Johnson, *Platforms*, 34.

171   "by our foes": Larry E. Nelson, *Bullets, Ballots and Rhetoric: Confederate Policy for the United States Presidential Election of 1864* (University: Univ. of Alabama Press, 1980), 113.

171   "Atlanta is ours": Nicolay and Hay, *Lincoln*, v. 9, p. 289.

172   "sorehead republicans": Donald, 536.

173   "think of anything else": Francis Fessenden, *Life and Public Services of William Pitt Fessenden*, vol. 1 (Boston: Houghton Mifflin, 1907), 343.

173   "Administration endorsed": Nicolay, *Oral*, 78.

173   "and rainy": Michael Burlingame, ed., *Lincoln Observed: Civil War Dispatches of Noah Brooks* (Baltimore: Johns Hopkins Univ. Press, 1998), 142.

173   "marked with great rancor": Hay, *Inside*, 243.

175   "but an *honorable* one": McPherson, 803–4.

175   "wearing his Sunday clothes": Porter, *Campaigning*, 218.

175   "has been universal": Joseph H. Twichell, "Army Memories of Lincoln," *Congregationalist and Christian World*, January 30, 1913, p. 154.

175   "men in the ranks": Brooks, *Washington*, 49–50.

175   "was a necessity": *CW*, v. 8, p. 101.

176   "treason and disunion": Nevins and Thomas, *Strong Diary*, v. 3, p. 511.

Chapter 8: With Malice Toward None

177   "the past against him": John Nicolay and John Hay, *Abraham Lincoln: A History*, vol. 9 (New York: Century, 1890), 377.

178   "rather Statesmanship": Brooks D. Simpson and Jean D. Berlin, eds., *Sherman's Civil War* (Chapel Hill: Univ. of North Carolina Press, 1999), 751.

178   "to decide": *CW*, v. 8, p. 182.

179   "Presidential maggots": Nicolay, *Oral History*, 152.

179   "other recommendations": Nicolay and Hay, *Lincoln*, v. 9, p. 392.

179   "statutes of limitations": Hay, *Inside*, 249.

180   "heard upon the question": *CW*, v. 8, p. 149.

180   "hard, keen intelligence": Charles A. Dana, *Recollections of the Civil War* (New York: D. Appleton, 1898), 174.

180   "a King's cure": *CW*, v. 8, p. 254.

181   "to deceive ourselves": *CW*, v. 8, p. 151.

181   "shall be adopted": *CW*, v. 8, p. 152.

181   "the two countries": *CW*, v. 8, p. 275.

181   "one common country": *CW*, v. 8, p. 221.

182   "unconditional submission": Dunbar Rowland, ed., *The Messages and Papers of Jefferson Davis*, vol. 6 (Jackson: Mississippi Department of Archives and History, 1923), 465.

182   "unhappy difficulties": *CW*, v. 8, p. 331.

182   "conferences or conventions": *CW*, v. 8, pp. 330–31.

183   "your military advantages": *CW*, v. 8, p. 331.

183   "jaded and weary": Joshua F. Speed, *Reminiscences of Abraham Lincoln* (Louisville: John P. Morton, 1884), 26.

183   "out of reach": Noah Brooks, "Personal Reminiscences of Lincoln," *Scribner's Monthly* 15 (March 1878): 673.

184   "sum of human misery": Hay, *Correspondence*, 139.

184   "anguish of soul": Thomas, 472.

184   "butcher's day": William O. Stoddard, *Inside the White House in War Times*, ed. Michael Burlingame (Lincoln: Univ. of Nebraska Press, 2000), 171.

184   "work out of him": Nicolay, *Oral History*, 69.

184   "loss of self-control": *CW*, v. 6, p. 538.

185 "blood running all around me": *Recollected Words*, 458.

185 "the altar of Freedom": *CW*, v. 8, pp. 116–17.

185 "should die": *Recollected Words*, 18.

185 "queer little conceits": Hay, *Inside*, 194.

185 "riskiest of story tellers": Hay, *Correspondence*, 136–37.

186 "nothing equals Macbeth": *CW*, v. 6, p. 392.

187 "different from theirs": *CW*, v. 5, p. 279.

187 "shall not end yet": *CW*, v. 5, pp. 403–04.

187 "no mortal could stay": *CW*, v. 7, p. 535.

187 "unclouded meridian splendor": Brooks, *Washington*, 235, 239.

188 "with all nations": *CW*, v. 8, pp. 332–33.

189 "keynote of this war": Worthington Chauncey Ford, ed., *A Cycle of Adams Letters* vol. 2 (Boston: Houghton Mifflin, 1920), 257.

189 "I have produced": *CW*, v. 8, p. 356.

189 "at home and abroad": *New York Herald*, March 4, 1865.

190 "swamped almost any other man": ibid.

190 "determined a decision": Allan Nevins, *The War for the Union*, vol. 1 (New York: Charles Scribner's Sons, 1959), 205.

190 "communicated nothing": Leonard Swett, *HI*, 168.

190 "as successfully as Mr. Lincoln": Gideon Welles, *Lincoln and Seward* (New York: Sheldon, 1874), 32.

191 "horses than oats": Leonard Swett, *HI*, 165.

191 "constitute a fair specimen": *CW*, v. 6, p. 559.

192 "who are not Republicans": *CW*, v. 5, pp. 494–95.

192 "splendid military despotism": *Littell's Living Age*, February 6, 1864, p. 284.

192 "coming to resolutions": ibid.

192 "might be": Dana, *Recollections*, 183.

192 "crushed at defeat": Michael Burlingame, ed., *Lincoln Observed: Civil War Dispatches of Noah Brooks* (Baltimore: Johns Hopkins Univ. Press, 1998), 215.

192 "his wiliest antagonists": *New York Herald*, March 4, 1865.

193 "sustain the faltering": John Nicolay and John Hay, *Abraham Lincoln: A History*, vol. 4 (New York: Century, 1890), 367–68.

193 "self-reliance": Welles, *Lincoln and Seward*, 32.

193 "no more bloodshed": Charles M. Segal, ed., *Conversations with Lincoln* (New York: G. P. Putnam's Sons, 1961), 382.

195 "subject of honesty": Justin G. Turner and Linda Levitt Turner, *Mary Todd Lincoln: Her Life and Letters* (New York: Alfred A. Knopf, 1972), 180.

195 "take care of myself": *CW*, v. 8, p. 385.

195 "let 'em up easy": *Recollected Words*, 182.

196 "be pressed": *CW*, v. 8, pp. 389, 392.

196 "our own soldiers": Ida M. Tarbell, *The Life of Abraham Lincoln*, vol. 2 (New York: McClure, Phillips, 1900), 161.

197 "the end at last": Frederick Seward, *Seward at Washington as Senator and Secretary of State*, vol. 3 (New York: Derby and Miller, 1891), 271.

198 "safely be prescribed": *CW*, v. 8, pp. 403–4.

199 "wild with exceeding joy": *New York Independent*, January 8, 1865.

199 "freedom from popular prejudice": Allen Thorndike Rice, ed., *Reminiscences of Abraham Lincoln* (New York: North American Review, 1888), 193.

199 "the black mans President": Draft of speech, June 1, 1865, Frederick Douglass Papers, Library of Congress.

200 "will ever make": William Hanchett, *The Lincoln Murder Conspiracies* (Urbana: Univ. of Illinois Press, 1983), 37.

200 "an emperor": Carpenter, 65.

200 "in danger": John W. Forney, *Anecdotes of Public Men*, vol. 2 (New York: Harper and Brothers, 1881), 425.

200 "would be availing": Joseph Gillespie, *HI*, 185.

201 "up to the occasion": Donald, 591.

201 "than with them": Gideon Welles, "Lincoln and Johnson," *Galaxy* 13 (April 1872): 526.

201 "had been sacrificed": ibid.

201 "been very miserable" Turner and Turner, *Mary Todd Lincoln*, 285.

202 "to the ages": Donald, 599.

202 "history has no parallel": E. D. Townsend, *Anecdotes of the Civil War* (New York: D. Appleton, 1884), 220–21.

BIBLIOGRAPHICAL ESSAY

The bibliographical notes for each chapter are mostly limited to books dealing with Abraham Lincoln. The best overview of the politics of the 1850s is David M. Potter's *The Impending Crisis, 1848–1861*, edited and completed by Don E. Fehrenbacher (New York: Harper and Row, 1976). For the Civil War, James M. McPherson, *Battle Cry of Freedom* (New York: Oxford Univ. Press, 1988), is a sound and thoughtful account. These works will refer the interested reader to important secondary works on a host of topics.

Chapter 1: A Son of the Frontier

Untangling the events of Abraham Lincoln's early life is a monumental challenge. The major sources for the years before 1837 are the interviews and recollections assembled by William Herndon, his law partner, after Lincoln's death. This material is finally available in a well-edited modern edition with a thorough index: Douglas L. Wilson and Rodney O. Davis, eds., *Herndon's Informants* (Urbana: Univ. of Illinois Press, 1998). These interviews are the basis for William H. Herndon and Jesse W. Weik, *Herndon's Life of Lincoln*, ed. Paul M. Angle (Cleveland: World Publishing, 1942). There are also some important recollections of Lincoln's early acquaintances in Walter B. Stevens, *A Reporter's Lincoln*, ed. Michael Burlingame (Lincoln: Univ. of Nebraska Press, 1998). The fullest study of Lincoln's years in Indiana is Louis Warren, *Lincoln's Youth: Indiana Years* (Indianapolis: Indiana State Historical Society, 1959). One of the most important books on Lincoln to appear in recent years is Douglas L. Wilson, *Honor's Voice: The Transformation of Abraham Lincoln* (New York: Alfred A. Knopf, 1998), which carefully examines his life in New Salem.

Chapter 2: Thwarted Ambition

The sources for Lincoln's life improve after his move to Springfield, though the Herndon interviews and recollections of acquaintances remain the major source for his career outside politics. Thus Wilson and Davis, eds., *Herndon's Informants*, and Angle's edition of *Herndon's Life of Lincoln* remain essential. There are additional interviews in Michael Burlingame, ed., *An Oral History of Abraham Lincoln* (Carbondale: Southern Illinois Univ. Press, 1996), which collects material from the John G. Nicolay Papers. John Simon, "Abraham Lincoln and Ann Rutledge," *Journal of the Abraham Lincoln Association* 11 (1990): 13–34, is a crucial contribution to this period of Lincoln's life. For Lincoln's marriage, see Wilson, *Honor's Voice*, and Michael Burlingame, *The Inner World of Abraham Lincoln* (Urbana: Univ. of Illinois Press, 1994). Jean H. Baker, *Mary Todd Lincoln* (New York: W. W. Norton, 1987), is the best biography of Lincoln's wife and has much material on their marriage. For the tangled chronology of Lincoln and Mary Todd's courtship and engagement, see Douglas Wilson, "Abraham Lincoln and 'That Fatal First of January,' " *Civil War History* 38 (1992).

Lincoln's legal career awaits a full-scale study, but John J. Duff, *A. Lincoln: Prairie Lawyer* (New York: Rhinehart, 1960), is a good introduction. John Evangelist Walsh, *Moonlight: Abraham Lincoln and the Almanac Trial* (New York: St. Martin's Press, 2000), discusses his most famous court-room effort. Lincoln's economic ideas are carefully examined in Gabor S. Boritt, *Lincoln and the Economics of the American Dream* (Memphis: Memphis State Univ. Press, 1978). For Lincoln's Whig loyalty, Daniel Walker Howe, *The Political Culture of the American Whigs* (Chicago: Univ. of Chicago Press, 1979) and Joel H. Silbey, " 'Always a Whig in Politics': The Partisan Life of Abraham Lincoln," *Papers of the Abraham Lincoln Association* 8 (1986): 21–42, are basic. David Donald, *Lincoln's Herndon* (New York: Alfred A. Knopf, 1948), examines Lincoln's partnership with Herndon. The two accounts of Lincoln's term in Congress are Donald W. Riddle, *Congressman Abraham Lincoln* (Westport, Conn: Greenwood Press, 1979), and Paul Findley, *A. Lincoln: The Crucible of Congress* (New York: Crown Publishers, 1979).

Chapter 3: Rise to Power

The most important study of Lincoln's political career in the 1850s is Don E. Fehrenbacher's *Prelude to Greatness: Lincoln in the 1850's* (Stanford, Calif.: Stanford Univ. Press, 1962), which is a gem of historical analysis. Robert W. Johannsen's *Lincoln, the South, and Slavery* (Baton Rouge: Louisiana State Univ. Press, 1991), is much more critical of Lincoln, but it asks probing questions that historians have too often glided over. There are many editions of the Lincoln–Douglas debates. I have relied on the edition edited by Robert W. Johannsen, *The Lincoln–Douglas Debates of 1858* (New York: Oxford Univ. Press, 1965). Edwin Earle Sparks, ed., *The Lincoln–Douglas Debates of 1858* (Springfield: Illinois State Library, 1908), includes valuable descriptions of campaign pageantry along with coverage in the press. Harold Holzer, ed., *The Lincoln–Douglas Debates* (New York: Harper Collins, 1993), highlights the problem of bias and distortion by printing alternative texts drawn from newspapers hostile to each candidate. For the 1860 campaign, William E. Baringer, *Lincoln's Rise to Power* (Boston: Little, Brown, 1937), and Reinhard H. Luthin, *The First Lincoln Campaign* (Cambridge: Harvard Univ. Press, 1944), are good accounts. William E. Gienapp, "Who Voted for Lincoln?," in John L. Thomas, ed., *Abraham Lincoln and the American Political Tradition* (Amherst: Univ. of Massachusetts Press, 1986), analyzes Lincoln's popular support in 1860.

Chapter 4: A People's Contest

For this and all subsequent chapters, Phillip S. Paludan, *The Presidency of Abraham Lincoln* (Lawrence: Univ. Press of Kansas, 1994), is basic. A much fuller account but more partisan in its defense of Lincoln is John G. Nicolay and John Hay, *Abraham Lincoln: A History*, 10 vols. (New York: Century, 1890).

Lincoln's activities as president-elect are covered in William Baringer, *A House Dividing: Lincoln as President Elect* (Springfield, Ill.: Abraham Lincoln Association, 1945). The best studies of Lincoln's handling of the Fort Sumter crisis are Kenneth M. Stampp, *And the War Came: The North and the Secession Crisis, 1860–1861* (Baton Rouge: Louisiana State Univ. Press, 1950), and Richard N. Current, *Lincoln and the First Shot* (Philadelphia: J. B. Lippincott, 1963), which reach similar conclusions. Mark E. Neely, *The Fate of Liberty: Abraham Lincoln and Civil Liberties* (New York: Oxford Univ. Press, 1991), offers an acute analysis of Lincoln's suspension of the writ of the habeas corpus during the war. For Lincoln's leadership during the early stages of the war, see Don E. Fehrenbacher's incisive "Lincoln's Wartime Leadership: The First Hundred Days" and William E. Gienapp, "Abraham Lincoln and the Border States." These essays are reprinted in Thomas F. Schwartz, ed., *"For a Vast Future Also": Essays from the Journal of the Abraham Lincoln Association* (New York: Fordham Univ. Press, 1999). In the same volume Norman B. Ferris offers a revisionist account of Lincoln and Seward in "Civil War Diplomacy: Their Relationship at the Outset Reexamined."

Chapter 5: From Limited War to Revolution

Mark E. Neely's *The Fate of Liberty* perceptively analyzes Lincoln's record on civil liberties in wartime. The fullest discussion of the war's constitutional issues is James G. Randall's old but still important *Constitutional Problems under Lincoln*, rev. ed. (Urbana: Univ. of Illinois Press, 1951). More recent constitutional scholarship is summarized in Harold M. Hyman and William M. Wiecek, *Equal Justice under Law* (New York: Harper and Row, 1982). Civil War diplomacy is discussed in Howard Jones, *Union in Peril: The Crisis over British Intervention in the Civil War* (Chapel Hill: Univ. of North Carolina Press, 1992).

T. Harry Williams offers a positive assessment of Lincoln's strategic ideas in his influential *Lincoln and His Generals* (New York: Alfred A. Knopf, 1952). My distinction about the components of war strategy is derived from James M. McPherson, *Abraham Lincoln and the Second American Revolution* (New York: Oxford Univ. Press, 1991).

Differing views of Republican factionalism are offered in T. Harry Williams, *Lincoln and the Radicals* (Madison: Univ. of Wisconsin Press, 1941), which is critical of the Radicals, and Hans Trefousse, *The Radical Republicans* (New York: Alfred A. Knopf, 1969), which is sympathetic. While Lincoln's biographers have given considerable attention to emancipation, historians have strangely neglected the topic. John Hope Franklin, *The Emancipation Proclamation* (Garden City, N.Y.: Doubleday, 1963), is a good short account of that subject. The best discussion of Lincoln and the colonization issue is Michael Vorenberg, "Abraham Lincoln and the Politics of Black Colonization," *Journal of the Abraham Lincoln Association* 14 (Summer 1993): 23–45.

Chapter 6: Midstream

T. Harry Williams, *Lincoln and His Generals*, skillfully examines Lincoln's relationship with his commanders in 1863. Lincoln's use of the unpopular Henry Halleck to deflect criticism from himself is discussed in Stephen E. Ambrose, *Halleck: Lincoln's Chief of Staff* (Baton Rouge: Louisiana State Univ. Press, 1962). For the concept of a home front, see Mark Neely's discussion in *The Last Best Hope of Earth* (Cambridge, Mass.: Harvard Univ. Press, 1993). The most important study of the opposition to the war in the North is Frank Klement's influential *The Copperheads in the Middle West* (Chicago: Univ. of Chicago Press, 1960), which unduly minimizes the threat posed by antiwar elements. V. Jacque Voegli, *Free but Not Equal: The Midwest and the Negro during the Civil War* (Chicago: Univ. of Chicago Press, 1967), demonstrates the strength of antiblack sentiment in the western states. The best study of Lincoln's political ideas, encapsulated in the Gettysburg Address, is Harry V. Jaffa, *A New Birth of Freedom* (Lanham, Md.: Rowman and Littlefield, 2000). Garry Wills, *Lincoln at Gettysburg: The Words That Remade America* (New York: Simon and Schuster, 1992), is a fuller account of this speech but is considerably overdrawn in its interpretation.

Chapter 7: To Finish the Task

Lincoln's reconstruction policy and his differences with the Radicals are carefully analyzed in William C. Harris, *With Charity for All: Lincoln and the Restoration of the Union* (Lexington: Univ. Press of Kentucky, 1997). Also useful is Herman Belz's *Reconstructing the Union* (Ithaca, N.Y.: Cornell Univ. Press, 1969), which pays particular attention to the constitutional basis of Reconstruction. The best study of the racial dimensions of Lincoln's reconstruction program is LaWanda Cox, *Lincoln and Black Freedom: A Study in Presidential Leadership* (Columbia: Univ. of South Carolina Press, 1981), which corrects some long-standing misimpressions.

David E. Long, *The Jewel of Liberty: Abraham Lincoln's Re-Election and the End of Slavery* (Mechanicsburg, Pa.: Stackpole Books, 1994), is a solid account of the

1864 presidential election. In some ways it has been superseded by Michael Vorenberg's *Final Freedom: The Civil War, the Abolition of Slavery, and the Thirteenth Amendment* (New York: Cambridge Univ. Press, 2001), which is a thoroughly researched account of the issue of emancipation that gives considerable attention to political developments in 1864. The fullest examination of the peace movement is Edward C. Kirkland's old but still useful *The Peacemakers of 1864* (New York: Macmillan, 1937). T. Harry Williams, *Lincoln and His Generals*, discusses Lincoln's continuing role in military matters after Grant assumed command. William C. Davis, *Lincoln's Men: How President Lincoln Became Father to an Army and a Nation* (New York: Free Press, 1999), examines Lincoln's special relationship with Union soldiers.

Chapter 8: With Malice Toward None

Michael Vorenberg's *Final Freedom* and Herman Belz's *Reconstructing the Union*, cited above, discuss the passage of the Thirteenth Amendment. Belz and William C. Harris, *With Charity for All*, examine the continuing issue of reconstruction and Lincoln's evolving views on this problem. Allen C. Guelzo sensitively analyzes Lincoln's religious ideas in *Abraham Lincoln: Redeemer President* (Grand Rapids, Mich.: William B. Eerdmans Publishing, 1999). Also see Nicholas Parrillo, "Lincoln's Calvinist Transformation: Emancipation and War," *Civil War History* 46 (September 2000): 227–53. William C. Harris, "The Hampton Roads Conference: A Final Test of Lincoln's Presidential Leadership," *Journal of the Abraham Lincoln Association* 21 (Winter 2000): 31–62, is the best account of that controversial subject. William Hanchett, *The Lincoln Murder Conspiracies* (Urbana: Univ. of Illinois Press, 1983), is a sound treatment of the assassination. Thomas Turner, *Beware the People Weeping* (Baton Rouge: Louisiana Univ. Press, 1982), surveys public reaction to the event. Aspects of Lincoln's leadership are examined in Gabor S. Boritt, ed., *Lincoln the War President* (New York: Oxford Univ. Press, 1992); David Donald, *Lincoln Reconsidered*, 2nd ed. (New York: Alfred A. Knopf, 1972); and James M. McPherson, *Abraham Lincoln and the Second American Revolution* (New York: Oxford Univ. Press, 1991). This chapter incorporates portions of my essay, "Abraham Lincoln and Presidential Leadership," in James M. McPherson, ed., *"We Cannot Escape History": Lincoln and the Last Best Hope of Earth* (Urbana: Univ. of Illinois Press, 1995), 63–85.

INDEX